WINE
BUYER'S
GUIDE

DORLING KINDERSLEY
LONDON • NEW YORK • STUTTGART

A DORLING KINDERSLEY BOOK

First published in Great Britain in 1994
by Dorling Kindersley Limited,
9 Henrietta Street, London WC2E 8PS
Copyright ©1994 Dorling Kindersley Ltd, London
Text and illustration copyright ©1994,
WINE Magazine.

A CIP catalogue record for this book is available from the
British Library.

ISBN 0 7713 0156 6

Printed and bound in Italy

CONTENTS

INTRODUCTION

Over the last few years, almost no one in Britain with even the most casual interest in what they drink can have failed to notice the plethora of labels and posters proclaiming the success of particular wines in *WINE Magazine's* annual International Wine Challenge.

There is of course, nothing new about wine competitions. Several Spanish producers still like to decorate their labels with medals won at events held over a century ago. What is new about the International Wine Challenge is its size – this year, over 7000 wines were tasted – its scope – from Liebfraumilch to Lafite – its authority and, most important of all, its direct relevance to the wines most of us regularly buy and drink.

——— A GUIDE THROUGH THE WINE MAZE ———

Britain is a uniquely fascinating place for a wine drinker. As this year's Challenge proved, and as you will see from the medal-winners on the following pages, nowadays you can buy wine here from just about every country on earth. But sometimes that breadth of choice can be daunting. How is anyone to choose between 20 or 30 different kinds of Chardonnay?

In the following pages, for the first time in book-form, you will find 2000 medal winners from the 1994 International Wine Challenge, listed by provenance and price. Whatever the style of wine you are looking for you will almost certainly find it here, complete with the tasters' description and information on where it can be bought in Britain.

THE CHALLENGE

For an event which has become such an international success, the International Wine Challenge started very small. In 1984, when *WINE Magazine* was just a few months old, Charles Metcalfe, the associate editor, and Robert Joseph, the editor, decided to set a team of English wines against a range of well respected bottles from other countries. Grandly titled 'The International Wine Challenge' this event involved 38 wines and 20 international tasters and was one of those sadly rare occasions where the English outsiders beat the fancied foreigners.

—— OVER 7000 ENTRIES ——

The surprise at that result was followed swiftly by questions in Parliament about government policy towards English winemakers and, more resoundingly, by a call for a return match.

Over the intervening decade the Challenge has grown annually to become the world's biggest, and most respected, wine competition.

Tasters gather from throughout the world

In 1994 it attracted over 7000 entries ranging from the humblest Vin de Table and Bag-in-Box to some of the most illustrious wines of the Old and New Worlds.

Challenge success can be attributed to a number of

A host of Challenge wines waiting to be tasted

factors. First, there is the fact that the tastings are held in Britain, a country whose wine drinkers are uniquely open-minded.

Over the last few years, major high street merchants have, for example, successfully introduced wines from such previously almost unknown winegrowing regions as the former Soviet republic of Moldova, Nitra in Slovakia and Mexico. These wines were not chosen for their cheapness – often they sell for more than rivals from France and Italy – nor, solely for their novelty value. To succeed in Britain, they have to represent value for money.

Equally important has been the participation of the British wine trade. Companies ranging from such traditional merchants as Berry Bros & Rudd, Averys and Justerini & Brooks submit wines, competing on level terms against high street chains like Marks and Spencer, Thresher and Sainsbury. It is the buyers from these companies, winemakers from Australia, France, California and Portugal and Britain's most respected wine writers

A team of over 20 prepare bottles for the tastings

who attend the two weeks of the Challenge as tasters. No other event can claim the participation of over three dozen Masters of Wine; members of an august body of whom there are fewer than 200 in the world. The wines are all tasted blind, by panels of five, in sets of 12–18 entries, grouped together by style and approximate price. Tasters are given the prerogative to give as many – or as few – medals as they think are deserved. In real terms this means that awards are made more meanly than in any other competition in the world.

This year, some 5000 of the entries received no medal; only 160 were given Gold Medals, less than three per cent of the entries.

If taking account of price – in effect judging the wines' value for money – is unusual, so is the way in which the Challenge ensures the automatic retasting of wines on which judges have disagreed.

——— A MILITARY OPERATION ———

These aspects of the event require the Challenge to be run like a full-scale military campaign. Preparations begin in January when invitations and entry forms are sent to some 4000 merchants and producers across the globe. During March, the returned entry forms, are meticulously deciphered and entered into the computers without which the event could never take place.

In April, a team of nearly 20 enthusiastic Challenge staff catalogue every bottle before camouflaging them in specially-produced tasting bags with tamper-proof plastic seals. 'Flights' of wines are carefully assembled to ensure that, as far as is possible, oaky blockbusters are not allowed to overshadow subtle, elegant wines.

Finally, at 10am on the first Tuesday of May, it is time for the first wines to confront their judges who have convened at Chelsea Harbour from throughout the world. By now, every flight has been prepared and replacement bottles set out so that corked samples can be replaced in moments. Sparkling wines are in the chiller, vintage ports decanted and bag-in-box wines transferred into bottles.

COLLATING THE RESULTS

From the moment the first sets of tasting notes are handed in, the Challenge staff are busy pumping results into the computers, creating a unique database to which will subsequently be added the details of where and at what price each successful wine is sold. Accuracy is paramount but experience counts; we have learned a great deal since we ran that little tasting back in 1984.

THE TROPHIES

Once the medals were awarded, a select group of judges, including Tim Atkin of *The Observer*, John Avery MW, Hew Blair of Justerini and Brooks, Oz Clarke, Rosemary George MW, Jane Hunt MW, Robert Joseph of *WINE* and *The Sunday Telegraph*, Maggie McNie MW, Charles Metcalfe of *WINE* and Granada TV's *This Morning*, Angela Muir MW, Michael Peace MW, Anthony Rose of *The Independent*, Derek Smedley MW, Jo Standen MW, Kit Stevens MW, Tom Stevenson, author of the *Sothebys World Wine Encyclopedia*, and Stuart Walton of *BBC Good Food Magazine* convened to decide which of the wines were the very best of their kind – the trophies

The first class to be judged, the CHARDONNAYS brought the tricky choice between the 1991 Puligny Montrachet la Truffière from Jean-Marc Boillot and the ultimate winner, a wine from the New World, the **1991 Swanson Vineyards Carneros Chardonnay**.

Next came the SAUVIGNON TROPHY, which, despite tough competition from the Loire and New Zealand, went to an Australian, Tim Knappstein for his **1993 Lenswood**

Sauvignon from a new region high in the hills above Adelaide.

The trophy for the best AROMATIC wine yet again went to the maker of last year's winner **Olivier Zind-Humbrecht**, for his wonderfully powerful-yet-complex **1989 Gewurztraminer Grand Cru Kessler.**

Having decided not to award a trophy in the Germanic class, when they came to the LATE HARVEST class, the judges recognised the skills of **Müller-Catoir**, one of that country's foremost new-wave winemakers whose **1992 Mussbacher Eselhaut Rieslaner Trockenbeer enauslese** showed what can be done with an unconventional grape variety.

Next came the reds, and the fight for the BURGUNDY-STYLE TROPHY, among wines from Mongeard-Mugneret, Perrot-Minot and Domaine de l'Arlot. But the winner went to another familiar Burgundy name, Drouhin, in the shape of a wine made on the other side of the world, the **1990 Domaine Drouhin Oregon Pinot Noir.**

The New World was just as successful in the RHONE-STYLE TROPHY, in which the **1991 Rosemount Show Reserve Syrah** squeaked ahead of such strong contenders as its compatriots, Henschke's Hill of Grace, Penfolds Grange and Rhônes from such producers as Marcel Juge, Guigal and

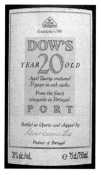

Chateau de Beaucastel. THE ITALY TROPHY offered some widely varying styles. Which is why it was decided to give awards both to the classic **1988 Amarone Capitel Monte Olmi, Azienda Agricola Tedeschi** and the new wave **1989 Marchese di Villamarina** from **Sella & Mosca** which took the prize from such potential champions as 1990 Solaia and 1990 Sassicaia.

Confronted with a set of BORDEAUX STYLE wines such as 1982 Latour, 1990 Lafite and Mouton Rothschild, 1990 Opus One, 1991 Wynns John Riddoch, 1990 Penfolds Bin 707 and 1991 Joseph Phelps Backus, some of the most conservative palates in Britain finally opted for the deliciously oaky-black-currranty **1990 Penfolds Bin 707 Cabernet Sauvignon.**

The Australians triumphed again in the MUSCAT CLASS, with the wonderfully christmas puddingy **Yalumba Museum Show Reserve Rutherglen Muscat.**

Back to the classics, with VINTAGE PORTS including 1985 Fonseca, 1977 Taylors, 1983 Warre's and 1966 Grahams. The winner was none of these; it was a **Quarles Harris** from the unfashionable **1980 vintage**, sharing the trophy with another previous Challenge success, the brilliantly consistent **Dow's 20 Year Old Tawny.**

There were no surprises among the sherries. **Gonzalez Byass** once again took the trophy with their nuttily intense **Matusalem Olo-roso Muy Viejo,** the wine which was awarded the overall FORTIFIED WINE TROPHY.

The Gold Medal SPARKLING WINES ranged from Champagnes such as 1988 Veuve Clicquot, 1983 Charles Heidsieck, Blanc Des Millenaires, 1986 Philiponnat Grand Blanc and 1985 Taittinger Comtes de Champagne, Blanc de Blancs to the 1990 Daniel Le Brun from New Zealand and the 1988 Schramsberg 'J' from California. It was a close race but the wine which scored the highest marks was the **Philip-onnat Grand Blanc, 1986.**

Having chosen the sparkling and fortified wine trophies, all that remained was to decide which of the trophy winners would take the award for overall white and red wine trophies. After long delibera tion, following last year's success by Burgundy, Bordeaux and Alsace, the judges this year awarded both awards to New World wineries on opposite sides of the Pacific. The WHITE WINE TROPHY went to the **1991 Swanson Vineyards Carn-eros Chardonnay,** while the RED WINE TROPHY was won by the **1990 Penfolds Bin 707 Cabernet Sauvignon.**

WINES OF THE YEAR

While selecting the Trophies in each class of the International Wine Challenge, the tasters also chose the WINES OF THE YEAR – a separate award which has been won in the past by such ground-breaking wines as the Montana Marlborough Sauvignon Blanc, Mumm Cuvée Napa Sparkling Wine and Tinto da Anfora from Portugal.

WINES OF THE YEAR are Gold and – in the case of the White and Sparkling wines – Silver medalists which fit the criteria of national availability (at least 10,000 cases) and affordability – (under £5 and £8 for still wines and under £10 for sparkling).

—— WHITE WINES OF THE YEAR ——

It is ironic that the first time the award has been won by a Sauvignon Blanc from France, it proved to be neither a Loire nor a Bordeaux, but the **1993 La Serre Sauvignon Blanc, Vin de Pays d'Oc, 1993** made by an Englishman, the ubiquitous Hugh Ryman.

A far less familiar style is to be found in the **1993 Cafayate Torrontes** by **Arnaldo Etchart**, a dry-but-grapey wine produced in

Argentina from the wonderful local Muscat-like Torrontes grape.

— RED WINES OF THE YEAR —

Australia did well again with both the **1990** and **1991** of the black-currranty **Penfolds Coonawarra Cabernet** having independently chosen, along with the **1993 Rosemount Cabernet-Shiraz**, a juicy-fruity wine which offers a very different style of wine from the Aussies most people will have encountered.

The mouth-wateringly strawberryish **1993 Solana Cencibel Valdepeñas** is not most people's immediate idea of a Spanish red, either, but this Gold Medal winner, jointly made by visiting Australian, Don Lewis of Mitchelton and the **Casa de la Viña** is a great example of the wine revolution now taking place in Spain.

The New World is rapidly mastering great value Champagne-method fizz with Australia and South Africa each producing a SPARKLING WINE OF THE YEAR. The **Bergkelder's Pongracz** is South Africa's second Sparkling Wine of the Year in a row, while **Yalumba** deserves to be congratulated for winning the same award twice with its biscuity-fruity **Cuvée 1 Prestige Pinot Noir-Chardonnay.**

HOW TO USE THIS BOOK

Every wine in this guide has been awarded a medal at the **1994 International Wine Challenge**. We have listed the winning wines by country and region with up to seven wine headings; red, dry white, medium white, sweet white, rosé, sparkling and fortified.

Under each of these headings the wines are listed in price order, from the least to the most expensive. Every wine carries the same range of information; the wine name (and vintage where applicable), the tasting note, the average retail price, the code for stockists (see page 282), and the medal the wine was awarded. Below is an example of how the wines are listed, showing the meaning of each column.

There is also a complete alphabetical index starting on page 290 and a listing of white and red wines under £5, and sparkling wines under £10 starting on page 272..

With all this information we are sure you will make the best decisions about which wines best suit your palate and wallet.

The wine name, vintage and region	*The average retail price*	*The Medals; G Gold, S Silver, B Bronze*	
ST AMOUR, SYLVAIN FESSY 1993 Beaujolais	*Fresh elegant mulberry fruit aroma with hint of spiciness. Positively overflowing with fruit.*	**£8.54**	LAV, WIN	S

The description provided by Challenge tasters.	*Codes for stockists (see page 282)*

THE
WINES

AUSTRALIA

Fast overtaking California as the most reliable source of New World wines, Australia is now surprising observers with its readiness to develop new regions and create new styles which stand alongside the ultra-fruity blockbusters with which it first made its name internationally. Clear regional styles do exist, but there is an increasingly wide range of wines being produced throughout the continent.

RED				
SOMERFIELD AUSTRALIAN DRY RED, PENFOLDS Southeast Australia	*Medium-bodied in a lighter, modern style with full fruit flavours and a long finish.*	£3.19	SMF, G	B
RYANS CREEK SHIRAZ/CABERNET, YALUMBA	*Mature, minty character to nose; good cabernet fruit flavours and length. Classy finish.*	£3.49	VW	B
ASDA SOUTH AUSTRALIAN SHIRAZ, ANGOVES 1991 South Australia	*Softly textured wine with complex oak flavours and mature ripe palate with gentle finish.*	£3.69	A	B
SOMERFIELD AUSTRALIAN CABERNET SAUVIGNON, PENFOLDS Southeast Australia	*Cedary and dusty, ripe, up-front fruit, richness of flavour. Soft and complex with clean finish.*	£3.99	SMF, G	B
PETER LEHMANN BAROSSA VALLEY GRENACHE 1989 Barossa Valley	*Fleshy fruit and lively acidity collide in a balanced, drinkable wine that is smooth and long.*	£3.99	OD, PLE, DBY	B
TESCO AUSTRALIAN MATARO, KINGSTON ESTATE Southeast Australia	*Sweet red berry fruit and toasty new oak flavours. An intense and drinkable wine.*	£3.99	TO	B

DRY PLAINS SHIRAZ CABERNET, BERRI ESTATES 1993 Murray Valley	*Rich, ripe peppery fruit, raspberry flavours and good acidity. Lively, young and balanced.*	£3.99	Widely available	B
HARDY'S NOTTAGE HILL CABERNET SAUVIGNON, BRL HARDY WINE CO 1992 South Australia	*Good soft fruit nose; young, clean, simple structure. Leafy fruit.*	£4.39	Widely available	B
MCWILLIAMS HANWOOD CABERNET SAUVIGNON 1991 New South Wales	*Good fruit extract and freshness. Complex flavours and tannins may all be found here.*	£4.39	MRN, DBY	B
PENFOLDS BIN 35 SHIRAZ/CABERNET 1992 South Australia	*Medium weight. Spicy wood and raspberry fruit flavours. Attractive and drinkable.*	£4.39	Widely Available	B
RYECROFT FLAME TREE CABERNET SHIRAZ 1993 McLaren Vale	*Fruit with oak influence and cherries galore. Full of character through to long finish.*	£4.49	HAD, BAR, HAL, GRT, BWI, DBY	S
PENFOLDS BIN 2 SHIRAZ-MOURVEDRE 1992 South Australia	*Aromatic, savoury nose, spicy summer fruit richness on palate. Strong finish. Big and beefy.*	£4.75	Widely Available	B
PENFOLDS ROWLANDS BROOK SHIRAZ 1991 South Australia	*Rich blackcurrant from well-defined palate. Natural fruit acidity. Balanced full flavours.*	£4.75	L&W, SHJ,	B
ROSEMOUNT CABERNET SAUVIGNON/SHIRAZ 1993 Southeast Australia	*Peppery and vegetal aromas; ripe in the mouth, well textured and soft tannins.*	£4.95	JS, SAV, BWC	G
ROSEMOUNT SHIRAZ/CABERNET SAUVIGNON 1993 Southeast Australia	*Lovely soft fruit, quite sweet but balanced by hints of spice and meat. Complex and rich.*	£4.99	TO, NUR, JN, CWS, FUL, GRT, WES, DBY	B

TOLLANA BLACK LABEL CABERNET SAUVIGNON, PENFOLDS 1991 Southeast Australia	*Red fruit and mint on nose; ripe, light fruit palate. Good structure.*	£4.99	TH, WR, BU, TDS	B
PEWSEY VALE VINEYARD CABERNET SAUVIGNON, S SMITH & SON 1990 Eden Valley	*Classic cedary, herbal, aromatic nose. Rich fruit and well balanced. Quite tannic, so needs ageing.*	£4.99	TO	B
DEAKIN ESTATE CABERNET SAUVIGNON, KATNOOK 1992	*Ripe cedar nose, rich, ripe fruit palate. Full and well structured.*	£4.99	VW	B
TOLLANA BLACK LABEL SHIRAZ, PENFOLDS 1991 South Australia	*Meaty fruit, good spice and weight with hint of oak. Rich and long, has a promising future.*	£4.99	TH, WR, BU, TDS	S
PARROT'S HILL SHIRAZ, BRL HARDY WINE CO/VALLEY GROWERS 1992 Barossa Valley	*Concentrated black cherry nose and palate, herby overtones and a silky finish.*	£4.99	WHC	B
LINDEMAN'S BIN 50 SHIRAZ 1992 Southeast Australia	*Well-made wine with good weight and struc- ture. Spice, pepper and fresh fruitcake flavours.*	£4.99	WSO, W, U, MRN, POR, BEF, DBY	B
ROUGE HOMME SHIRAZ/CABERNET 1991 Coonawarra	*Good earthy nose, spicy wood aromas, fruit and plum-pudding flavours. A delicious mouthful.*	£4.99	HAM, CHH, RBS, SAN, H&H, FUL, DBY	G
ROO'S LEAP SHIRAZ CABERNET, MILDARA 1992 Coonawarra	*Dark crimson/red wine, plummy and liquorice aromas with some sweet oak. Powerful, meaty.*	£4.99	JTD, P&R, THP, PHI, GRT	S
MILDARA CHURCH HILL SHIRAZ/CABERNET 1991 Southeast Australia	*Full range of flavours, from spicy onion soup aroma, to rich, dark chocolate and spicy fruit.*	£4.99	MWW, PHI, GS, AUC, GRT	B

ST. MICHAEL McLAREN VALE SHIRAZ, ANDREW GARRETT 1992 McLaren Vale	*Tart, brambley fruit and rich coconut sweetness. Big wine with glorious length and minty tones.*	£4.99	M&S	B
KRONDORF SHIRAZ/CABERNET 1991 South Australia	*Lovely colour, good fruit concentration and a subtle use of oak.*	£5.00	GS, PHI, AUS	B
MONTARA `M' SHIRAZ PINOT NOIR 1992 Ararat	*Mature, raspberry jam nose of full ripe fruit is followed by spicy tannins in a refined finish.*	£5.00	ADN, SOM, CHF, BOO, AMW	B
DAVID WYNN SHIRAZ CABERNET 1993 Eden Valley	*Lovely, smokey berry fruit. Young and attractively free of oak.*	£5.20	SOM, JAR	B
LEASINGHAM DOMAINE CABERNET MALBEC 1992 Clare Valley	*Good black colour. Plenty of opulent smoky oak and fresh berry fruit. Great wine for a fiver.*	£5.45	OD, DBY	B
LEASINGHAM DOMAINE SHIRAZ 1992 Clare Valley	*Rich vanilla on nose, berry and bramble fruit concentration follows. Demands to be drunk.*	£5.45	OD	S
WYNDHAM ESTATE BIN 444 CABERNET SAUVIGNON 1992 Southeast Australia	*Dark centre and intense ruby rim. Mint and redcurrant jelly on nose. Perfectly balanced.*	£5.49	MWW, MRS, HAL, A&A, WCO, DBY	S
YALDARA SHIRAZ 1992 Southeast Australia	*Elegant, with good weight, ripe blackcurrants, salt and pepper savouriness. Lean finish.*	£5.49	BTH, MIT, WON, RWW, PLA	B
PENFOLDS KOONUNGA HILL SHIRAZ-CABERNET 1992 South Australia	*Sweet chestnut aroma, complex berry fruit flavours, good acid bite and dryish tannins.*	£5.49	Widely Available	B

PETER LEHMANN SHIRAZ 1990 Barossa Valley	*Integrated oak flavours on nose. Excellent mid-palate. Refreshing and totally enjoyable.*	**£5.49**	OD, JMC, GNW, PLE, DBY, DIO	**S**
WYNNS COONAWARRA ESTATE SHIRAZ 1992 Coonawarra	*Huge density of fruit on nose. Firm tannins suggest will develop further. A sleeping beauty!*	**£5.50**	TH, VW, OD, WR, BV, DBY	**S**
BASEDOWS SHIRAZ 1990 Barossa Valley	*Tomato and raspberry flavours with soft vanilla oak. Can stand alone or turn supper into a meal.*	**£5.50**	BI	**S**
WINDY PEAK CABERNET MERLOT, DE BORTOLI 1992 Victoria	*Deep garnet colour. Opulent, minty, blackcurrant on nose. Long fragrant finish.*	**£5.69**	SAF	**S**
D'ARENBERG D'ARRY'S ORIGINAL SHIRAZ GRENACHE 1991 McLaren Vale	*Rich dense nose, full blackcurrant fruit and a tannic finish. Ideal with full-flavoured food.*	**£5.82**	WS, WES	**B**
MOONDAH BROOK CABERNET SAUVIGNON 1991 Western Australia	*Good Cabernet nose with soft spicy fruits. Plummy, rich, with good length and balance.*	**£5.89**	SAF, DBY, DIO	**B**
ROTHBURY ESTATE SHIRAZ 1992 Southeast Australia	*Huge nose. Full ripe blackcurrant flavours that are well-balanced. Long rich finish.*	**£5.95**	D, ABY, GRT, DBY	**G**
HARDY'S CHATEAU REYNELLA CABERNET MERLOT 1992 South Australia	*Strong, spicy Cabernet nose with toasty, vanilla new oak. Deep, rich palate.*	**£5.99**	JMC, NVN, CWS, OD, WHC, NRW, DBY	**G**
HOUGHTON GOLD RESERVE CABERNET SAUVIGNON 1988 Western Australia	*Dark, rich and oaky. Vegetal, ripe character on nose with impression of some maturity.*	**£5.99**	IRV, CWN, AR	**B**

PARROT'S HILL SHIRAZ, BRL HARDY WINE CO-OP, 1992, VALLEY GROWERS, Barossa Valley	*Concentrated, Black-cherry nose and palate, with herby overtones. Good balance.*	**£5.99**	IVY	**B**
PREECE CABERNET SAUVIGNON, MITCHELTON,1992, Southeast	*Minty, eucalyptus nose, leading to spiced fruits in the mouth. Good depth and length.*	**£5.99**	OD, JMC, GNW, HOU, DBY	**B**
MOODAH BROOK CABERNET SAUVIGNON, 1992	*Soft, perfumed berry nose. Hint of mint and blackcurrant fruit. Good length.*	**£5.99**	SAF	**B**
MOUNT HURTLE CABERNET SAUVIGNON/MERLOT, GEOFF MERRILL 1989 McLaren Vale	*Deep mulberry colour, soft wood and raisiny fruit nose. Gently oaky with great finesse.*	**£5.99**	G, PLE	**B**
ROSEMOUNT CABERNET SAUVIGNON 1992 Southeast Australia	*Brooding, black cherry colour. Blackcurrant, tar and tobacco on the nose. Soft mulberries on palate.*	**£5.99**	Widely Available	**S**
HARDY'S CHATEAU REYNELLA CABERNET SAUVIGNON, BRL HARDY WINE CO 1991 South Australia	*Purple black. Concentration of blackcurrants on nose with sweet berry flavours and new oak.*	**£5.99**	G, WB, DU, WHC, NRW, DBY	**B**
MICHELTON PREECE CABERNET SAUVIGNON 1992 Southeast Australia	*Deep, rich colour. Complex, nose and spiced fruits in the mouth. Good depth and length.*	**£5.99**	OD, JMC, PHI, GNW, HOU, DBY	**B**
GRAMPS CABERNET SAUVIGNON/MERLOT/CABERNET FRANC, 1989 Southeast Australia	*Blackcurranty nose with a hint of maturity. Sweet, rich and fruitcakey with a toasty oaky finish.*	**£5.99**	WTR, DIO, GSH, JCK, PEA, CAX, DIO	**B**

MOUNT HURTLE SHIRAZ, GEOFF MERRILL 1991 McLaren Vale	*Huge mouthful of berry fruit and black pepper spice. Well-balanced with real potential to develop into a classic.*	£5.99	OD, PLE	S
SALTRAM METALA SHIRAZ/CABERNET 1992 Longhorne Creek	*Touch of tar and oak on nose, juicy, ripe berries. Chunky texture. Teeth-coating tannins.*	£5.99	OD	B
CHATEAU REYNELLA BASKET-PRESSED SHIRAZ, BRL HARDY WINE CO 1991 South Australia	*Ripe, peppery spicy nose with fruit flavours and a touch of sweet oak. Good new world style.*	£5.99	W, OD, R, WHC	B
PETER LEHMANN CABERNET SAUVIGNON 1992 Barossa Valley	*Closed at first, develops in the glass. Oak and berry fruits with marzipan. Quite rich and long.*	£6.00	W, OD, HN, PLE, DBY	B
ROTHBURY ESTATE SHIRAZ 1993 Hunter Valley	*Gamey flavours with clove and pepper. Fruit flavour finish.*	£6.00	L&W, GRT, DBY	G
DAVID WYNN SHIRAZ 1992 Eden Valley	*Ripe, juicy fruit under spicy, peppery flavours. Not finely balanced but delicious all the same.*	£6.10	ADN, MRT, WL, SOM, DBY	B
ROWAN CABERNET MERLOT, ROTHBURY 1992 Northeast Victoria	*A vegetal, slightly smoky nose. Big in the mouth, with coffee flavours.*	£6.25	VW	B
TRENTHAM ESTATE MERLOT 1992 New South Wales	*Some maturity. Spicy, herbaceous nose with overlaying soft berry fruits. Drinking now.*	£6.29	SK, PAL	B
HARDY COLLECTION COONAWARRA CABERNET SAUVIGNON 1992 South Australia	*Deep, inky colour. Minty, nose with vanillary new wood. Sweet cassis fruit and soft tannins.*	£6.35	OD, JMC, HOU, WHC	B

CHATEAU TAHBILK CABERNET SAUVIGNON 1989 Goulburn Valley	*Concentrated chocolate and eucalyptus nose. Complex, warm, full middle palate.*	**£6.39**	OD, DBY	**B**
PENFOLDS BIN 28 KALIMNA SHIRAZ 1991 South Australia	*Spicy wood flavours and rich fruit dominate full-bodied wine of excellent depth and length.*	**£6.39**	Widely Available	**B**
GOUNDREY LANGTON CABERNET SAUVIGNON 1992 Mount Barker	*Good full colour. Faintly burnt nose of oak and berry fruit. Jammy palate with aromatic finish.*	**£6.49**	AD, RHV, WON, WWN, GRT	**B**
SALTRAM MAMRE BROOK CABERNET 1993 Barossa Valley	*Ruby red. Ripe, black fruits on nose with substantial oak. Sweet on palate with long finish.*	**£6.49**	OD	**S**
SALTRAM PINNACLE SELECTION CABERNET 1993 Barossa Valley	*Deep red colour. Fine nose with complex coffee and vanilla aromas. Full and ripe in the mouth.*	**£6.49**	OD	**S**
BRIDGEWATER MILL MILLSTONE SHIRAZ, PETALUMA 1991 South Australia	*Tremendous, vibrant colour, sweet marzipan nose. Will become more generous with age.*	**£6.49**	OD	**B**
SIMON HACKETT CABERNET/SHIRAZ 1990	*Soft fruit and delicate spice. Lots of ripe berry fruit flavours; good definition. Spicy oak.*	**£6.50**	MWW, DBY	**B**
YALDARA CABERNET/MERLOT 1990 Barossa Valley	*Brick-red colour. Good old Bordeaux nose. Long, rich, oaky palate. Drink now.*	**£6.50**	MIT, VDV, SW	**S**
WYNNS COONAWARRA ESTATE CABERNET SHIRAZ 1990 Coonawarra	*Rich, plummy nose. Good concentration of ripe fruit and soft tannins - very attractive.*	**£6.50**	SAF, DBY	**B**

BROWN BROTHERS KING VALLEY SHIRAZ 1991 Northeast Victoria	*Eucalyptus and mint nose, full intense fruit flavours on palate with well-constructed finish.*	**£6.50**	MWW, OD, THP, GRO, CPW, NRW, DBY	**B**
PENFOLDS BIN 128 COONAWARRA SHIRAZ 1991 Coonawarra	*Meaty nose. Weighty palate of minty fruit and vanilla oak, plenty of tannins. Solid stuff.*	**£6.50**	FUL, MWW, MAR, TO, WL, ABY, BEF, DBY	**B**
BAILEY'S CLASSIC SHIRAZ 1992 Northeast Victoria	*Intense, ripe, berry fruit nose. Mouthfilling, rich cherry/raspberry taste. Medium finish.*	**£6.75**	OD	**B**
RYMILL WINERY, THE RIDDOCH RUN COONAWARRA SHIRAZ 1991 Coonawarra	*Concentrated black fruit nose. Cherry and black-currant fruit. Well rounded and balanced.*	**£6.89**	L&W, SHJ,	**S**
LANGI CABERNET, MOUNT LANGI GHIRAN 1991 Victoria	*Deep, opaque ruby. Slight green leaves on the nose. Good depth.*	**£6.99**	OD, WCE, DBY	**S**
YALUMBA FAMILY RESERVE CABERNET MERLOT 1990 Southeast Australia	*Well-made with good fruit and structure, this is attractive and should develop well.*	**£6.99**	WOC, CAC, JN, DBY	**B**
THE MENZIES CABERNET SAUVIGNON, YALUMBA 1991 Coonawarra	*Black-red colour. Cigar box and chocolate nose. Strong flavours of cher-ry and blackcurrant.*	**£6.99**	LAV, WIN, JN, OD, JS	**G**
GOUNDREY LANGTON CABERNET MERLOT 1992 Mount Barker	*Full colour. Forward bouquet of vanilla oak and red fruit. Cherry and strawberry palate.*	**£6.99**	AD, CEB, W, WON, LV, CEB	**B**
ROUGE HOMME CABERNET SAUVIGNON 1991 Coonawarra	*Very New World minty cassis style. Full-bodied with lots of sweet fruit.*	**£6.99**	Widely Available	**B**

FOREST HILL CABERNET SAUVIGNON, VASSE FELIX 1991 Mount Barker	*Deep garnet coloured wine with overt cedary bouquet; very claret-like perfume. Slightly earthy*	£6.99	LAV, WIN	**B**
ST HALLETT'S CABERNET SAUVIGNON/CABERNET FRANC/MERLOT 1992 Barossa Valley	*Deep purple. Complex fruit-packed nose. Good extract, full, rich fruit and herby character. Good balance.*	£6.99	JS, AUC, RD, DBY, SUM	**S**
DELATITE MERLOT 1992 Victoria	*Minty nose. Peppery with vanillary new oak. Give it three to five years.*	£6.99	AUC	**B**
TIM KNAPPSTEIN CABERNET/MERLOT 1991 South Australia	*Mint chocolate and black-currant nose. Absurdly fruity and minty on the palate. Easy drinking.*	£6.99	OD	**B**
RIDDOCH CABERNET SHIRAZ, KATNOOK PTY LTD 1991 Coonawarra	*Red fruit and vanilla on the palate, Rioja style. Delicate in the mouth. Good length.*	£6.99	TH, WR, BU, GSH, NRW, BI	**S**
BROKENWOOD CABERNET SAUVIGNON 1991 Hunter Valley	*Rich, spicy nose. Oaky sweet fruit with hint of coffee. Concentrated and elegant.*	£6.99	NY, LV, RES, WH, H&H	**B**
MITCHELTON RESERVE CABERNET SAUVIGNON 1991 Southeast Australia	*Deep coloured. Cassis/ raspberry flavours - creamy and fine. Good length and clean finish.*	£6.99	BWL, DBY, COK, RAM, GRT, DBY	**S**
MILDARA COONAWARRA CABERNET SAUVIGNON 1991 Coonawarra	*Blackberry fruit with a good balance of tannins. A warm and jammy style.*	£6.99	OD, PHI, LUV, GSH	**B**
WIRRA WIRRA CHURCH BLOCK RED 1992 McLaren Vale	*Classy Bordeaux-style nose. Juicy and concentrated with raspberry and chocolate. Rich and soft.*	£6.99	WSO, D, WOI, SOM, THP, DBY	**S**

WOLF BLASS YELLOW LABEL CABERNET SAUVIGNON 1992 Southeast Australia	*Fruity, intense wine; full, elegant nose, well-balanced with sweetish raspberry flavour.*	£6.99	Widely Available	**B**
ROTHBURY SHIRAZ 1991 Hunter Valley	*Curranty liquorice aromas, tannic structure with strong oak flavours. A wine for the future.*	£6.99	VW, DBY	**B**
PRIMO ESTATE SHIRAZ 1991 Adelaide Plains	*Mature fruit nose, savoury mincemeat flavours and smooth chocolate texture.*	£6.99	AUC	**B**
TALTARNI SHIRAZ 1991 Victoria	*Nicely balanced Syrah characteristics - good interplay between fruit, acidity, and tannins.*	£6.99	RD, LAY, TP	**B**
YALUMBA FAMILY RESERVE SHIRAZ 1990 Barossa Valley	*Herbaceous/balsamic aromas, chewy red fruit on palate, elegant acidity, good tannins.*	£6.99	AUC, CAC, WOC, JN	**B**
WATER WHEEL BENDIGO SHIRAZ 1992 Bendigo	*Deep colour with almost leathery, shoe polish aromas. Gutsy and concentrated with body.*	£6.99	AUC	**S**
PETER LEHMANN CLANCY'S AUSTRALIAN RED 1991 Barossa Valley	*Creamily textured with savoury oak and spiced cooked fruit flavours of plums and damsons.*	£6.99	OD, JS, PLE, DBY	**B**
MITCHELL'S CABERNET SAUVIGNON 1991 Clare Valley	*Spicy with mint and blackcurrant aroma. Lots of fruit and tannin. Drink now or keep.*	£7.00	L&W, SHJ, G&M, LS, HOT,	**S**
WYNNS COONAWARRA ESTATE CABERNET SHIRAZ 1989 Coonawarra	*Deep, dark and mysterious. Massive fruit flavours and good length. Very nice.*	£7.00	SAF	**B**

WYNNS COONAWARRA ESTATE CABERNET SHIRAZ 1988 Coonawarra	*Blackcurrant, sweet, rich and lovely fruit flavours. Soft and ready. Some oak.*	£7.00	VW, OD	B
JAMIESONS RUN RED, MILDARA 1991 Coonawarra	*Clean and fresh character brilliantly structured. Plenty of fruit flavours and lots of length.*	£7.00	VW, THP, D, GRT, FUL, DBY	G
EDEN RIDGE CABERNET SAUVIGNON, ADAM WYNN 1992 Eden Valley	*Mint and blackcurrant nose. Concentrated, almost fat fruit flavours with a soft, long finish.*	£7.00	ADN, CHF, BOO, VER, HPD, DBY	B
BUCKLEYS BAROSSA VALLEY GRENACHE 1992 Barossa Valley	*Meaty, rich and spicy with rustic nose, blackcurrant flavours, oaky finish. Young but accomplished.*	£7.00	AUC	B
MITCHELL PEPPERTREE SHIRAZ 1992 Clare Valley	*Peppery nose with aromas of new oak. Rich, chewy fruit. Characterful wine giving good value.*	£7.00	L&W, SHJ, G&M, LS, HOT,	S
TALTARNI SHIRAZ 1990 Pyrenees, Victoria	*Rich dark plummy hue, aromatic spice and full fat fruit flavours. Herbaceous, warm and generous.*	£7.00	RD, LAY, TP, DBY	G
ROCKFORD DRY COUNTRY GRENACHE 1992 Barossa Valley	*Medium-bodied with a light, toasty oak nose, pleasant jammy fruit and some spicy tannins.*	£7.20	ADN	B
CABERNET MERLOT, HUNTINGTON ESTATE 1989 Mudgee	*Big, rich, beefy, nose. Good length of ripe, burnt, sweet fruit on palate. Great class.*	£7.25	ORG	S
SEPPELT HARPERS RANGE CABERNET SAUVIGNON 1991	*Full-bodied with sweet cassis and vanilla flavour. Good balance; drink now.*	£7.30	OD, VW, DBY	B

KRONDORF CABERNET SAUVIGNON 1990 Barossa	*Rich, ripe, oakey. Touch of blackcurrant. Traditional Austrian style.*	£7.30	GS, PHI	**B**
KRONDORF LIMITED RELEASE CABERNET SAUVIGNON 1989	*Good intensity; blackcurranty and jammy. Concentrated with good acidity.*	£7.39	VW	**B**
SHAREFARMERS BLEND, PETALUMA 1990 Coonawarra	*Vanilla, oak and blackcurrant nose with full blackcurrant flavour. Stylish and light.*	£7.39	LAV, WIN	**B**
TIM KNAPPSTEIN CABERNET/MERLOT 1992 South Australia	*Fine, strong, cedar nose, with nice sweet fruit, quite tannic. Rich texture.*	£7.49	OD	**B**
CAMPBELLS BOBBIE BURNS SHIRAZ 1992 Rutherglen	*Magnificent bouquet of tar, leather and peppery Syrah character. Sweet fruit balanced by good tannins.*	£7.49	PHI, CPW, GNW, LKN, H&H	**G**
ST HALLETT'S BAROSSA SHIRAZ 1992 Barossa Valley	*Exotic tangerine nose. Plenty of ripe fruit fleshiness and soft tannic structure.*	£7.49	WR, AUC	**S**
WYNNS COONAWARRA ESTATE CABERNET SAUVIGNON 1991 Coonawarra	*Rich, Port-like palate, capsicum character and light, red-berry fruit nose. Strong fruit flavours.*	£7.50	VW, OD, DBY	**G**
HILL-SMITH ESTATE CABERNET SAUVIGNON/SHIRAZ 1991 Eden Valley	*Good fruit and gentle oak treatment. Quite long and well balanced. Has potential.*	£7.50	ADN, RAC, W	**B**
STONIER'S PINOT NOIR 1992 Mornington Peninsula	*Raspberry boiled-sweet nose with palate full of fruit balanced by soft tannins. Long with depth.*	£7.50	WAW, HOL, PV	**G**

PENLEY ESTATE HYLAND SHIRAZ 1992 Coonawarra	*Rich oak flavours, minty spice and zesty raspberry/redcurrant fruit.*	£7.50	WTR, AUC, L&W	B
EDEN RIDGE SHIRAZ, ADAM WYNN 1992 Eden Valley	*Solid dark cherry fruit flavours with minimal spice and touch of oak. Good structure and texture.*	£7.50	CHF, RAM, DBY, CWI, JAR, DBY	S
PENLEY ESTATE CABERNET SAUVIGNON 1991 Coonawarra	*Lovely strawberry jam sweetness and simple blackcurrant flavours; nice balance.*	£7.65	AUC, WTR, L&W	B
DAVID WYNN PATRIARCH SHIRAZ 1992 Eden Valley	*Ripe berry fruit, hints of chocolate and white pepper spice with soft, leathery tannins. Excellent.*	£7.85	ADN, TDS, BOO, AMW, CHF	S
TUNNEL HILL PINOT NOIR, TARRAWARRA VINEYARDS 1993 Yarra Valley	*Strawberries and cherries on nose with ripe, open fruit. Round and rich, with good balance.*	£7.89	AUC, PHI, DBY	S
MONTARA VINEYARD SHIRAZ 1992 Victoria	*Tarry nose, spice and Port-like fruit; good oak balance and long finish. A huge character.*	£7.95	ADN, BOO	B
HUNTINGTON ESTATE CABERNET SAUVIGNON, 1990 Mudgee	*Sweet, rich and full nose; spicy blackcurrant flavour. Real potential. Needs two to three years.*	£7.95	LSI	B
PENFOLDS COONAWARRA CABERNET SAUVIGNON 1991 Coonawarra	*Deep colour. Oaky character, almost Port-like in texture. Woodland-berry nose. Very well focused.*	£7.99	SAF, VW, TH, JS, WR, D, NRW, DBY, OD	G
PENFOLDS COONAWARRA CABERNET SAUVIGNON 1990 Coonawarra	*Full and flavoursome. Young, fresh berry and wood character with good depth of flavours.*	£7.99	SAF, VW, TH, JS, WR, NRW, ABY, DBY,OD	G

CAPE MENTELLE CABERNET SAUVIGNON 1991 Margaret River, West Australia	*Full, rich, blackcurrant. Medium tannins with ripe fruit. Long finish.*	**£7.99**	ADN, SEL, CON, TAN	**B**
WYNNS COONAWARRA ESTATE CABERNET SAUVIGNON 1990 Coonawarra	*Inky black, deep purple. Intense fruit flavours and clean blackcurrant/ eucalyptus nose.*	**£7.99**	VW, OD	**S**
PENFOLDS BIN 389 CABERNET-SHIRAZ 1991 South Australia	*Deeply coloured wine, vanilla and blackcur- rants. Ripeness and tannins.*	**£7.99**	Widely Available	**B**
WOODSTOCK CABERNET SAUVIGNON 1991 McLaren Vale	*Strong, morello cherry, almost Port-like nose, with new oak. Warming and peppery on palate.*	**£7.99**	BAR	**B**
HOLLICK COONAWARRA RED 1991 Coonawarra	*Sweet pepper and ripe blackberry aromas. Touch of oak, well integrated with jammy stewed fruit.*	**£7.99**	MMW, F&M, WWI, R	**S**
ST HUGO CABERNET SAUVIGNON, ORLANDO WINES 1989 Coonawarra	*Complex, spicy nose with mint and vanilla. Plummy, blackberry fruit palate.*	**£7.99**	JS, U, JSN, AUC, MHW, CAX, SPR, DBY	**B**
TALTARNI MERLOT 1991 Pyrenees	*Nice fruity nose with some wood. Dry, acidic tawny wood tannins. Good long finish.*	**£7.99**	RD, FSW, CAC	**S**
TALTARNI CABERNET SAUVIGNON 1988 Pyrenees	*Nice fruit and wood bouquet; cassis and cedar. Good, fruity, ripe flavours on mid-palate.*	**£7.99**	TP, T&W, LAY	**S**
BROKENWOOD SHIRAZ 1991 Hunter Valley	*Unusually fragrant, chocolatey and spicy with ripe berry fruit flavours. Full bodied.*	**£7.99**	NY, LV, RES, WH, H&H	**S**

MOUNT LANGI GHIRAN, LANGI SHIRAZ 1991 Victoria	*Elegant, minty aromas, peppery spice and subtle raspberry flavours. Great depth and complexity.*	**£7.99**	OD, WCE, H&H, SEB, DBY	**S**
CHAPEL HILL SHIRAZ 1991 McLaren Vale	*Minty, creamy palate with damson fruit and soft tannins. Nicely structured. Smooth finish.*	**£7.99**	TO, WR	**B**
CAPE MENTELLE CABERNET MERLOT 1991 Margaret River, West Australia	*Nice, complex oak and fruit body; rhubarb. Lovely sweet fruit and firm tannins.*	**£7.99**	THP, EUR, HHC, MMW, FTH	**B**
ORLANDO LAWSONS PADTHAWAY SHIRAZ 1989 Padthaway	*Cedar and dark cherry aromas, fresh minty palate and fine tannic finish. Full-flavoured.*	**£7.99**	WTR, PEA, JCK, HN, OD, SPR, CAX, DIO	**B**
ST HUGO CABERNET SAUVIGNON, ORLANDO WINES 1990 Coonawarra	*Good ripe, blackcurrant fruit, flavoursome with soft tannins.*	**£8.00**	JS, U, JSN, AUC, MHW, SPR, CAX	**B**
PIKES POLISH HILL CABERNET SAUVIGNON 1991 Clare Valley	*Sweet, ripe cassis and new wood on nose. Incredible density and concentration of jammy red fruit.*	**£8.00**	ADN, RAM, UBC, DBY, PAV	**G**
WIRRA WIRRA R S.W SHIRAZ 1992 McLaren Vale	*Clean, fresh and vibrant. Ripe, concentrated fruit, minty aromas and tarry, tannic texture.*	**£8.00**	OD, BBR, WOI, FUL	**S**
PENFOLDS BIN 407 CABERNET SAUVIGNON 1991 South Australia	*Young brambley nose. Rich luscious fruit with good tannins. Well-balanced and good depth.*	**£8.10**	WR, TH, BU, CEL, BTH	**B**
PLATT'S CABERNET SAUVIGNON 1991 Mudgee	*Intense colour. Nose of plums and cherries, lightly oaked. Clean and crisp with a firm finish.*	**£8.35**	TP, LSI	**B**

CAPE MENTELLE SHIRAZ 1991 Margaret River	*Chewy, berry fruit, full oak style and youthful green tannins. Full of leather and minty spice.*	**£8.35**	JAR, J&B, HN, BAB, N&P, H&H, DBY, CEB	B
SHOTTESBROOKE VINEYARD CABERNET MERLOT, 1990 McLaren Vale	*Good depth of minty, blackcurrant fruit, a light touch of oak, soft tannin and good length.*	**£8.49**	AUC	B
THOMAS HARDY COONAWARRA RESERVE CABERNET SAUVIGNON 1989 South Australia	*Strong oak and ripe blackberry fruit lifted by a bouquet of mint and blackcurrant leaves.*	**£8.49**	WHC	S
ROSEMOUNT SHOW RESERVE COONAWARRA CABERNET SAUVIGNON 1990 Coonawarra	*Inky colour. Rich, chocolatey, eucalyptus character. Cherry and blackcurrant fruit. Long finish.*	**£8.50**	TO, BU, WR, GRT, DBY, BWC	B
COLDSTREAM HILLS CABERNET MERLOT 1992 Yarra Valley	*Creamy, cedary, plummy fruit, good balance and ripe tannins.*	**£8.50**	PAG, ZAC, OD, W, BWC, DBY	S
COLDSTREAM HILLS PINOT NOIR 1993 Yarra Valley	*Closed nose, but full and round on the palate with long finish.*	**£8.50**	PAG, ZAC, OD, BWC, DIO, DBY	B
HENSCHKE KEYNETON ESTATE SHIRAZ/CABERNET 1991 Adelaide Hills	*Dark purple colour signals full blackcurrant aromas to follow. Dense and weighty.*	**£8.50**	L&W, AUC, WCE, SEB, DBY	S
TYRRELLS VAT 9 SHIRAZ 1990 Hunter Valley	*Starts as it finishes - with lively, fresh fruit flavours and smoky touch of oak. Honest and direct.*	**£8.50**	AV, DBY, CEB, LV	S
R B J THEOLOGICUM, GRENACHE/MOURVEDRE 1993 Barossa Valley	*Warm, luxuriant ripe style with full fruit flavours and concentrated length.*	**£8.69**	AUC	B

D'ARENBERG IRONSTONE PRESSINGS 1991 McLaren Vale	*Nice fresh fruit flavours; high acidity. Nice palate at back and finish. Good wood.*	£8.75	TP, WES	**B**
YALUMBA SIGNATURE RESERVE CABERNET SAUVIGNON/SHIRAZ 1989 South Australia	*Minty, open eucalyptus nose; nice weight with excellent potential. Full, soft palate, warm.*	£8.99	WIN	**S**
CHAPEL HILL CABERNET SAUVIGNON 1992 McLaren Vale	*Inky purple. Sweet, oak-dominated nose. Full-bodied, big and chewy. A cracker.*	£8.99	AUC,	**S**
THE ANGELUS CABERNET SAUVIGNON, WIRRA WIRRA VINEYA 1992 McLaren Vale	*Smooth and supple with a big cherry nose. Soft fruit mid palate and an old oaked character.*	£8.99	OD, BBR, WSO, WOI, SOM, FUL, AUC	**S**
STONIER'S CABERNET 1991 Mornington Peninsula	*Capsicum, wood, cassis and violet bouquet; substantial fruit flavours. An elegant wine.*	£8.99	WAW, HOL, RES, SAC, PV	**S**
PLANTAGENET CABERNET SAUVIGNON 1989 Mount Barker	*Soft oaky nose; fruit flavours. Nice acidity and tannins.*	£8.99	GI	**S**
CHAPEL HILL CABERNET SAUVIGNON 1991 McLaren Vale	*Open, deep plummy nose. Mint, chocolate and black forest fruits on palate. Long and leathery.*	£8.99	AUC, TO	**B**
MICK MORRIS CABERNET SAUVIGNON 1989 Rutherglen	*Scented, soft mint nose. Clean, warm and gently balanced with nice oak.*	£8.99	PEA, WTR, EGL, CDE, DBW, CAX	**S**
PENFOLDS BIN 407 CABERNET SAUVIGNON 1990 South Australia	*Deep colour. Closed nose but hints of dark treacle. Lots of spicy fruit and tannin - good potential.*	£8.99	Widely Available	**B**

HEGGIES VINEYARD CABERNET, S SMITH & SON 1989 Eden Valley	*Nice nose. Juicy fruit and ripe mint flavour on palate. Nice length.*	**£8.99**	LAV, WIN	**B**
EBENEZER CABERNET/ MERLOT/MALBEC 1991, BRL HARDY WINE CO Barossa Valley	*Soft fruity nose and complex flavour. Good fruit on mid-palate. Nice finish and good length.*	**£8.99**	WHC	**S**
CABERNET/SAUVIGNON, GEOFF MERRILL 1988 South Australia	*Deep ruby. Nice mint and fresh fruit. Good mid-palate. Nice finish.*	**£8.99**	OD, PLE	**B**
GEOFF MERRILL CABERNET SAUVIGNON 1989 South Australia	*Medium weight with fruit and gentle oaky character. Light with long finish.*	**£8.99**	OD, PLE	**B**
YALUMBA SIGNATURE RESERVE CABERNET SAUVIGNON/SHIRAZ 1990 South Australia	*Blackcurrant aromas; richness and balance. Well structured wine, fine tannins. Very long.*	**£8.99**	ADN, AUC, DBY, JN	**B**
GOUNDREY WINDY HILL CABERNET SAUVIGNON 1990 Mount Barker	*Raspberries and cream nose. Plenty of sweet fruit and lots of new oak.*	**£8.99**	OBC, GRT	**B**
GOUNDREY WINDY HILL CABERNET SAUVIGNON 1989 Mount Barker	*Good, deep colour and strong oak nose. Complex. Elegant with good length.*	**£8.99**	A, GRT, RWW	**G**
LINDEMAN'S ST GEORGE CABERNET SAUVIGNON 1990 Coonawarra	*Minty, eucalyptus nose. Sweet, ripe fruit. Good acidity and structure.*	**£8.99**	OD, BU, TH, WR, AUC	**B**
LINDEMAN'S ST GEORGE CABERNET SAUVIGNON 1991 Coonawarra	*Strong blackcurrant perfume. Good, ripe fruit and soft tannins. Lingering finnish.*	**£8.99**	OD, BU, TH, WR, AUC, DBY	**S**

PLANTAGENET SHIRAZ 1990 Mount Barker	*Unusual, tarry nose, nice, spicy fruit flavours with a touch of oak and a long finish.*	**£8.99**	GI	**B**
EBENEZER SHIRAZ, BRL HARDY WINE CO/ VALLEY GROWERS 1991 Barossa Valley	*Bold wine, raisiny rich-ness and coffee aroma. Sweet cherry, zippy acid-ity and good structure.*	**£8.99**	WHC	**S**
ROSEMOUNT ESTATE SHOW RESERVE SYRAH 1991 McLaren Vale	*Full-bodied, warm, gutsy Rhône style wine with long smoky flavours and fruit.*	**£8.99**	WR, BU, GRT, BWC	**G**
TIM ADAMS SHIRAZ 1990 Clare Valley	*Great raspberry and cherry flavours and good soft fruit tannins. Long, luscious and lively.*	**£8.99**	BWS, MG, SEL, P&R	**S**
WOLF BLASS PRESIDENT'S SELECTION SHIRAZ 1990 South Australia	*Toffee and plum-pud-ding aromas, sultana and mincemeat flavours. Hugely impressive.*	**£8.99**	CD, BKW, SAF, DBY, DBY, CEB	**G**
COLDSTREAM HILLS CABERNET SAUVIGNON 1990 Yarra Valley	*Forthcoming, developed aroma. Wonderful nose; touch of mint and euca-lyptus. Mature and soft.*	**£9.25**	M&S, BWC, DBY	**B**
DEVIL'S LAIR CABERNET SAUVIGNON 1991 Margaret River	*A classy wine. Berry aromas, blackberries and violets. Quite a heavy palate. Well made.*	**£9.45**	JS, FUL	**G**
BALGOWNIE ESTATE CABERNET SAUVIGNON 1988 Victoria	*Almost black. Nearly Porty nose with a hint of chocolate. Superbly tarry. Needs about four years.*	**£9.49**	PHI	**G**
KATNOOK CABERNET SAUVIGNON 1990 Coonawarra	*Serious nose; sweet, soft fruits. Good upright structure, creamy oak character. Long finish.*	**£9.50**	PON, ELV, AUC, GSH, BI	**B**

Wolf Blass President's Selection Cabernet Sauvignon 1989 Langhorne Creek	*Elegant with light, fruity nose. Complex flavours. Sweet ripe mid-palate. Superb, a joy to drink.*	**£9.50**	CD, BKW, SAF, ABY, SEA, DBY	**G**
St Hallett's Old Block Shiraz 1991 Barossa Valley	*Vibrant, youthful colour with cherry and strawberry fruit flavours. A subtle yet long finish.*	**£9.50**	WR, TO, F&M, L&W, RD, DBY, AUC	**G**
Rothbury Estate Reserve Shiraz 1993 Hunter Valley	*Minty, mulberry fruit with a touch of New World oak and a hint of spice.*	**£9.95**	OD	**S**
St Hubert's Cabernet Sauvignon 1992 Yarra Valley	*Ripe fruit nose; blackcurrants and oak. Balanced huge fruit flavours. Well made with long future.*	**£9.95**	LAV	**S**
Bailey's 1920s Block Shiraz 1992 Northeast Victoria	*Already showing good tannic structure, firm, spicy fruit and dark chocolate richness.*	**£9.95**	BWS	**B**
Lindeman's Pyrus 1990 Coonawarra	*Super-rich cassis and new-oak nose. Structured but soft, with ample fruit and power.*	**£9.99**	OD, JS, TH, WR, BU, ABY, DBY	**S**
Petaluma Coonawarra Red 1990 Coonawarra	*Soft, very ripe cherry fruit, creamy middle, good weight and balance. Hint of mint.*	**£9.99**	OD, TH, ADN, AUC, ROB	**B**
Lindeman's Pyrus 1991 Coonawarra	*Intense deep blackcurrant character; sweet, jammy nose. Well structured and good length.*	**£9.99**	OD, JS, TH, WR, BU, DBY	**B**
Lindeman's Limestone Ridge Shiraz-Cabernet 1991 Coonawarra	*Spice, oak and berry nose; sweet, syrupy berry fruit character. Rich and ripe.*	**£9.99**	OD, BU, TH, U, MWW, DBY	**B**

TARRAWARRA PINOT NOIR, TARRAWARRA VINEYARDS 1991 Yarra Valley	*Strong almond nose. Strawberries, almonds and spice on palate. Well balanced, softens at end.*	£9.99	AUC, PHI, TO	**B**
ROCKFORD BASKET PRESS SHIRAZ 1990 Barossa Valley	*Ripe cherry flavours from start to finish accompanied by firm tannins.*	£9.99	QR, ADN, WSO, AUC, NY, H&H, LV, DBY	**G**
HARDY'S EILEEN HARDY RESERVE SHIRAZ, BRL HARDY WINE CO 1991 South Australia	*Cedar and blackberry on nose. Damsons and plums on palate. Very appealing.*	£9.99	OD, SAF, WHC, DBY	**S**
KINGSTON ESTATE RESERVE SHIRAZ 1991 South Australia	*Ripe, characterful nose, plummy stewed fruit flavours and a soft, velvety texture.*	£9.99	TO	**B**
PENFOLDS ST HENRI SHIRAZ/CABERNET 1990 South Australia	*Deep purple. Sensational morello cherry flavour. Full succulent finish in a wine that lasts for ages.*	£9.99	MWW, MAR, HAR, F&M, AUC, NRW, DBY	**G**
PENLEY ESTATE SHIRAZ CABERNET 1991 Coonawarra	*Rich, sweet curranty, chocolate aromas. Powerful, good concentration with clean, minty finish.*	£9.99	AUC, WTR, L&W, DIO	**B**
BANNOCKBURN PINOT NOIR 1990 Geelong	*Scarlet. Elegant sweet nose. Light-bodied, with a soft palate of ripe fruits with citric tones.*	£10.00	ADN, BEN, ROB, AUC, ABY	**B**
VASSE FELIX CABERNET SAUVIGNON 1991 Margaret River	*Dry, oaky, vegetal nose. Well-balanced fruit and oak flavours, lovely softness. Developing nicely.*	£10.50	LAV, OD, BEN, ADN, MWW, DBY	**S**
HENSCHKE MOUNT EDELSTONE SHIRAZ 1990 Adelaide Hills	*Big open jammy nose, strawberry fruit flavours, tarry tannins and an agreeable bite of acidity.*	£10.65	L&W, AUC, BOO, GSH, SEB, DBY	**G**

HENSCHKE MOUNT EDELSTONE SHIRAZ 1991 Adelaide Hills	*Syrah fruit and minty eucalyptus with spicy tannins. As delicious as it is well structured.*	£10.65	L&W, AUC, WCE, LV	S
CYRIL HENSCHKE CABERNET SAUVIGNON, 1989 Adelaide Hills	*Medium intensity with mahogany and cherry aromas. Vanilla flavours.*	£10.95	L&W	B
PENLEY ESTATE CABERNET SAUVIGNON 1990 Coonawarra	*Attractive bouquet. Fruity palate with smoky oak. Great length and balance. Has grip and vigour.*	£10.95	WTR, D, SEB	G
ELDERTON COMMAND SHIRAZ 1987 Barossa Valley	*Bread-sauce nose of cloves and milk and peppery fruit palate. Drink it now!*	£10.95	ALL	B
CULLEN'S CABERNET SAUVIGNON/MERLOT 1992 Margaret River	*Herbaceous, spicy and curranty. Intense rich, chocolatey fruit. Excellent finish.*	£10.95	ADN, LWE, DIR, WCE, AMA, ACH, HN	S
PETALUMA COONAWARRA CABERNET/MERLOT 1990 Coonawarra	*Deep purple/black. Soft fruit. Good balance of mint and oak.*	£10.99	AVA, JN, DBY	S
TARRAWARRA PINOT NOIR, TARRAWARRA VINEYARDS 1992 Yarra Valley	*Beautiful bouquet of elegant fruit. Palate is full of character. Long warm finish. Still developing.*	£10.99	AUC, PHI, DBY, TO	S
MITCHELTON PRINT LABEL SHIRAZ 1991 Southeast Australia	*Concentrated, earthy richness with full fruit and stalky tannins. Will smooth its edges with time.*	£10.99	OD, GRT, DBY	B
HOLM OAK VINEYARDS CABERNET SAUVIGNON 1992 Tasmania	*Concentrated fruit nose. Deeply flavoursome but retains freshness. Rich, ripe finish.*	£11.00	DBY, JN, CHF	S

CYRIL HENSCHKE CABERNET SAUVIGNON, 1988 Adelaide Hills	*Brilliant concentrated blackberry cabernet with complexity that goes beyond the oak.*	£11.50	L&W, AUC, GSH, BOO, HVW, SEB, DBY	S
MOSS WOOD CABERNET SAUVIGNON 1992 Margaret River	*Richly textured, deep flavoured and packed with fruit. Vibrant, rich and balanced.*	£11.50	ADN, MIT, F&M, DBY, LV, H&H, DBY, LV	G
CULLEN'S CABERNET SAUVIGNON/MERLOT RESERVE 1991 Margaret River	*Very ripe, curranty, chocolatey style, good, gutsy, cedary with lots of staying power.*	£11.60	DIR	S
PIPER'S BROOK VINEYARD PINOT NOIR 1992 Tasmania	*Complex vegetal and spicy nose. Ripe, spicy fruit on the full palate. Great smooth finish.*	£11.89	AUC, ADN, WTP, DBY, BEN	B
MOUNTADAM PINOT NOIR, ADAM WYNN 1992 Adelaide Hills	*Geranium leaf nose and strawberry fruit flavours. Excellent fruit/tannin.*	£11.90	TDS, DBY, BOO, MRT, BH	B
HENSCHKE ABBOTT'S PRAYER MERLOT/ CABERNET, LENSWOOD 1990 Adelaide Hills	*Spicy, blackcurrant nose and vanilla character. Great length, lovely finish. A very good bottle.*	£11.95	L&W, GSH, SEB, DBY	G
STONIER'S RESERVE PINOT NOIR 1992 Mornington Peninsula	*Full complex nose of raspberry jam. Lots of strawberry fruit on palate.*	£11.95	WAW, LWE, PV	S
COLDSTREAM HILLS RESERVE PINOT NOIR 1992 Yarra Valley	*Strong fruit character, fresh and balanced with strawberry flavours right through to long finish.*	£11.99	PAG, OD, BWC	B
BALGOWNIE ESTATE PINOT NOIR 1989 Victoria	*Open, cherry nose. Full and soft with a long, dry finish. Good drinking now and ages well.*	£11.99	PHI	S

DALWHINNIE SHIRAZ 1991 Pyrenees	*Subtle with chocolate richness, and ripe straw-berry flavours. Firm tannins and complex finish.*	**£12.95**	WTR, SEB	**B**
PETER LEHMANN CABERNET SAUVIGNON/MALBEC 1990 Barossa Valley	*Fruit and mint bouquet; young fruit on palate. Nicely made.*	**£12.99**	OD, PLE	**S**
E&E BLACK PEPPER SHIRAZ, BRL HARDY WINE CO/VALLEY GROWERS 1991 Barossa Valley	*Intense oaky nose, some lively spice with sweet fruit. Maturing, earthy wine with intense long lasting flavours.*	**£12.99**	WHC, D, DBY, CEB	**S**
PETER LEHMANN STONEWELL SHIRAZ, CELLAR COLLECTION 1988 Barossa Valley	*Rich, ripe, juicy wine with luscious fruit, balanced by firm tannins. Direct, and generous.*	**£12.99**	OD, PLE	**S**
PENFOLDS MAGILL ESTATE SHIRAZ, 1990, South Australia	*Lovely, juicy fruit flavours. supple and rounded.*	**£12.99**	OD, TH, WR, BU, ADN, DBY	**B**
JAMES IRVINE GRAND MERLOT 1989 Eden Valley	*Bitter coffee aromas, ripened fruit on palate. Slightly closed but will open up.*	**£13.99**	HVW, GSH, OBC	**S**
MESHACH SHIRAZ, GRANT BURGE 1990 Barossa Valley	*Classic Rhone style of intense perfumed fruit, toasty oak flavours. Huge wine with a big future.*	**£13.99**	FSW, POM, GSH, LWE, DBY, LV	**S**
WYNNS COONAWARRA ESTATE MICHAEL SHIRAZ 1991 Coonawarra	*Warm inviting nose with spicy orange overtones. Ripe damson flavours. Complex, subtle finish.*	**£13.99**	OD, DBY	**B**
MOUNTADAM 'THE RED', ADAM WYNN 1991 Adelaide Hills	*Rich, maturing nose of mint, berries and cassis. Full, lightly oaky palate with soft berry fruit.*	**£14.00**	CHF, PLA, ADN	**S**

PENFOLDS BIN 707 CABERNET SAUVIGNON 1990 South Australia	*Vanilla, coconut character and soft berry and tar flavours. Closed nose. Good length. Excellent.*	**£14.99**	Widely Available	**G**
WYNNS COONAWARRA ESTATE JOHN RIDDOCH CABERNET SAUVIGNON 1991 Coonawarra	*Attractive nose of vanilla and dark fruit. Excellent rich fruit flavours, spicy and forthcoming.*	**£14.99**	VW, OD, LV, DBY	**G**
WOLF BLASS BLACK LABEL CABERNET SAUVIGNON/MERLOT 1985 Southeast Australia	*Powerful stuff! Massive minty style with ripe rich, cakey character. Lovely balance.*	**£14.99**	CD, ABY, SEA, DBY	**B**
WOLF BLASS BLACK LABEL CABERNET SAUVIGNON/MERLOT, 1987 South Australia	*Mint, chocolate and Cabernet nose. Fruit and oak well mixed . Sweetness and plenty of tannin.*	**£14.99**	OD, DBY	**B**
WYNNS COONAWARRA ESTATE JOHN RIDDOCH CABERNET SAUVIGNON 1990 Coonawarra	*Rich, plummy oak palate. Intense berry fruits. Incredibly rich. Big wine with good potential.*	**£15.50**	VW, OD, SEB, LV	**S**
RAVENSWOOD CABERNET SAUVIGNON, HOLLICK WINES 1990 Coonawarra	*Medicinal, oaky nose. Light and minty. Nice balance of fruit, with touch of sweetness.*	**£15.99**	NY, GSH, SK, WWI, R	**B**
JACARANDA RIDGE CABERNET SAUVIGNON, ORLANDO WINES 1989 Coonawarra	*Lovely style of wine, ripe and attractive. Soft, lush mouthfull. Long and flavoursome.*	**£16.25**	PEA, OD, MHW, WTR, CEN, CAX	**G**
JACARANDA RIDGE CABERNET SAUVIGNON, ORLANDO WINES 1990 Coonawarra	*Minty and spicy nose; good cassis and blackberry fruit character. A sweet, wonderful mouthful.*	**£16.25**	OD, PEA, MHW, WTR, EGL, CAX	**S**
PARKER ESTATE FIRST GROWTH 1990 Coonawarra	*Beautiful ripe cassis nose. Good fruit freshness and spice on palate. Great in five years.*	**£17.82**	C&B, WIA	**S**

HENSCHKE HILL OF GRACE SHIRAZ 1990 Adelaide Hills	*A wine of serious stature with ripe fruit nose. Concentrated finish gives intense blackberry flavour.*	£21.50	L&W, AUC, SEB, GSH, JTS	G
PENFOLDS GRANGE BIN 95 1988 South Australia	*New world spicy tannins with minty flavour. Already impressive, will develop still further.*	£39.99	Widely Available	G
DRY WHITE				
TOLLANA DRY WHITE, PENFOLDS 1993 Southeast Australia	*Good juicy tropical fruit. Ultra Australian style.*	£3.49	TH, WR, BU, TDS	B
PENFOLDS BIN 21 SEMILLON-CHARDONNAY 1993 South Australia	*A nutty nose with floral tones gives way to lots of apricot fruit.*	£3.99	Widely Available	B
PETER LEHMANN BAROSSA VALLEY DRY WHITE 1993 Barossa Valley	*Good up-front lemon nose, fine appley taste. Refreshing finish.*	£3.99	OD, DBY	B
OLD TRIANGLE RIESLING, S SMITH & SON 1993 Barossa Valley	*Fresh, fruity nose, clean and light, with some floral overtones. Delicate and soft on palate. Clean finish.*	£4.40	A, W	B
ANGOVE'S CHARDONNAY 1993	*Pineappley flavour, full with lots of fruit on palate. A big wine.*	£4.49	MWW	B
DAVID WYNN, DRY WHITE 1992 Eden Valley	*Grassy and nutty on nose, with hints of tropical fruit. Interesting finish of honey and praline.*	£4.50	ADN, WL, CHF, JAR, NY	S
JACOB'S CREEK CHARDONNAY, ORLANDO WINES 1993 Southeast Australia	*Good clean, fresh nose. Round mulberry flavours. Good balance and length.*	£4.69	Widely Available	B

QUELLTALER ESTATE RIESLING 1993 South Australia	*Soft, broad, quite attractive creamy nose with touches of citrus. A good structure and well made.*	£4.75	AUC	**B**
HOUGHTON SWAN VALLEY DRY WHITE 1991 Western Australia	*A lively developed bouquet, delicate and quite floral. Rounded and well-balanced wine.*	£4.79	CWS, JEH, DBY	**B**
LINDEMAN'S BIN 65 CHARDONNAY 1993 Southeast Australia	*New wood style with a touch of sweetness. Ripe and buttery palate.*	£4.99	M&S	**B**
HARDY'S MOONDAH BROOK ESTATE CHENIN BLANC, BRL HARDY WINE CO 1993 Western Australia	*Resinous oak and fresh lemons, plus lime fruit on the palate. Good balance and great length.*	£4.99	JMC, WL, JS, R, TDS, DBY, CWS	**B**
PENFOLDS KOONUNGA HILL CHARDONNAY 1993 South Australia	*Sound, ripe, smooth and buttery. Balanced upfront flavours. Lovely wine satisfies in all departments.*	£4.99	Widely Available	**B**
RED CLIFFS ESTATE CHARDONNAY 1993 Mildura	*A good full-length wine with sweet tropical fruit flavour. Lovely, big and generous. Superb.*	£4.99	TH, BU, BI	**B**
BRIDGEWATER MILL RIESLING 1993 South Australia	*Oily and petrolly but rather more refreshing than four star with a creamy mouthfeel.*	£4.99	TH	**B**
MARIENBERG COTTAGE CLASSIC, MARIENBERG WINES 1993 McLaren Vale	*Golden yellow. Boasts a spicy, Riesling nose. The good fruit contains slightly tropical flavours.*	£4.99	THP	**B**
POACHERS BLEND, WHITE, ST HALLETT 1993 Barossa Valley	*Good and gluggable. An attractive scented nose, good acidity and touch of sweetness on finish.*	£4.99	WR, AUC	**B**

WHITE CLARE, WAKEFIELD WINES 1991 Clare Valley	*Sweetish, almost oaked nose with some full citrus fruit and good acid on the palate.*	£4.99	BTH, HAR, RAE, U, W	B
ORLANDO RF CHARDONNAY 1992 Southeast Australia	*Sweet, ripe, rich fruit balanced well with good oak flavours; a lovely light finish. Gorgeous.*	£4.99	Widely Available	S
PENFOLDS SOUTH AUSTRALIAN SEMILLON-CHARDONNAY 1993 South Australia	*Tones of spice and vanilla. May need year or so for fruit and wood characters to integrate.*	£4.99	Widely Available	S
SIMON HACKETT MCLAREN VALE SEMILLON 1993 McLaren Vale	*Open lemony nose with a touch of smokiness. Appealing flavours of lime juice and fruit salad.*	£4.99	CPW, CAC, WRW, BFV, GAR	S
EDEN RIDGE DRY WHITE, ADAM WYNN 1993 Eden Valley	*Some youthful spritz and grassy flavours with ripe, clean fruit on palate make this quite a classy wine.*	£5.00	H&D, RAM, ADN, SOM, CWI	B
BASEDOWS BAROSSA VALLEY SEMILLON, GRANT BURGE 1993 Barossa Valley	*Attractive aromatic nose, tangy and spiced with liquorice. Exotic fruit softened by some nutty oak.*	£5.00	VW, BI	S
HARDY'S BAROSSA VALLEY CHARDONNAY, BRL HARDY WINE CO 1993 Barossa Valley	*Tingly tang of pineapple fruit. Deep, complex, spicy and oaked.*	£5.25	SAF, WHC	B
LEASINGHAM DOMAINE CHARDONNAY 1993 Clare Valley	*Complex nose of spices, honey, orange and ripe fruit. Good lasting flavours and intensity.*	£5.25	OD	S

Pinpoint who sells the wine you wish to buy by turning to the stockist codes
If you know the name of the wine you want to buy, use the alphabetical index
If price is your motivation, refer to the invaluable price guide index; red and
white wines under £5 and sparkling wines under £10. Good hunting!

WINDY PEAK CHARDONNAY, DE BORTOLI 1992 Victoria	*Clean, fresh nose. Lemon zest, honey, rich spices, pineapples. Attractive and nicely balanced.*	**£5.29**	JS	**B**
PETER LEHMANN, BAROSSA VALLEY SEMILLON 1993 Barossa Valley	*Restrained waxy lemon aroma. Ripe fruit offset by subtle oak tannins. Vibrant and delicious.*	**£5.35**	JS, OD, BAL, PLE, DBY, DIO	**B**
HOUGHTON GOLD RESERVE VERDELHO, HOUGHTON 1993 Western Australia	*Full on nose with lots of grapefruit and passion-fruit. Light and clean with good acidity and fruit.*	**£5.49**	AR, DBY	**S**
McWILLIAMS MOUNT PLEASANT CHARDONNAY 1992 Southeast Australia	*Clean, ripe, soft and but-tery. Rich fruit palate and clean finish. Big, com-plex, rounded and fun.*	**£5.59**	OD, WAV, AUC, DBY	**B**
GOLDEN HILL CHARDONNAY 1993 McLaren Vale	*Lots of wonderful exotic fruit. Firm but elegant flavour. Medium length.*	**£5.75**	C&B, BWS, PON, SEL	**B**
HARDY'S MOONDAH BROOK ESTATE VERDELHO, BRL HARDY WINE CO 1993 Western Australia	*Fruity, elegant nose of gooseberries. Good weight of grapey, peachey fruit. Well-made wine.*	**£5.79**	OD, JMC, TO, VW, GMN, DIO, DBY	**S**
BROWN BROTHERS KING VALLEY RIESLING 1993 Northeast Victoria	*Real bottle age character gives this wine depth and length: light, clean and very likeable.*	**£5.95**	W, AWC, WWT	**B**
ROSEMOUNT CHARDONNAY 1993 Hunter Valley	*Attractive aromas, but-tery, ripe oaky nose, plenty of flavour and fruity body. Clean and balanced .*	**£5.99**	SAF, D, BWC, HHC, CEB, WES, DBY	**B**
MITCHELTON CHARDONNAY 1992 Southeast Australia	*Very clean, attractive wine, ripe and well-balanced. Lemon meringue-pie.*	**£5.99**	OD, CEL, DBY, COK, JMC, GRT, DBY	**B**

Bridgewater Mill Chardonnay, Petaluma 1992 South Australia	*Round, soft character. A wine of good length and clean flavours.*	**£5.99**	VW, OD	**B**
Cowra Vineyards Chardonnay, Richmond Grove Wines 1993 Cowra, NSW	*Soft, fresh fruit with some complexity. Gentle peach and melon style, gentle oak.*	**£5.99**	EUR, MAR, WTR, PEA, CDE	**B**
Gramps Chardonnay, Orlando Wines 1993 Southeast Australia	*Elegant appley nose with a touch of vanilla. Well integrated fruit and oak. Balanced with clean finish.*	**£5.99**	SEL, MAR, PEA, CLS, WTR, CAX, DIO	**B**
Wirra Wirra Church Block White 1993 McLaren Vale	*Lightly reminiscent of smoky bacon, a wine in excellent balance.*	**£5.99**	FLM, SOM, WOI, FUL	**B**
David Wynn Chardonnay 1993 Eden Valley	*A herbaceous nose showing peaches and green apple fruit; good balance. Flinty acid finish.*	**£6.00**	H&D, OD, JAR, WL, CHF, DBY	**B**
Mitchelton Marsanne, Mitchelton 1993 Goulburn Valley	*Aromatic bouquet. Delicious honeydew melon flavours in mouth. Juicy, with lively acid.*	**£6.00**	OD, A, PHI, DBY	**B**
Pikes Polish Hill Sauvignon Blanc 1993 Clare Valley	*Distinct richness of citric fruit, with a little spice. Clean and well made with plenty of length.*	**£6.20**	PLA	**B**
Rowan Chardonnay, St. Hubert's Wines 1993 Victoria	*Honey, spice and soft sweet wood nose. Lemony and weighty. Quite 'zingy'.*	**£6.25**	VW, DBY	**B**
Simon Hacket Semillon	*Peachy citrus fruit nose. Fine full melon, lemon palate. Refreshing lingering finish.*	**£6.30**	CPW, HVW, GAR, FSW	**S**

HENSCHKE. TILLY'S VINEYARD SEMILLON-CHARDONNAY 1991 Barossa Valley	*Lots of lemony oak and honeyed fruit lend complexity and weight to this impressive wine.*	£6.49	L&W, MOR	**B**
TERRA WHITE, HOLLICK WINES 1993 Coonawarra	*Hints of grass and vanilla pod on the nose. Some nice, rich fruit which lasts well on the finish.*	£6.49	PAL, WWI, GSH, R	**B**
WYNDHAM ESTATE OAK CASK CHARDONNAY 1992 Southeast Australia	*Clean, bright, buttery, oak-flavoured wine with lots of fruit, and a lovely dry finish. Classy.*	£6.49	MWW, MRS, HS, SG, WCO, D, DBY	**S**
ROTHBURY ESTATE BARREL FERMENTED CHARDONNAY 1993 Hunter Valley	*Soft and easy Chardonnay flavour, with a touch of vanilla and nice toasty aged character.*	£6.50	NIC, CLP, D, GRT, DBY	**B**
BASEDOWS CHARDONNAY 1990 Barossa Valley	*Complex, oaky bouquet with excellent marriage of fruit and acidity on the palate. Nice drinking.*	£6.50	BI, CWM	**S**
WOLF BLASS CHARDONNAY 1993 South Australia	*Full-nosed wine; oaky, rich, creamy, with a hint of lemon. Full-bodied with a nice spiciness.*	£6.50	BKW, THP, SEA, DBY	**S**
BROWN BROTHERS KING VALLEY SAUVIGNON BLANC 1993 Northeast Victoria	*Clean with slightly mineral flinty style. Backdrop of ripe gooseberry. Lots of clean, fresh acidity.*	£6.60	TH, GNW, CPW, MHC, DBY	**B**
PLANTAGENET OMRAH VINEYARD CHARDONNAY 1993 Mount Barker	*Youthful with green tones. Leafy, lychee nose, fresh, zippy green apple fruit. Finishes cleanly.*	£6.95	GI	**S**
BOTOBOLAR VINEYARD MARSANNE, 1992 Mudgee	*Complex with peaches, apricots and limes on the nose. Succulent and limey on palate. Dry finish.*	£6.95	VR, ORG	**S**

CHATEAU TAHBILK CHARDONNAY 1992 Victoria	*Creamy, coconut bouquet. Concentrated fruit flavours with balanced acidity and good length.*	**£6.99**	OD, PLE, DBY	B
MOUNT LANGI GHIRAN CHARDONNAY 1992 Great Western	*Well-balanced nose with controlled use of oak and nice toasty character. Not too heavy.*	**£6.99**	WCE	B
HILLSTOWE CHARDONNAY, MCLAREN VALE 1991 McLaren Vale	*Soft barley sugar nose with fresh palate. Nice with good acidity and fruit. Full oaky finish.*	**£6.99**	MYS	B
MITCHELTON RESERVE CHARDONNAY 1992 Southeast Australia	*Superb, full appley nose. Full flavoured with good fruit and acidity. A mouthful of good stuff.*	**£6.99**	OD, JMC, BWL, GRT, DBY	B
ST HALLETT'S CHARDONNAY 1993 Barossa Valley	*Nice soft ripe fruit nose with fullish palate. Well made.*	**£6.99**	WR, AUC, RD, DBY, SUM	B
JAMIESONS RUN CHARDONNAY, MILDARA 1993 Coonawarra	*Powerful, spicy apple nose. Full pineapple palate. Clean finish.*	**£6.99**	OD, WL, G, PHI, VW, THP, GRT, DBY	B
HENSCHKE ADELAIDE HILLS DRY RIESLING 1991 Adelaide Hills	*Rich lemon jelly cube nose with hint of peaches and cream. Fresh clean melon and soft fruits on palate.*	**£6.99**	L&W, DBY	B
HEGGIES VINEYARD RIESLING, S SMITH & SON 1992 Eden Valley	*Clean, ripe, petrolly. Good mouthful with orange and apple flavour and generous length.*	**£6.99**	ADN	B
MITCHELL WATERVALE RIESLING 1992 Clare Valley	*A big, rich, petrolly wine - long and intense; good ripe New World style with apple and apricot flavours.*	**£6.99**	TAN	B

PENFOLDS SEMILLON 1993 South Australia	*Smoky bacon sprinkled with lime juice. Rich, full, very creamy, almost caramelly style.*	£6.99	OD	**B**
BRIDGEWATER MILL SAUVIGNON BLANC, PETALUMA 1993 South Australia	*Fresh and clean with lots of gooseberry and elder-flower aromas. Rich and juicy with honey flavour.*	£6.99	OD, BAR	**B**
ST HALLETT SEMILLON/SAUVIGNON BLANC, 1993 Barossa Valley	*Fresh, open, fruity bouquet and good balance of fruit and acidity. Nice weight with long finish.*	£6.99	TO	**B**
ST HALLETT'S SEMILLON/SAUVIGNON BLANC 1992 Barossa Valley	*Clean and aromatic with hint of sweetness. Quite rich. Should be drunk now.*	£6.99	TO	**B**
ROUGE HOMME CHARDONNAY 1992 Coonawarra	*Full of fruity flavours and a lovely spicy finish; well-oaked with good length and weight.*	£6.99	WSG, CHH, SD, HOU, H&H, DBY	**S**
PENFOLDS CHARDONNAY 1993 South Australia	*Fine, great class, and subtle, complex flavours; lovely depth. Nice.*	£6.99	TH, OD, FUL, MWW, WR, NRW	**S**
PENFOLDS CHARDONNAY 1992 South Australia	*Terrific wine with a complex, nutty and oaky nose. A lovely balance of flavours.*	£6.99	Widely Available	**S**
GRANT BURGE BAROSSA VALLEY OLD VINE SEMILLON 1993 Barossa Valley	*A clean crisp wine with elegance that takes time to emerge. Classy with plenty of intensity.*	£6.99	GSH, LV, MS, PIM, C&H, AUC	**S**
YALUMBA MUSEUM SHOW RESERVE RUTHERGLEN MUSCAT Rutherglen	*Nutty nose. Fruity, caramel flavour with faint orange tone. Rich and full-bodied.*	£6.99	TH, TO, VW, BEN, SOM, LV	**G**

MITCHELL CLARE VALLEY SEMILLON 1992 Clare Valley	*A lovely ripe mouthful of fruit with instant spice, acidity and zip.*	**£7.00**	L&W, SHJ, BLS, WOA, MOK	**B**
MOUNTADAM RIESLING, ADAM WYNN 1990 Adelaide Hills	*Has a fruity, oily character and good length. Stylish with herbal and lime touches, crisp acidity.*	**£7.35**	ADN, RBS	**B**
TIM KNAPPSTEIN CLARE VALLEY/LENSWOOD CHARDONNAY 1991 South Australia	*Ripe melon nose; full and buttery. Straight-forward wine. Like drinking a glass of sunshine.*	**£7.49**	OD	**B**
MITCHELTON GOULBURN VALLEY RESERVE MARSANNE 1991 Southeast Australia	*Intense oily nose with lots of flavour. Warm fruit meets firm new oak.*	**£7.49**	W, JS, JMC, OD, BWL, GRT, DBY	**B**
TIM KNAPPSTEIN LENSWOOD VINEYARD SAUVIGNON BLANC 1993 South Australia	*Appealing asparagus and blackcurrant aromas. Sauvignon flavour in New Zealand style. Excellent.*	**£7.49**	LAV. OD	**G**
MCWILLIAMS MOUNT PLEASANT MOUNTAIN CHARDONNAY 1992 Hunter Valley	*Nice bouquet; fleshy ripe palate with oakiness coming through. Well integrated and nicely styled.*	**£7.49**	WAV, TO	**B**
WYNNS COONAWARRA ESTATE CHARDONNAY 1992 Coonawarra	*Oaky bouquet; quite complex. Simple, clean fruit palate, well-balanced.*	**£7.50**	TH, VW, OD, WR, BV, DBY	**B**
STONIER'S CHARDONNAY 1992 Mornington Peninsula	*Delicate lemony green nose with fantastic palate. Balanced acidity and good length.*	**£7.50**	WAW, HOL, PV	**B**
WYNNS COONAWARRA ESTATE CHARDONNAY 1991 Coonawarra	*Oak and mango bouquet; rich and buttery, attractive, easy drinking wine. A real mouthful.*	**£7.50**	TH, VW, OD, WR, BV	**B**

TUCKS RIDGE CHARDONNAY 1992 Mornington Peninsula	*Honey, caramel and wood character. Fresh with good richness and length. Pleasant.*	**£7.50**	BOO	**B**
EDEN RIDGE CHARDONNAY, ADAM WYNN 1992 Eden Valley	*Sweet nose. Attractive palate of tropical fruit flavour. Balanced finish with nice acid backbone.*	**£7.50**	ADN, JAR, VER, CHF, HW	**B**
PLATT'S SEMILLON 1992 Mudgee	*Fresh nose. Medium dry, with lots of acid and some rich oiliness. Full-bodied. Delicious stuff.*	**£7.75**	TP	**B**
STEVENS SEMILLON, TYRRELLS VINEYARDS 1993 Hunter Valley	*Full, rich gooseberries on an open nose. Of medium length, plenty of fruit - a refreshing style.*	**£7.75**	AV	**B**
TUNNEL HILL CHARDONNAY, TARRAWARRA VINEYARDS 1993 Yarra Valley	*Faint floral nose. Good balance and mainly complex red fruit character. Long rich lemony finish.*	**£7.89**	AUC, PHI, BWB, DBY	**B**
PEWSEY VALE VINEYARD RIESLING, S SMITH & SON 1993 Eden Valley	*Mouthwatering nose of citrus fruits. Lovely ripe apricot fruit. Very well put together.*	**£7.95**	LV	**S**
BROKENWOOD CHARDONNAY, HUNTER VALLEY 1993 Hunter Valley	*Peachy, light lemony nose. A very good wine with excellent balance and a dry finish.*	**£7.99**	NY, LV, RES, WH, H&H	**B**
BROWN BROTHERS KING VALLEY CHARDONNAY 1992 Northeast Victoria	*Fresh fruit nose and complex, lovely bright fruit palate.*	**£7.99**	OD, MWW, TAN, ROD, CPW, THP, DBY	**B**
STAFFORD RIDGE LENSWOOD CHARDONNAY 1991 South Australia	*Appealing, restrained style with delicate nose, yet quite complex. Fruit rather than peel flavours.*	**£7.99**	AUC	**B**

St Hilary Padthaway Chardonnay, Orlando Wines 1992 Padthaway	*Soft delicate wine, nice balance - not too sharp or oaky. Full lychee/ lemon fruit flavours.*	**£7.99**	A, WTR, CDE, DIO, SPR, CAX, DBY	**B**
Krondorf Show Reserve Chardonnay 1992 South Australia	*Good mouthwatering acidity and fruit. Full and mouthfilling.*	**£7.99**	THP, D, DBY	**B**
Yarra Ridge Chardonnay, Victoria 1993 Yarra Valley	*Clean, modern fruit; pineapple and vanilla nose. Gentle toasty finish.*	**£7.99**	PHI	**B**
Stafford Ridge Chardonnay 1990 South Australia	*Buttery and toasty with up-front fruit flavours. Full, fat style with good acidity and flavours.*	**£7.99**	AUC	**B**
Tim Adams Riesling 1993 Clare Valley	*A pleasantly fruity nose and nice strawberry fruit with touches of apples. Quite austere but elegant.*	**£7.99**	ENO, AUC	**B**
Wirra Wirra Chardonnay 1992 South Australia	*Strong, buttery, new-oak flavours make it smooth and full, with a spicy character and good length.*	**£7.99**	WSO, OD, BBR, WOI, AUC	**S**
Brokenwood Cricket Pitch Sauvignon Blanc/Semillon 1993 Hunter Valley	*Delicious flavour with a good level of classic Sauvignon. Produces a really enjoyable glassfull.*	**£7.99**	NY, LV, RES, WH, H&H	**S**
Shaw & Smith Sauvignon Blanc 1993 Adelaide Hills	*Good juicy asparagus aroma with some class and complexity. An eminently gluggable wine.*	**£7.99**	OD, WCE, H&H, NRW, SEB, DIO	**S**
Cape Mentelle Semillon Sauvignon 1993 Margaret River	*Super citrus fruit on the nose of this well-made wine. Well-balanced with a lovely finish.*	**£7.99**	Widely Available	**S**

TIM ADAMS SEMILLON 1993 Clare Valley	*Fresh, crisp with pineapple and lemon aromas. Beautifully balanced. Should develop superbly.*	**£7.99**	AUC	G
HENSCHKE SEMILLON 1992 Adelaide Hills	*Shows lots of style; lively lime fruit and fine acidity supported by elegant toasty oak.*	**£8.00**	L&W, AUC, WCE	B
JASPER HILL GEORGIA'S PADDOCK RIESLING 1992 Bendigo	*The bottle age shines through in the buttery kerosene nose. Palate retains fresh appley fruit.*	**£8.15**	ADN	B
TASMANIA WINE COMPANY CHARDONNAY, PIPER'S BROOK VINEYARD 1993 Tasmania	*Herbaceous and faintly pebbley nose with buttery lemon fruit and citric acidity. Dry and very appealing.*	**£8.25**	FUL, FSW, JS, HN, LEA, DBY	B
HENSCHKE EDEN VALLEY RIESLING 1990 Adelaide Hills	*Nice and full bodied with good length. Blessed with ethereal spicy aromas with lemon hints.*	**£8.29**	L&W, AUC, SEB, WCE	B
PLATT'S MUDGEE CHARDONNAY 1992 Mudgee	*Clean, bright colour. Good upfront fruit. Quite intense fruit flavours. Good acidity and length.*	**£8.35**	TP, LSI	B
GEOFF MERRILL SEMILLON-CHARDONNAY 1989 South Australia	*Big and uncompromising, buckets of rich buttery wood flavour and honey suckle fruit.*	**£8.35**	OD	B
ROSEMOUNT ESTATE SHOW RESERVE CHARDONNAY 1992 Hunter Valley	*Thickish vanilla nose; body and fruit with just enough acidity. Melony flavour and lemony finish.*	**£8.50**	JS, SAF, W, WR, BU, GRT, FUL, DBY, BWC	B
ORLANDO FLAXMANS TRAMINER, ORLANDO WINES 1990 Eden Valley	*A viscous but upbeat wine with heady aromas of lemons and limes. Good weight in mid-palate.*	**£8.50**	AUC, CUM, PEA, CDE, WTR, CAX	S

PENLEY ESTATE CHARDONNAY, COONAWARRA 1992 Coonawarra	*Young Chardonnay fruit and soft oak. Attractive ripeness of fruit. Good weight and acidity.*	**£8.60**	WTR	**B**
CHAPEL HILL RESERVE CHARDONNAY 1993 McLaren Vale	*Refined and classy. Clean and elegant. Most attractive. Sweet ripe fruit flvours.*	**£8.99**	AUC	**B**
GOUNDREY WINDY HILL MOUNT BARKER CHARDONNAY 1991 Mount Barker	*Rich, ripe, oaked nose with good weight. Full rich, ripe fruit and oak flavours. Solid.*	**£8.99**	AD, GRT, RWW	**B**
CHAPEL HILL RESERVE CHARDONNAY 1991 South Australia	*Good graphite nose with toasted oak and tropical fruit. Firm, well-developed fruit.*	**£8.99**	ENO	**B**
EBENEZER CHARDONNAY, BRL HARDY WINE CO/VALLEY GROWERS 1993 Barossa Valley	*Oak and spice; fine, rich, full fruit flavours and a clean, dry crisp finish. A show stopper.*	**£8.99**	WHC	**S**
CHAPEL HILL RESERVE CHARDONNAY 1992 South Australia	*Ripe, big bodied wine of good style and long finish. Clean fruit flavours and citrus aromas.*	**£8.99**	AUC	**S**
PETALUMA CLARE RIESLING 1993 Clare Valley	*Rich and concentrated, almost spicy, nose. Palate full of lingering fruit and tingling acidity.*	**£9.21**	ADN, AUC, F&M, HAR	**B**
BANNOCKBURN CHARDONNAY, GEELONG 1992 Geelong	*Honeyed nose; light buttery oak and fruit flavours. A ripe full wine, rewarding to drink.*	**£9.85**	ADN, LEA, ROB, BEN	**S**
WELLINGTON CHARDONNAY, TASMANIA 1992 Tamar Valley, Tasmania	*Light and clean, with mild elegant oak character. Lovely balance and excellent length.*	**£9.90**	NI	**B**

KINGSTON RESERVE RIVERLAND CHARDONNAY 1991 South Australia	*Buttery and full, cream and spice on bouquet. Fat, rich palate with a lot of spice. Elegant acidity.*	£9.99	TO	**B**
SHAW & SMITH RESERVE CHARDONNAY 1992 Adelaide Hills	*Well integrated oak character and well-balanced flavours. A touch of spice with a long, clean finish.*	£9.99	OD, WCE, SEB	**B**
HENSCHKE EDEN VALLEY CHARDONNAY 1991 Adelaide Hills	*Ripe peach and citrussy fruit flavours. Nicely balanced nose and palate which will develop further.*	£9.99	L&W, AUC, BOO, DBY	**S**
KATNOOK ESTATE CHARDONNAY, COONAWARRA 1991 Coonawarra	*Soft, ripe fruit with excellent buttery character that carries through. Rich and flavoursome.*	£9.99	RAM, BI	**S**
STONIER'S RESERVE CHARDONNAY, MORNINGTON PENINSULA 1992 Mornington Peninsula	*Rich, creamy, toasty, pineappley flavour. Intense, perfumed with a fine finish.*	£10.00	WAW, PV	**B**
CULLEN'S SAUVIGNON BLANC 1993 Margaret River	*Lovely grassy nose. Rich, ripe, fruit; gooseberries and blackcurrants.*	£10.45	ADN	**G**
HENSCHKE LENSWOOD VINEYARD CROFT CHARDONNAY 1991 Adelaide Hills	*Fresh fruit salad nose, with pineapple palate. Good fruit and wood character with dry finish.*	£10.95	L&W, BOO	**S**
AMBERLEY ESTATE MARGARET RIVER SEMILLON 1993 Margaret River	*Warm and ripe candied lemon and honey on the nose with a flavour of rich fruit and buttery oak.*	£10.95	NI	**S**
BRANDS LAIRA CHARDONNAY, McWILLIAM'S/BRANDS 1992 Coonawarra	*Tropical fruit nose and a soft, clean balance of acidity and smoothness. Pleasantly long.*	£10.99	WAV	**B**

PETALUMA CHARDONNAY 1991 Picadilly Coonawarra	*Clean, ripe, with fruity aromas. Strong palate. Well-balanced, spicy with long fruit flavours.*	£10.99	AVA, JN, DBY, OD, TH, FUL, ADN	S
MOUNTADAM CHARDONNAY, ADAM WYNN 1992 Adelaide Hills	*Light fresh oak palate with soft balance and long fruit flavours. Good and not too heavy.*	£10.99	TDS, ADN, CHF, PAV, BOO, DBY	S
TYRELL'S VAT 47 CHARDONNAY 1993 Hunter Valley	*Butter and citrus peel nose. Slight sweetness. Good balance, complexity with clean varietal style.*	£11.00	AV, DBY, CEB	G
MOSS WOOD CHARDONNAY, MARGARET RIVER 1993 Margaret River	*Tangy lime flavours and lively acidity create a firm, racy style. Lovely balance of flavours.*	£11.50	Widely Available	S
COLDSTREAM HILLS RESERVE CHARDONNAY 1992 Yarra Valley	*Classy fruit flavours with good palate and nice acidity. Should develop further.*	£11.99	PAG, OD, BWC	B
MOONDAH BROOK SHOW RESERVE CHENIN BLANC, BRL HARDY WINE CO 1987 Western Australia	*Lemon curd on warm buttery toast. Deliciously creamy and a little nutty. Terribly moreish. Bravo.*	£12.95	WHC	S
PIPER'S BROOK VINEYARD CHARDONNAY 1992 Tasmania	*Toasty, buttery palate with quite high acidity and good length.*	£12.99	AUC, ADN, WTP, DBY, BEN	B
DALWHINNIE CHARDONNAY 1992 Pyrenees	*Aromatic, with smoky flavours and slightly steely nose. Good balance of fruit and oak.*	£14.50	WTR	G
LEEUWIN ESTATE ART SERIES CHARDONNAY 1988 Margaret River	*Savoury, oaky toasty 'big nosed' wine. Good fruit concentration and fresh palate. Good toasty finish.*	£14.99	DD	B

MEDIUM WHITE

BROWN BROTHERS LATE-PICKED MUSCAT BLANC 1993 Northeast Victoria	*Lightly, fruity nose; lemons and oranges. Mouthwatering flavoured palate with long finish.*	£5.99	D, MWW, TO, THP, NRW, DBY	B

SWEET WHITE

LINDEMAN'S BOTRYTIS SEMILLON 1987 South Australia	*Lemons and limes on the nose. Pure tasting, oranges and lemons. Well-balanced with sherbety aftertaste.*	£5.99	OD	S
LINDEMAN'S BOTRYTIS SEMILLON 1989 South Australia	*Pungent nose of orange marmalade with honey and burnt caramel. Long dry finish.*	£5.99	OD	B
KATNOOK ESTATE BOTRYTIS CHARDONNAY 1989 Coonawarra	*Pale yellowy/gold; soft medium sweetness. Burnt caramel nose with soft, smooth middle.*	£6.99	AUC, BI	B
TESCO BOTRYTIS SEMILLON, WILTON ESTATE 1992 Riverina	*Rich, tropical fruit and botrytis on nose. Intense flavour of honey and marmalade, with long clean grapefruit finish.*	£6.99	TO	S
PRIMO ESTATE BOTRYTIS RIESLING 1993 South Australia	*Pungent tinned peaches on nose and grapey fruit flavours. Sweet and long lasting.*	£6.99	AUC	S
CRANSWICK ESTATE BOTRYTIS SEMILLON 1993 New South Wales	*Sweet, tropical and peachy fruit. Honeyed, toffee and marmalade flavour. Finishes well.*	£6.99	GAR	G
YALUMBA FAMILY RESERVE BOTRYTIS SEMILLON 1991 Barossa Valley	*Sweet fruit. Clean, ripe, rich and vibrant with oaky overtures. Good length and dryish finish.*	£6.99	LAV, WIN, JN, LV	G

PEWSEY VALE VINEYARD AUTUMN BOTRYTIS RIESLING, S SMITH & SON 1991 Eden Valley	*Warm nose and palate. Round and full-bodied. Full of intense fruit flavours. Lightly sweet.*	£7.99	LAV, WIN, TO	S
CHAPEL HILL RESERVE BOTRYTIS 1993	*Good botrytised nose; stylish and spritzy. Full orange fruit on palate.*	£7.99	AUC	B
HENSCHKE NOBLE RIESLING 1992 Eden Valley	*Soft, Seville-orange nose, aromatic and honeyed. A citrus palate.*	£8.00	L&W	S

ROSE

MOUNT HURTLE GRENACHE ROSE, GEOFF MERRILL 1993 Southeast Australia	*Well-extracted and deeply coloured, full of jammy fruit with a touch of sweetness. Clean finish.*	£4.99	PLE, JS, DBY	B

SPARKLING

KILLAWARRA BRUT, PENFOLDS	*Broad, fat style of well-made fizz with a grapey taste that is part of its overall complexity.*	£5.00	FUL, D, MAR, BTH, L&W, DBY	B
ANGAS BRUT NON-VINTAGE CUVEE ROSE, YALUMBA	*Fruity nose with hint of acidity. Has length and depth lacking in many other wines at this price.*	£5.90	VW, OD, JS, TH, TO, D, FUL, DBY	B
SEPPELT PINOT ROSE CUVEE BRUT	*Yeasty nose, good fruit flavours and balancing acidity. A beauty.*	£7.00	LWE, LEA, MHW, OD, HAM	B
SEAVIEW PINOT NOIR-CHARDONNAY, PENFOLDS 1990	*Good yeasty, fruity nose; biscuit taste with fruit and length. Excellent value.*	£7.99	TH, WR, BU, U, MAR, DBY, DIO	B
CUVEE PRESTIGE PINOT NOIR/CHARDONNAY, YALUMBA, BAROSSA VALLEY, 1991, South Australia	*Fruit and yeast on the palate. A full finish, but overall dryness means this is definitely one to try.*	£7.99	OD, JS, MWW, D, ADN	S

YALDARA VINTAGE BRUT PINOT NOIR CHARDONNAY 1990	*Soft, creamy nose leads to similar taste with a green-apple overlay. Shortish finish.*	**£7.99**	PLA, WOI, MIT, OBC	B
DAVID WYNN BRUT, ADAM WYNN Eden Valley	*Scented, almost incense-like; a nose with manageable fruit and a reasonable finish.*	**£7.99**	CHF, ADN, SHB, PHI, NY	B
YALUMBA CUVEE PRESTIGE PINOT NOIR CHARDONNAY	*Clean nose and taste. Fruit and yeast in the palate with full finish. Definitely one to try.*	**£7.99**	OD, JS, MWW, D, ADN	S
YALUMBA CUVEE PRESTIGE CABERNET SAUVIGNON	*Nose that is oaky with spicy tones. Sweetish tone in the complex palate. Long finish.*	**£7.99**	OD, ADN, TO, JN	S
MICK MORRIS RUTHERGLEN SPARKLING SHIRAZ DURIF Rutherglen	*Raspberry tones and sweeter than most; redolent of Port. Intensely evocative.*	**£8.50**	CAX	B
ROSEMOUNT BRUT 1990 Southeast Australia	*No aggressive mousse; an even-tempered beast, camel-coloured, a clean nose and a light bite.*	**£8.75**	VW, SAL, BSE, COK, FEN, GRT, WES	B
SEPPELT SPARKLING SHIRAZ 1990 Barossa Valley & Padthaway	*Deep-red colour. Sweet and rich, with a savoury finish. Ideal for puddings.*	**£8.99**	OD, VW, SAF, ABY, H&H, TO	B
SEPPELT SPARKLING SHIRAZ 1991	*Dark-red colour and cherry aroma announce a big, concentrated style, tinged with sweetness.*	**£9.00**	OD, VW, SAF, ABY, TO, H&H	B
YALUMBA D 1991	*Yeast and biscuit on the nose. Delightful creamy flavour. Bottle age has led to good length.*	**£9.99**	OD, ADN, SOM, JN	B

SEPPELT SALINGER, SEPPELT 1990	*Fresh, clean, sparkling nose with lemon tart taste of reasonable length. Not for Demi-Sec fanciers.*	**£10.50**	Widely Available	**B**
SEPPELT SHOW SPARKLING SHIRAZ 1985	*Rich, soft, not oversweet. The vintage Australians are still waiting for in their shops. Buy it now.*	**£11.50**	OD, DBY	**S**
HEEMSKERK JANSZ BRUT 1990 Tasmania	*Fresh, green fruit on soft palate; a balance that is hard to fool.*	**£13.25**	ADN, OD, JN	**B**
MOUNTADAM EDEN VALLEY SPARKLING WINE 1990 Eden Valley	*Onion-skin tone, pleasant-drinking, rosé style with an underlying sweetness.*	**£16.95**	H&D	**S**

FORTIFIED

MORRIS LIQUEUR MUSCAT Rutherglen	*Good bouquet with some alcohol coming through. Sweet palate.*	**£8.99**	Widely Available	**B**
SALTRAM PICKWICK BAROSSA VALLEY FORTIFIED WINE Barossa Valley	*Pungent, burnt nose; sweet and rich on palate balanced by acidity. Quite complex and long.*	**£9.95**	OD	**S**
CHAMBERS-ROSEWOOD RUTHERGLEN LIQUEUR MUSCAT Rutherglen	*Woody, walnutty nose. Sweet orange/toffee flavours coming through on palate. Good length.*	**£9.99**	AUC, ADN, TAN, CRL, NY, H&H, LV	**B**
RUTHERGLEN LIQUEUR MUSCAT, STANTON AND KILLEEN Rutherglen	*Milk-chocolate-orange nose, and coffee and burnt toffee flavours. Delightfully sweet.*	**£9.99**	Widely Available	**S**
BROWN BROTHERS RESERVE TAWNY Northeast Victoria	*Deep, mahogany brown with currants and rich, sweet caramel palate. Lots of spirit with the sweet fruit.*	**£10.25**	AWC, WWT	**B**

BAILEY'S FOUNDER LIQUEUR TOKAY Northeast Victoria	*Suggestions of caramelised lychees and toffee. Quite rich, with some nuttiness; a classic liqueur tokay.*	£10.49	WWT, DBY	S
CAMPBELLS RUTHERGLEN LIQUEUR MUSCAT Rutherglen	*Lightish nose with oranges and Muscat bouquet. Full, rich caramelly fruit character.*	£10.95	CPW, GNW, RIB, CRL, SD, H&H, DBY	B
RUTHERGLEN SHOW MUSCAT DP 63, B SEPPELT & SONS Rutherglen	*Beautiful colour; with lifted raisin concentration. Soft, sweet and syrupy.*	£10.95	M&V, AUC, NI, VD, NY, H&H, THP, LV	S
BAILEY'S FOUNDER LIQUEUR MUSCAT Northeast Victoria	*Dark brown/red. Interesting long flavours. Good sweet palate.*	£10.99	NI, GHL, DBY	B
BROWN BROTHERS LIQUEUR MUSCAT Northeast Victoria	*Good brown/red colour. Peppery overtones on a sweetish palate. Rich concentration.*	£12.99	AWC, WWT, NRW, DBY	B

AUSTRIA

Making a remarkable comeback after the 'anti freeze' scandal of a decade ago, Austria's winemakers are teaching their neighbours across the German border a lesson in flavoursome winemaking. The most dazzling styles are the late-harvest wines, but the warmish climate is enabling the Austrians to make red and dry white wines which ought to be the envy of some of the big-name estates in the Rheingau.

RED					
WINZERHAUS BLAUER ZWEIGELT, NIEDER-ÖSTERREICHISCHER WINZERVERBAND 1993 Weinviertel	*Enticing spicy nose of white pepper and capsicums. Lovely clean acidity leaves you refreshed. Good length.*	**£3.85**	TO, U, DIO, WTR, PEA, CAX		B
BLAUFRANKISCH & ZWEIGELT 'BLEND II' KRACHER 1992 Neusiedlersee	*Well-balanced with deep rich purple colour. Soft black cherry fruit. Good length and spicy finish.*	**£7.99**	NY		B
BLAUFRANKISCH & ZWEIGELT 'BLEND 1', KRACHER 1992 Neusiedlersee	*Ripe depth of flavour to fruit. Soft and spicey new oak character. Jammy fruit.*	**£8.99**	NY		B
SOUVERANER MALTESER RITTERORDEN KOMMENDE MAILBERG 1990 Weinviertel	*Dark crimson wine with nice cedar/leather and dark fruit. Full flavoured and complex fruit.*	**£11.50**	LWE		B
GEORG STIEGELMAR PINOT NOIR BARRIQUE TROCKEN 1990 Burgenland	*Beautiful ruby wine. An attractive nose, ripe and spicy. Lots of mouthfilling oaky fruit. Elegant.*	**£15.00**	HAR, SEL, HN		S
GEORG STIEGELMAR PINOT NOIR 1991 Burgenland	*Vibrant fruity nose. Good weight of juicy fruit on palate. Lively and elegant.*	**£16.00**	SEL		B

GEORG STIEGELMAR CUVEE ST GEORG 1990 Burgenland	Well made, mid-weight plummy and raspberry-ish wine. Lovely clean flavours.	£16.00	RNW	B

DRY WHITE

KREMSER WACHTBERG TRAMINER, WEINGUT UNDHOF, FRITZ SALOMAN 1990 Krems	Pungent and scented with marshmallow and pear fruit. Touch of lavender and lively acidity.	£6.50	HAR, WTR, PEA, DIO, EGL, CAX	B
STEINER HUND RIESLING KABINETT, FRITZ SALOMON 1990 Krems	Ripe, exotic, lychee characters precede full, spicy, smoky fruit. Clean and honeyed. Good stuff.	£6.95	HAR, WTR, PEA, DIO, EGL, CAX	B
WEISSER SCHILFMANDL, SCHILFWEIN VIN PAILLE, WILLI OPITZ 1992 Neusiedlersee	Honeyed, perfumed aromas, with raisins on palate. Flavours of orange blossom. Long finish.	£30.95	T&W	G

SWEET WHITE

LENZ MOSER RIESLING & SYLVANER TROCKEN-BEERENAUSLESE 1976 Neusiedlersee-H, gelland	Orange coloured wine with rich peaches and cream character. A little spice on palate.	£9.95	W, LV	B
KRACHER SÄMLING 88 BEERENAUSLESE 'ZWISCHEN DEN SEEN' 1991 Neusiedlersee	Golden. Lots of botrytis on nose. Light, but with good depth of fruit. A nice, clean finish	£12.85	HOL, H&H	B
SÄMLING 88 BEERENAUSLESE, KRACHER 1987 Neusiedlersee	Honeyed botrytis nose. Rich, fruity, toffee-flavoured. Good acidity, long finish. Delicious.	£15.00	NY	G
KRACHER MUSKAT OTTONEL BEERENAUSLESE 'ZWISCHEN DEN SEEN' 1991 Neusiedlersee	Slightly earthy and sweet, with subdued, tropical, nutty nose. Christmas cake flavours.	£15.99	NY	S

KRACHER MUSKAT OTTONEL BEERENAUSLESE 'ZWISCHEN DEN SEEN' 1988 Neusiedlersee	*Deep gold with orange highlights. Clean nose with vegetal hints. Sweet ripe, concentrated fruit on palate. Dryish finish.*	£17.99	NY	S
WELSCHRIESLING EISWEIN, 1990 Neusiedlersee	*Rich and intense, with a curranty-baked apple flavour. Wonderfully well-balanced.*	£17.99	NY	S
KRACHER TRAMINER BEERENAUSLESE 'NOUVELLE VAGUE' 1989 Neusiedlersee	*Bright, rich, golden, with noticeable botrytis on nose. Delicate fruity flavours. Lots of richness.*	£18.99	NY, HOL	B
KRACHER TRAMINER BEERENAUSLESE 'NOUVELLE VAGUE' 1991 Neusiedlersee	*Pale yellow, with some oakiness on nose. Complex flavours of sweet peaches and butteriness.*	£18.99	NY	B
GRAND CUVEE BEERENAUSLESE, KRACHER 1991 Neusiedlersee	*Lots of botrytis on nose Raisin flavours. Rich and sweet,but cleaned by zingy acidity.*	£18.99	HOL, H&H	S
CHARDONNAY/WELSCH -RIESLING BEERENAUSLESE 'NOUVELLE VAGUE' 1992 Neusiedlersee	*Complex, apricot nose. Youthful and vibrant, syrupy and rich, with a citric-in-toasted-wood flavour. Good length.*	£18.99	NY, H&H	G
KRACHER TROCKENBEERENAUSLESE 'ZWISCHSEN DEN SEEN' 1992 Neusiedlersee	*Soft, with dried fruits on nose. Woody and smoky flavours well moulded with raisins and sultanas.*	£19.00	NY, H&H	B
KRACHER CHARDONNAY & WELSCHRIESLING BEERENAUSLESE 1991 Neusiedlersee	*Young and grapey, fragrant with a hint of oak. Citrus fruits on palate, fresh with lovely acidity and long finish.*	£19.00	NY, HOL, H&H	B

Wine	Notes	Price	Supplier	Medal
KRACHER SÄMLING 88 TROCKENBEERENAUSLESE 'ZWISCHEN' 1991 Neusiedlersee	*Ripe, honeyed, orange blossom nose with noticeable botrytis. Sweet citrus acidity, full-bodied and lush.*	£19.00	HOL, H&H	S
KRACHER BOUVIER TROCKENBEERENAUSLESE 1984 Neusiedlersee	*Honeyed on nose and palate. Flavours of marmalade, peaches and apricot.*	£20.00	NY	B
KRACHER WELSCHRIESLING BEERENAUSLESE 1981 Neusiedlersee	*Ripe, complex nose; warm, fruity palate.*	£20.00	NY	B
KRACHER WELSCHRIESLING TROCKENBEERENAUSLESE 'ZWISCHEN DEN SEEN' 1988 Neusiedlersee	*Figgy nose with barley-sugar aromas and hint of golden syrup. Liquorice flavours. Intense with raisins on finish.*	£21.00	NY	S
BLAUBERGER EISWEIN, WILLI OPITZ 1992 Neusiedlersee	*Extraordinary intense red fruit and almost Christmas pudding flavours. Blockbuster.*	£23.20	T&W	B
GRÜNER VELTLINER TROCKENBEERENAUSLESE, WILLI OPITZ 1993 Neusiedlersee	*Deep apricot gold. Powerful aroma of barleysugars and honeyed raisins. Luscious fruit on palate.*	£27.50	T&W	S
KRACHER MUSKAT OTTONEL TROCKENBEERENAUSLESE 1981 Neusiedlersee	*Unctuous with a marmalade nose. Fruity and nutty. Palate full of rich toffee and cream.*	£28.00	NY	S
KRACHER WELSCHRIESLING TROCKENBEERENAUSLESE 1981 Neusiedlersee	*Fruity nectar with lovely thick, oily nose and complex, opulent sweetness. Flavoured with caramel and syrup.*	£28.00	NY	G

WEISSER SCHILFMANDL, WILLI OPITZ 1992 Neusiedlersee	*Fascinating raisiny wine with an almost red fruit flavour. Delicate but curranty.*	£30.95	T&W	G
BLAUBERGER RED TROCKENBEERENAUSLESE, WILLI OPITZ 1991 Neusiedlersee	*Orangey brown. Sweet, with raisins and cinnamon on nose and summer fruits on palate.*	£35.30	T&W	G

PERSONAL TASTING NOTES

SIGHT	Clear Bright Hazy Cloudy Colour
SMELL	Fresh Musty Floral Fruit Vegetal Animal Wood/Oak Others
TASTE	Weight Sweetness Dryness Acidity Fruit Vegetal Wood/Oak Balance
SUMMARY	Age Maturity Location Vintage

EASTERN EUROPE

THE ADVENT OF PRIVATISATION and the arrival of flying winemakers on behalf of British retailers is helping to transform the face of Eastern European wine. Inevitably, however, development varies enormously from one country and region to another and it is impossible to generalise about trends, other than to say that, over the next few years, the challenge will often be between indigenous grape varieties and the 'international' styles demanded in the west.

—— BULGARIA ——

BLEND				
CABERNET SAUVIGNON/ MERLOT COUNTRY WINE, VINCOM BURGAS Burgas	*Burnt tobacco aromas and cassis bouquet. Fruit palate. Light, tannic and well balanced.*	£2.49	A, JMC, WL, BOY, WRT	**B**
SPAR CABERNET SAUVIGNON & CINSAULT COUNTRY WINE, RUSSE WINERY Northern Region	*This red is pleasant and easy, full of fresh, jammy, red-fruit flavours and a Southern French character.*	£2.79	SPR	**B**
SAFEWAY YOUNG VATTED MERLOT 1993 Russe	*Soft plumb fruit, light to medium bodied with a touch of tannin.*	£2.85	SAF	**B**
ORIACHOVITZA VINTAGE BLEND RESERVE MERLOT/CABERNET SAUVIGNON 1990 Oriachovitza	*Full blackcurrant, spicy flabour. Nice oak and rich berry fruit flavour. Good finish.*	£2.75	JS, BLW, G&J, WOW, WES, FUL	**B**
CABERNET SAUVIGNON/ MERLOT RESERVE, LOVICO SUHINDOL 1989 Suhindol	*Oak and berry aromas; followed by full, gentle palate. Good.*	£2.99	SAF, THP, FUL	**B**

LOVICO SUHINDOL RESERVE MERLOT 1990 Suhindol	*Spicy, open nose; full and rich. Nice light, soft fruit style, good length and finish.*	£2.99	A, KS, OD, FUL, THP, DIO, CWS	B
SLIVEN BULGARIAN CABERNET SAUVIGNON, VINI SLIVEN 1989 Sliven	*Mature red colour. Sweet vanilla oak and rich fruit aromas. Rich smoky, black fruits in mouth.*	£3.29	TDS, VW, AB, BUD	B

— HUNGARY —

RED				
NAGYREDE ROUGE, SZOLOSKERT CO-OPERATIVE 1993 Nagyrede Region	*Fresh, almost Beaujolais-like fruity young wine.*	£1.99	I, SAF	B
MERLOT, MINOSEGI, SZARAZ VOROS BOR 1993 Villany	*There is a ripe fruit on the nose of this fresh, young, light wine.*	£2.95	A, SAF, TH, HAG	B
DRY WHITE				
RIVER DUNA SAUVIGNON BLANC, NESZMELY 1993	*Rich, rounded wine full of lovely soft gooseberry fruit and fresh citric flavour.*	£2.99	SAF	B
NAGYREDE SAUVIGNON BLANC, KYM MILNE/NAGYREDE 1993	*Clean, dry, gooseberry, appley fruit. Decent weight with ripe, refreshing finish.*	£3.99	SAF	B
SWEET WHITE				
TOKAY 5 PUTTONYUS, INTERCONSULT 1988 Tokaji	*Concentrated, nutty-raisiny wine with a hint of spice.*	£6.49	VER	B

TOKAJI ASZU 4 PUTTONYOS, TOKAJI WINE TRUST 1988 Tokaji	*Deep gold colour. Botrytis aroma on nose. Raisin palate with treacle and toffee. Lovely acidity.*	**£7.95**	W	**B**
TOKAJI ASZU 5 PUTTONYOS, TOKAJI HEGYALJA 1981 Tokaji	*Bright, clear, golden brown. sweetness and good acidity, almost toffee-like flavours.*	**£12.75**	BAR, SEL	**S**
TOKAJI ASZU 6 PUTTONYOS, HETSZOLO 1981 Tokaji	*Nutty and biscuity on nose. Resinous and piney with flavours of mangoes and rich Dundee cake.*	**£19.95**	GRO, POM, SOB, RWW	**G**

— MOLDOVA —

DRY WHITE				
SAUVIGNON BLANC, HINCESTI 1993	*Rich flavour of mango lifted by tones of grape-fruit. Very impressive in this price bracket.*	**£2.99**	OD, TH, WR, BU, MWW, HHR	**B**

— ROMANIA —

RED				
SAFEWAY ROMANIAN SPECIAL RESERVE PINOT NOIR 1989 Dealul Mare	*Ripe, soft, plummy, easy going. A delight.*	**£2.99**	SAF, HA	**B**

ENGLAND

IMPROVING WITH EVERY HARVEST, today's English wines often have more in common with the dry wines of the Loire and the aromatic whites of Northern Italy than with anywhere else in the world. Thankfully, England's winemakers have mostly given up their efforts to make mock-German wines and begun to develop an identity for themselves.

RED			
BEENLEIGH CABERNET SAUVIGNON/MERLOT, BEENLEIGH MANOR VINEYARD 1991 Devon	*This red shows a dark, rich, purple colour and bags of rich, flavoursome, chewy fruit. Classy, full-bodied stuff.*	**£12.75**	NI, HWM, WR, BU	B

DRY WHITE			
SHAWSGATE VINEYARD MULLER THURGAU/ SEYVAL BLANC 1992 East Anglia	*The gooseberry bouquet is very clean and dry. Good acidity on the palate, with good length.*	**£4.25**	SHA	B
BACCHUS, EAST SUTTON VINE GARDEN, 1992 Kent	*Possessed of a fragrant, perfumed nose, this attractive wine has plenty of sweet ripe fruit.*	**£4.50**	BGV, ESG	B
WYKEN BACCHUS, WYKEN VINEYARDS 1991 Suffolk	*Fresh grapes and leaves. Spritzy, clean, fresh and dry. Well-balanced, with touches of green apple.*	**£4.65**	WKV	B
HERITAGE FUME, HARVEST WINE GROUP 1993 Southern England	*Stylish citrus nose with a hint of lanolin, gooseberry, appley flavours and zippy green acid.*	**£4.99**	EMV, WR, BU, TH	B

NUTBOURNE VINEYARD HUXELREBE 1992 West Sussex	*Lively lemon fruit on the nose. Nice, full limey fruit on the palate, with good balancing acidity.*	£4.99	PI, FS, NBV	B
BARKHAM MANOR SCHONBURGER, BARKHAM MANOR VINEYARD 1990 East Sussex	*With its smoky nose and good, ripe aromas, this is a full-bodied and fairly pleasant wine, with a dryer finish.*	£5.20	BAK	B
BARKHAM MANOR SCHONBURGER/RIVANER 1991 East Sussex	*Light, clean and fresh acidity with lemony, grassy nose.*	£5.85	BAK	B
WARDEN VINEYARD, ENGLISH WHITE WINE, WARDEN ABBEY VINEYARD 1992 Bedfordshire	*Elderflowers and grass on the nose of this young wine. Clean and fresh. Medium finish.*	£5.90	SV, HW, WR, BV	B
OATLEY VINEYARD KERNER/KERNLING 1991 West Sussex	*Crisp and fresh with a zippy grapefruit acidity alongside some soft, clean fruit. Very drinkable.*	£6.00	WOT, OAT	B
CHANCTONBURY CLASSIC, CHANCTONBURY VINEYARD 1992 Sussex	*Fresh nose of tropical fruits and pear drops, with an almost muscatty dimension. Faintly spritzy, with softish fruit.*	£6.99	SAF, PAL, LW, CVY	B
DENBIES BACCHUS 1992 Surrey	*Elderflower and orange blossoms on the nose. Spicy, honeyed fruit, with good weight. Great length and clean acid.*	£6.99	DBS	S
BACCHUS MEDIUM, LAMBERHURST VINEYARDS 1993 Kent	*Very pale colour. Clean, fresh, ripe fruit nose. Sauvignon-style fruit and spice, with light, crunchy, gooseberry acidity. Finishes clean.*	£7.00	LAH	S

SHAWSGATE VINEYARD, BACCHUS 1991 East Anglia	*Elegant, with rich, green apple fruit on the palate. Nice and bracing.*	£7.50	SHA	B
CHANCTONBURY CLASSIC, CHANCTONBURY VINEYARD 1993 Sussex	*Grassy and slightly biscuity nose, with delicate melon fruit. The palate shows a slight petillance and finishes crisply.*	£7.50	CVY	B
SHARPHAM BARREL-FERMENTED WHITE 1993 Devon	*Very gentle lime and pineapple fruit, with a hint of vanilla from the subtle oak.*	£7.95	NI, HWM, WR, BU	B

SWEET WHITE

DENBIES WINE ESTATE NOBLE HARVEST 1992 Surrey	*Ripe apricot nose of good intensity. Very rich and extremely well lasting.*	£17.50	DBS, RWW, SEL, HAR	B

ROSE

SUSSEX SUNSET, HIDDEN SPRING VINEYARD 1993 Sussex	*Clean fruit acidity gives this wine a mouthwatering quality: lovely elegant fruit.*	£5.95	HSV, HWM, SAF	B

SPARKLING

CARR TAYLOR NV SPARKLING WINE East Sussex	*Aromas of elderflower and grapefruit, reminiscent of Alsace. Clean, lively characters make this good and refreshing.*	£9.50	CTV, EWC, WIL, SAS	B

FRANCE

Still the heartland of the wine world, despite the increasingly eager efforts of contenders throughout the world. A glance through the following pages, however, reveals how Burgundy, Bordeaux and the Rhône, for example, are all looking far more competitive against the New World than the Loire. As for France's hidden strengths, just look at those new wave medal winners from regions in the south which once did little more than tip their harvests into the wine lake.

— BORDEAUX —

RED				
Waitrose Good Ordinary Claret, Ginestet Bordeaux	*This youthful, ruby-coloured wine has a light and grapey palate.*	**£2.99**	W	**B**
Chateau La Foret, Barton & Guestier 1993 Bordeaux	*Attractive, herbaceous, leafy bouquet with sweet, juicy, gulpable fruit.*	**£3.49**	SAF	**S**
Somerfield Oak-Aged Claret, Louis Eschenauer 1990 Bordeaux	*Good colour and bouquet. Fresh fruity and slightly sweet. Drinking well.*	**£4.45**	SMF, G	**B**
Waitrose Special Reserve Claret, Ginestet 1990 Bordeaux	*Good colour and quite nice supple merlot finish. Soft, good drinking. Light and approachable.*	**£4.75**	W	**B**
Chateau Saint Robert, Graves, Credit Foncier 1988 Bordeaux	*Rich, ripe fruit nose with tannins. Balanced with length.*	**£4.99**	SMF, G	**B**
Collection Anniversaire, Special Reserve Claret, Yvon Mau 1990 Bordeaux	*Powerful, woody aromas and good colour to this wine. Good tannins and massive fruit flavours.*	**£4.99**	U	**B**

CHATEAU MINGOT, COTES DE CASTILLON, YVON MAU 1990 Bordeaux	*Much soft fruit nose; some good tobacco aromas. Generous palate with nice flavours.*	**£4.99**	U	**B**
CHATEAU MEAUME, BORDEAUX SUPERIEUR, ALAN JOHNSON-HILL 1990 Bordeaux	*Lovely rich colour and quite classy bouquet; generous. Good fruit flavours and tannins.*	**£4.99**	MWW	**B**
CHATEAU PEYROU, COTES DE CASTILLON, C PAPON 1989 Bordeaux	*Praised for its well-matured concentration of flavours and medium length. Good value.*	**£5.29**	WL	**B**
CHATEAU LAMARTINE, BORDEAUX ROUGE, COMPAGNIE MEDOCAINE 1990 Bordeaux	*Classic Cabernet aroma tempered with spicy oak. Extract of blueberry and raspberry fruit.*	**£5.29**	PF	**B**
CHATEAU DE PIC, 1ERES COTES DE BORDEAUX 1990 Bordeaux	*Ripe, rich cedar fruit. Fine palate. Nice structure.*	**£5.49**	DBY	**B**
MEDOC, BARTON & GUESTIER 1990 Bordeaux	*Round, sweet grapey fruit flavours; green tannins, good structure and well balanced.*	**£5.50**	DVC, OD, CWW, DH	**B**
DOMAINE LA GRAVE, BORDEAUX ROUGE 1990 Bordeaux	*Juicy fruit nose; sweet and full. Rounded fruit, casssis flavoured palate with good balance.*	**£5.70**	GH	**S**
MICHEL LYNCH BORDEAUX ROUGE, COMPAGNIE MEDOCAINE 1990 Bordeaux	*Soft style of wine with good structure. Clean full nose; green light fruity character.*	**£5.99**	SAF, HN, OD, VW, DBY	**B**
SIRIUS BORDEAUX ROUGE, PETER A SICHEL 1989 Bordeaux	*Highly developed, deep, fruity character sporting solid, curranty fruit. A good lunch wine.*	**£5.99**	TH, WL, WR, BU, F&M	**B**

CHATEAU RICHOTEY, FRONSAC, ETS J P MOUEIX 1990 Bordeaux	*Soft and easy drinking, clean, fresh fruit and nice tannins.*	£5.99	C&B, WIA	B
CHATEAU DE BELCIER, COTES DE CASTILLON 1990 Bordeaux	*Very quaffable. The herbaceous nose has some perfume. Good concentration of flavours.*	£5.99	DBY, D	B
CHATEAU BONNET RESERVE, BORDEAUX 1992 Bordeaux	*Young, blueish colour. Vibrant cherry fruit on the nose. Still a little closed but good structure.*	£5.99	TH, DBY	B
CHATEAU LAMOTHE DE HAUX, PREMIERES COTES DE BORDEAUX, FABRICE NEEL 1990 Bordeaux	*This wine is ruby red, with a fruity, vegetal nose. Youthful.*	£6.00	CAR, FSW, FIN, ND, CHH, BGC	B
DOMAINE DU BALARDIN, BORDEAUX SUPERIEUR, R ZUGER (CHATEAU MALESCOT) 1990 Bordeaux	*Nice maturity and complexity on the nose. Good blackcurrant fruit lingers on the finish.*	£6.99	CRL, HER, TRE, HC	B
CHATEAU CARIGNAN, 1ER COTE DE BORDEAUX 1988 Bordeaux	*Strong bouquet followed by quite fat flavours. Slightly biting in mouth.*	£6.99	VW	B
CHATEAU DE SOURS, BORDEAUX ROUGE 1990 Bordeaux	*Raspberry nose; slight green, stalky aromas; capsicum. Well structured.*	£6.99	MWW, C&B, PLA, IRV, FUL, HHR	B
CHATEAU POITOU, LUSSAC ST-EMILION 1986 Bordeaux	*Deep, ruby red wine; soft nose followed by quite tannic fruity palate.*	£7.20	M&V, ACH	B
CHATEAU DU CARTILLON, HAUT-MEDOC, R GIRAUD SA 1990 Bordeaux	*Concentrated colour with good weight of fruit on palate. Vanilla character; firm tannins but supple.*	£7.50	SEL, PAT	B

CHATEAU LA PRADE, BORDEAUX COTES DE FRANCS, PATRICK VALETTE 1990 Bordeaux	Woody nose; a little closed at first. Good depth to palate, soft jammy fruit flavours and tannins.	£7.60	RR	B
CHATEAU BEL-AIR ORTET, ST-ESTEPHE 1986 Bordeaux	High bouquet, slightly stalky merlot character. Good cassis fruit to nose. Excellent tannins.	£7.99	SMF, G	B
CHATEAU DE FRANCS, COTES DE FRANCS 1990 Bordeaux	Bright red coloured wine with mature nose. Easy, good fruit flavours, young.	£7.99	TH, WR, BU	B
ST-JULIEN TRADITION, BARTON & GUESTIER 1990 Bordeaux	Ripe, plummy, oaky bouquet; rich palate, quite hot.	£7.99	OD, SAF, CWW	B
LE MOULIN DE LUDON, HAUT-MEDOC, CHATEAU LA LAGUNE 1990 Bordeaux	Red brick coloured wine. Soft ripe fruit flavours. Lovely structure, youthful, sweet oak and spice.	£7.99	MWW	S
CHATEAU DES ANNEREAUX, LALANDE DE POMEROL 1990 Bordeaux	Warm to savoury bouquet. Soft floral fruit. Good feel inthe mouth with soft tannins.	£8.00	ABY, DBY	B
CHATEAU LA ROUSSELIERE, ST-ESTEPHE, 1990 Bordeaux	Sweet, leathery palate with good structure; ripe spicy fruit and full furry tannins.	£8.90	SUM	S
CHATEAU LA TOUR DE BY, MEDOC 1989 Bordeaux	Good, intense varietal Cabernet Sauvignon nose with hints of chocolate. Pleasant and spicy.	£8.99	U, THP	B
LA FERME D'ANGLUDET, MARGAUX, PETER A SICHEL 1990 Bordeaux	Leafy, cedary, bell pepper nose with ripe fruit flavours and a hint of coffee on the finish.	£8.99	WL, MWW, FIN	B

CHATEAU CARTEAU, COTES DAUGAY, SAINT-EMILION GRAND CRU 1989 Bordeaux	*Good, soft sweet edge; mild creamy oak. Good fruit and lovely ripe tannins. Good potential.*	£9.25	WSO	**B**
CHATEAU FOURCAS-LOUBANEY, LISTRAC 1989 Bordeaux	*Lovely, warm, baked beans nose. Soft and scented with lovely fruit. Light and balanced.*	£9.40	J&B	**B**
CHATEAU LES ORMES DE PEZ, ST-ESTEPHE 1991 Bordeaux	*Consistant purple colour to edge. Young vintage, cloves, stalky fruit and good tannins.*	£9.99	SAF	**B**
CHATEAU LAPLAGNOTTE-BELLEVUE, ST-EMILION GRAND CRU 1990 Bordeaux	*Deep rich colour with strong berry nose, some wood. Fruit mid palate. Good potential.*	£9.99	J&B, THP	**B**
CHATEAU DU BREUIL, HAUT-MEDOC, LOUIS VIALARD SARL 1989 Bordeaux	*Supple, medium-bodied wine, ripe and sweetly oaky with a little tannin and nice length.*	£10.00	PLA	**B**
DOMAINE DE BIGARNON, ST-JULIEN, CHATEAU LEOVILLE LAS CASES 1983 Bordeaux	*Hot nose and deep fruit character; medium weight, quite dry.*	£10.50	VW, BI	**B**
CHATEAU CISSAC, HAUT-MEDOC 1990 Bordeaux	*Good nose; young fresh fruit with good tannins on palate.*	£10.99	ELV, EP, J&B, BEF, SUM, DBY	**B**
RESERVE PAUILLAC, DOMAINES BARON DE ROTHSCHILD 1990 Bordeaux	*Soft rounded, curranty aromas, cedary light redcurrant fruit. Nice concentration.*	£10.99	TH	**B**
CHATEAU DE LAMARQUE, HAUT-MEDOC 1990 Bordeaux	*Slightly green medicinal character; ripe fruit with slight pepperiness, nice minty finish.*	£11.20	C&B, WIA	**S**

CHATEAU BELGRAVE, HAUT-MEDOC 1990 Bordeaux	*Good fruit nose; varietal character with a touch of spice. Soft, easy drinking.*	**£11.25**	BWS	B
PAUILLAC, CHATEAU LATOUR 1991 PAUILLAC Bordeaux	*Nice nose; good, rich and jammy. Soft, well-balanced. Lots of tannins.*	**£11.55**	WL	B
L'ESPRIT DE CHEVALIER, PESSAC-LEOGNAN, DOMAINE DE CHEVALIER 1990 Bordeaux	*Jammy fruit nose; spice and full Cabernet flavours. Good length and balance. Fairly light.*	**£11.75**	ADN	B
CHATEAU TOUR PIBRAN, PAUILLAC 1990 Bordeaux	*Ripe, blackcurrant palate; slightly bitter. Developed fruit flavours.*	**£12.00**	PF	B
CLOS DU MARQUIS, ST-JULIEN, CHATEAU LEOVILLE-LAS-CASES 1988 Bordeaux	*Good deep red colour with a clean bramble fruit nose. Quite elegant, plummy fruit.*	**£12.00**	TH, WR, BU, BWI	B
FORTNUM & MASON ST-EMILION GRAND CRU, CHATEAU GRAND MAYNE 1989 Bordeaux	*Mid deep red wine with attractive mint and sweet fruit.*	**£12.50**	F&M	B
CHATEAU MOULIN PEY-LABRIE, CANON FRONSAC, G HUBAU 1989 Bordeaux	*Slightly stalky nose followed by quite tannic palate. Slightly metallic.*	**£12.58**	WL	B
AMIRAL DE BEYCHEVELLE, ST-JULIEN, CHATEAU BEYCHEVELLE 1989 Bordeaux	*Serious cedary Bordeaux. Clear mid-red colour with good fruit structure and firm wood tannins.*	**£12.99**	SHB, DBY, GNW, POM, WCE, GRT	B
CHATEAU BEYCHEVELLE, ST-JULIEN 1991 Bordeaux	*Beautifully integrated with fine, mellow liquorice and tannic flavours. Good balance.*	**£13.95**	GRT	S

CHATEAU LA LAGUNE, HAUT-MEDOC 1990 Bordeaux	*Clean, ruby coloured wine, aromatic with an attractive nose of rich and intense fruit.*	£13.99	THP, H&H, TBW, DBY, D	S
CHATEAU LASCOMBES, MARGAUX 1989 Bordeaux	*Reddish brown wine. Deep concentration of fruit, with firm tannins. Good, long fruity finish.*	£14.00	GBA, RBS, THP, MAY, N&P, SUM, CHL	B
CHATEAU CHASSE-SPLEEN, MOULIS 1990 Bordeaux	*Beautiful depth. Soft, curranty fruit nose; slight coffee and tobacco flavours.*	£14.00	JS	S
CHATEAU GAZIN, POMEROL 1989 Bordeaux	*A big mouthful of spice and fruit, well-balanced, good tannins and slightly sweet wood flavours.*	£14.00	M&S, DBY, BWI	S
CHATEAU MOUTON BARONNE PHILIPPE, PAUILLAC 1985 Bordeaux	*Pleasant strawberry nose with good balance of fruit and rich flavours. Well-balanced.*	£14.99	WMK, GRT, DBY	S
CHATEAU GRAND MAYNE, ST-EMILION GRAND CRU 1985 Bordeaux	*Unusual combination of fruit and cooked vegetables on the nose. Light bodied and fruity.*	£14.99	M&S	S
CHATEAU MALESCOT-ST-EXUPERY, CHATEAU MALESCOT 1990 Bordeaux	*Deep purple, youthful coloured wine. Spicy aroma. Future potential.*	£15.00	PF, LV	B
CHATEAU HAUT MARBUZET, ST-ESTEPHE, DUBOSCQ 1988 Bordeaux	*Good deep colour. Slightly vegetal nose with a dusty, earthy edge. Plenty of fruit.*	£15.00	SMF, G, DBY	B
CHATEAU LASCOMBES, MARGAUX 1988 Bordeaux	*Complex aroma and spicy palate with nice balance. Good finish.*	£15.00	GBA, RBS, THP, MAY, N&P, H&H, CHL, SUM	S

CHATEAU HAUT-MARBUZET, ST ESTEPHE 1990 Bordeaux	*Deep blackcurrant colour; fresh and juicy blackcurrant aromas; vanilla and oak.*	**£15.00**	DBY	**S**
CHATEAU LEOVILLE BARTON, ST-JULIEN 1989 Bordeaux	*Rich purple colour with fine mulberry fruit palate. Incredible vanilla bouquet.*	**£15.00**	L&W, SUM, BI, BWI, D	**G**
CHATEAU FIGEAC, ST-EMILION 1988 Bordeaux	*Porty, sweet palate, ripe, round, chocolatey and spicy. Will be very good in five to 10 years.*	**£16.00**	BGC, WCS, DBY	**G**
CHATEAU D'ARMAILHAC, PAUILLAC, BARON PHILIPPE DE ROTHSCHILD SA 1989 Bordeaux	*Complex oak, cedar on fruit aromas; firm, spicy ripe fruit. Broad tannin finish. Well-balanced.*	**£16.29**	LAY, A&N, POR, BNK, MRC, DBY	**B**
CHATEAU HAUT MARBUZET, ST. ESTEPHE, 1989, Bordeaux	*Lovely, ripe, oaky Medoc, with lots of flavour. Will improve with time.*	**£16.79**	DBY	**B**
CHATEAU GRAND PUY DUCASSE, PAUILLAC 1986 Bordeaux	*Deep, rich, concentrated tobacco and blackcurrants. Warm, full ripe fruit. Fine finish.*	**£17.95**	WMK	**B**
LES FORTS DE LATOUR, PAUILLAC, CHATEAU LATOUR 1986 Bordeaux	*Very good colour; nice oaky, soft attack. Ripe mid palate; well made and beautifully balanced.*	**£19.00**	WL, GRT	**B**
CHATEAU TALBOT, ST-JULIEN 1985 Bordeaux	*Excellent nose; minty, mature and complex. Lovely wine on the palate with dry finish.*	**£19.00**	THP, H&H, BWI, BI	**S**
CHATEAU LYNCH-BAGES, PAUILLAC 1987 Bordeaux	*Deep bouquet with good fruit and nice tannins. Ripe, rich concentration.*	**£19.99**	M&S, ABY, SEB	**B**

LES FORTS DE LATOUR, PAUILLAC, CHATEAU LATOUR 1987 Bordeaux	*Classy wine; cloying, stylish red currants. Good weight and length to finish. Nice drinking.*	£19.99	JS, TO	**B**
PAVILLON ROUGE, MARGAUX, CHATEAU MARGAUX 1990 Bordeaux	*Rich, ripe fruit with nice oak treatment. Very attractive and warm with a chocolatey texture.*	£22.99	DIR, DUW, TO	**S**
CHATEAU COS D'ESTOURNEL, ST-ESTEPHE 1989 Bordeaux	*Attractive vanilla and spice nose with concentrated smooth, rich fruit flavours. Good tannins.*	£22.99	THP, D, TBW, DBY, BWI	**S**
CHATEAU LYNCH-BAGES, PAUILLAC 1989 Bordeaux	*Spicy, frangipan aroma Dark inky fruit, quite austere. Good long finish. Concentrated style.*	£25.00	BWI, D	**B**
CHATEAU LATOUR, PAUILLAC 1983 Bordeaux	*Delicate fruit aroma. Vanilla wood and a hint of eucalyptus. Firm tannins, ripe finish.*	£49.99	VW, ABY	**B**
CHATEAU MOUTON ROTHSCHILD, PAUILLAC 1990 Bordeaux	*Intense and complex, chocolatey, fruit nose, lovely, rich and flavoursome. Excellent.*	£50.00	THP, BI, LV	**G**
CHATEAU LAFITE-ROTHSCHILD, PAUILLAC 1990 Bordeaux	*Powerful rich mint/cassis and berry, lingering tannins. Great now, great in the future.*	£59.00	THP, BI, SEB	**G**
CHATEAU LATOUR, PAUILLAC 1982 Bordeaux	*Powerful fruit aromas, cassis and fruit, mature, spicy, raspberry-rich and fleshy. Great potential.*	£99.99	VW, BUT, BI	**G**

Pinpoint who sells the wine you wish to buy by turning to the stockist codes. If you know the name of the wine you want to buy, use the alphabetical index. If price is your motivation, refer to the invaluable price guide index; red and white wines under £5 and sparkling wines under £10. Good hunting!

DRY WHITE

MARQUIS D'ALBAN BORDEAUX BLANC, DULONG 1993 Bordeaux	*Very floral with masses of fruit and a slight petillance.*	£3.95	NRW, EOO, WWI, VEX	B
CHATEAU LES VIEILLES SOUCHES BORDEAUX SAUVIGNON, JEAN GUILLOT 1992 Bordeaux	*A round, complete nose, suggesting aniseed and gooseberry. Soft, gentle and ripe with lots of fruit.*	£3.99	CWW	B
ANGELICO, BORDEAUX BLANC, CALVET 1993 Bordeaux	*A tropical fruit nose with good, rounded fruit on the palate. Good concentration and length.*	£3.99	OD	B
GRAVES BLANC, COLLECTION ANNIVERSAIRE, YVON MAU 1993 Bordeaux	*Classic Sauvignon characters on the nose with penetrating blackcurrant leaf and nettle aromas.*	£4.99	U	B
CHATEAU BONNET, ENTRE-DEUX-MERS, A LURTON 1992 Bordeaux	*Distinctive fresh peaches on the nose. Herbs and gooseberries on the palate and a long finish.*	£4.99	DBY	B
CHATEAU THIEULEY, ENTRE-DEUX-MERS 1993 Bordeaux	*Lots of fresh good fruit, whiffs of asparagus and grass on the nose. Highly vigorous fruit acid.*	£5.00	MWW, H&H, HHC	B
CHATEAU BAUDUC BORDEAUX BLANC LES TROIS HECTARES 1992 Bordeaux	*A fresh nose of pineapple and fat ripe peaches. New oak barrels lend a creamy vanilla flavour.*	£5.72	CVR, SUM	B
CHATEAU THIEULEY BORDEAUX BLANC, F COURSELLE 1993 Bordeaux	*Fresh grassy nose with piercing fruit and lots of varietal character. Crisp and clean. Stylish.*	£5.99	WL, H&H, GRT	B

CHATEAU DE SOURS BORDEAUX BLANC 1992 Bordeaux	Good and tangy. A combination of rich zingy fruit and integrated oak.	£5.99	Widely Available	B
CHATEAU COUCHEROY, GRAVES, A LURTON 1992 Bordeaux	Golden-hued, with a well-filled, flowery aroma and clean, soft fruit. Quite intense stuff.	£5.99	TH, WR, BU, TDS	S
CHATEAU RESPIDE, GRAVES BLANC, PIERRE BONNET 1992 Bordeaux	A delicately perfumed nose with good, grapey flavours on the palate. Good length and finish.	£6.99	NIC	B
CHATEAU THIEULEY BORDEAUX, CUVEE BARRIQUE 1992 Bordeaux	Spicy fruit salad. Evidence of Semillon in the subtle, soft, ripe fruit and plenty of gentle oak.	£7.95	MWW, H&H	S
GRAVES TRADITION, BARTON & GUESTIER 1990 Bordeaux	Rather spicy, woody nose with a hint of glycerine. Rich tropical fruit is off-set against weighty oak.	£7.99	OD	B
CHATEAU CHARMES GODARD, BORDEAUX BLANC, M. THIENPONT 1990 Bordeaux	Lovely nose of smoky, nutty oak. Zesty citrus fruit layered with nuts, biscuits and cream.	£8.00	THP	S
CHATEAU MAGNEAU, BORDEAUX BLANC, CUVEE JULIEN 1990 Bordeaux	Plenty of up-front new American oak supported by a wealth of rich buttery fruit. Good length.	£8.95	TO	B
CHATEAU COUHINS LURTON, PESSAC-LEOGNAN 1990 Bordeaux	Well integrated oak and rich pineapple fruit with hints of citrus fruit, mint and apples.	£12.00	THP, DBY	B
CHATEAU LA TOUR-MARTILLAC, PESSAC-LEOGNAN 1989 Bordeaux	Soft and creamy new oak reminiscent of a good white Burgundy, packed with rich flavour.	£16.50	PON	S

SWEET WHITE

Sauternes Baron de Fontenilles, Ginestet Bordeaux		£4.39	MRN	B
Chateau De Berbec, Premieres Cotes de Bordeaux 1990 Brun Camille Bordeaux	*Attractive and luscious grapefruit fruitiness balanced by soft acidity. Elegant with great length.*	£6.00	TDS, SAF, R&I, NRW	S
Les Cypres de Climens, Sauternes, Chateau Climens 1984 Sauternes	*A bright wine with a pungent floral and honey nose. Very classy with nutty tones.*	£10.29	VW	S
Sainte Croix du Mont, Baron Philippe de Rothschild 1990 Bordeaux	*An almondy nose, full of soft creamy fruit, weighty with good structure. Smoky finish.*	£10.39	HPD, RAC, WBR, WSW	B
Chateau Haut Caplane, Sauternes, D Milhade 1990 Bordeaux	*Honey on nose followed by luscious fruit balanced by gentle acidity and ripe sweetness.*	£12.00	ABY	B
Chateau Bastor-Lamontange, Sauternes 1989 Bordeaux	*Citric and almondy aromas. Honeyed fruit on the palate with nice balancing acidity.*	£15.95	SMF, G	B
Chateau Climens, Barsac 1991 Bordeaux	*Full-bodied with luscious fruit flavours accompanied by charred oak. Nicely balanced.*	£21.49	TH, WR, BU	S

ROSE

Michel Lynch Bordeaux Rose, Compagnie Medocaine 1992 Bordeaux	*Vividly coloured with delicious berry flavour and a soft ripe nose. A well-balanced wine.*	£5.89	PF	B

CHATEAU BONNET BORDEAUX CLAIRET 1993 Bordeaux	*An attractive fresh young nose. Light and elegant fruit. Balanced with fresh acidity.*	**£6.29**	TH	**B**
CHATEAU DE SOURS BORDEAUX ROSE 1993 Bordeaux	*Smooth jelly fruit and a cherry bouquet rounded off with a pleasing dash of fresh acidity.*	**£6.50**	MWW, C&B, PLA, IRV, FUL, HHR, D, BEF, BWI	**B**

— BURGUNDY —

RED

MACON ROUGE SUPERIEUR LES TRUFFIERES, HONORE LAVIGNE 1992 Burgundy	*Bright, clean strawberry/cherry fruit character. Soft silky smooth texture in the mouth.*	**£4.15**	MHV	**B**
MACON SUPERIEUR LES EPILLETS, CAVE DE LUGNY, 1993 Burgundy	*Toasted fruit nose, juicy raspberry fruit on the palate, and some green, stalky tannins to finish.*	**£4.65**	W, RWL, BKT	**B**
JULIENAS LES FOUILLOUSES, DOMAINE M PELLETIER, EVENTAIL DE VIGNERONS PRODUCTEURS, 1993 Burgundy	*Hardy, fresh, green-pepper aromas. Good acidity and dry fruit flavours.*	**£5.90**	EP	**B**
BURGUNDY PINOT NOIR, LABOURE ROI 1991 Burgundy	*Good, long rich wine with full raspberry flavours and a subtle use of oak.*	**£5.99**	BKW	**B**
MACON-BRAY, DOMAINE DE LA COMBE, HENRI LAFARGE 1992 Burgundy	*Described by many tasters as 'stylish'. Excellent spiced plum/berry fruit. Good length.*	**£6.49**	TH, WR, BU	**B**

HAUTES COTES DE NUITS, CAVE DES HAUTES COTES 1990 Burgundy	*Rich, ripe and fruity on the nose but also earthy and vegetal with lots of rich fruit on the palate.*	£6.99	TH, WR, BU, TO	B
BEAUNE, LES CAVES DES HAUTES-COTES 1991 Burgundy	*A young wine, clean fruit definition, weight and balance, and a dry, tannic finish.*	£6.99	WL	B
BOURGOGNE ROUGE COTE CHALONNAISE LE DIGOINE, A & P DE VILLAINE 1992 Burgundy	*Bright, attractive and fragrant, a touch herbaceous. Warming sweet berries on the palate.*	£7.15	ABY	B
BEAUNE, LUC JAVELOT 1991 Burgundy	*A light, attractive style of wine with a lovely strawberry nose, very elegant and fresh.*	£7.29	SAF	B
BOURGOGNE ROUGE BONS BATONS, DOMAINE PATRICE & MICHELE RION 1992 Burgundy	*Strawberry fruit with good definition on the palate; juicy, tones of eucalyptus and great length.*	£7.50	M&V, SAN, ACH	B
PINOT NOIR, DOMAINE PARENT 1990 Burgundy	*Light violet-coloured wine, very upfront with a fruity and sappy nose.*	£7.80	OD, F&M, WSO, TAN	B
MERCUREY 'LES MAUVARENNES', MAISON J FAIVELEY 1991 Burgundy	*Clean fresh cherry aromas, ripe fruit concentration and a dry, acidic finish.*	£8.99	MWW, DBY	B
FIXIN, DOMAINE FOUGERAY DE BEAUCLAIR 1992 Burgundy	*Pale and soft, with aromatic raspberry fruit on the nose which promises to open further.*	£9.00	BBR, FW	B
MONTHELIE, JAFFELIN 1989 Burgundy	*A slightly grassy, powerful and fragrant nose which shows its age.*	£9.46	JAV	G

BEAUNE, VAUCHER 1988 Burgundy	*Cherries and toasty bouquet; depth on palate of peppery soft fruit. Well balanced .*	£9.99	SMF, G	**B**
NUITS-ST-GEORGES, GEORGES DESIRE 1991 Burgundy	*Vanilla bouquet; nice supple character to palate, vanilla and fruit. Good length.*	£9.99	SMF, G	**B**
SAVIGNY LES BEAUNE, DOMAINE MAILLARD 1990 Burgundy	*Powerful liquorice nose with a rich, fruity flavour on the palate and good use of oak.*	£9.99	BU	**G**
BOURGOGNE HAUTES COTES DE NUITS, CUVEE DES DAMES DE VERGY 1990 Burgundy	*Positive Pinot nose, gamey, farmyard characteristics and some fresh acid astringency.*	£10.00	NIC	**B**
MERCUREY, JUILLOT 1990 Burgundy	*A nose of toffees and roses. Good balance of tannin, fruit and acidity.*	£10.15	DD	**B**
BOURGOGNE HAUTES COTES DE NUITS, DOMAINE A-F GROS 1989 Burgundy	*Goats' cheese and straw on the nose, followed by a pleasant sweet fruit attack.*	£10.35	B&B, CAC, GHL, AWV, HEY, DBY	**B**
MARSANNY LES ST-JACQUES, DOMAINE FOUGERAY-BEAUCLAIR 1992 Burgundy	*Marzipan nose and cassis flavours from a wine of strong, tannic structure.*	£10.50	CAC, FW, B&B	**B**
VOSNE ROMANEE 1ER CRU LES BEAUX-MONTS, DOMAINE DANIEL RION 1989 Burgundy	*Oak on the nose with cooked, jammy fruit concentration to follow. Great depth.*	£10.99	M&V	**B**
CHOREY LES BEAUNE, EDMOND CORNU 1990 Burgundy	*Smoky, slightly meaty, aromas with further time in bottle recommended for fuller fruit.*	£11.00	CAR, GI	**S**

SAVIGNY LES BEAUNE, J M PAVELOT 1989 Savigny Les Beaune	*A delicate green, herbal, flinty nose. Full of rich cherry fruit.*	£11.45	D	S
CHAMBOLLE-MUSIGNY, C MASY-PERIER 1991 Burgundy	*Balanced raspberry fruit and a dry finish that will benefit from further ageing.*	£11.99	SAF	B
BOURGOGNE HAUTES COTES DE NUITS, LECHENEAUT 1992 Burgundy	*Bright raspberry flavours with herbal influence and savoury saltiness. Intense but accessible.*	£11.99	ENO	B
SAVIGNY LES BEAUNE, JOSEPH DROUHIN 1990 Burgundy	*Bright cherry-coloured wine, with a geranium-leaf nose. Woody over-tones and grapey fruit.*	£11.99	OD	S
BEAUNE 1ER CRU TEURONS, DOMAINE ROSSIGNOL TRAPET 1991 Burgundy	*Deep ruby. A warm nose of summer fruits, soft juicy fruits on the palate.*	£12.51	ABY	B
BEAUNE 1ER CRU 'LES SCEAUX', BOUCHARD AINE & FILS 1988 Burgundy	*Deep scarlet. Inviting minty and eucalyptus nose. Ripe, sweet fruit, great balance.*	£12.89	WWT, CAC	S
GEVREY CHAMBERTIN, ANTONIN RODET 1983 Burgundy	*Powerful nose; good burnt, animally bou-quet and mature fruit. Well balanced acidity.*	£12.95	JS	B
SANTENAY CLOS DE LA CONFRERIE, VINCENT GIRARDIN 1992 Burgundy	*A powerful bouquet of blackcurrant cordial with intense, smoky wood. Drinking well now.*	£12.95	TAN, HW, TAN, POR, FSW, BEL, EBA	G
NUITS-ST-GEORGES, DOMAINE DE L'ARLOT 1991 Burgundy	*Deep scarlet. Very smooth and concentrat-ed with summer fruits on the palate.*	£13.00	ABY	S

MOREY ST-DENIS 'EN LA RUE DE VERGY', DOMAINE HENRI PERROT-MINOT 1990 Burgundy	*Garnet-coloured wine with perfumed violets on the nose; well-balanced with a long finish.*	£13.89	WTR	B
GEVREY-CHAMBERTIN, LABOURE ROI 1991 Burgundy	*Deep-scarlet wine, with a fruity nose, hinting at cherries. Soft tannins and light acidity .*	£14.00	BAR	B
SANTENAY BEAUREPAIRE 1ER CRU, JOSEPH DROUHIN 1989 Burgundy	*Pale-scarlet wine with a minty, vegetal nose and hints of strawberries. Very full and fruity.*	£14.39	VW	B
BEAUNE 1ER CRU, DOMAINE DU CHATEAU DE MEURSAULT 1992 Burgundy	*A stalky and grassy young wine, both sweet and savoury, with an open nose.*	£15.00	HAR, BTH, PAT	B
BEAUNE 1ER CRU, DOMAINE PARENT 1990 Burgundy	*Attractive fruity and oaky nose. Light-weight fruit on the palate; soft, elegant, nicely balanced.*	£15.00	MJW, AWV, GHL, CAC	B
VOSNE-ROMANEE, MONGEARD-MUGNERET 1990 Burgundy	*Tawny red. A soft, spicy, vegetal nose. Nicely balanced. Delicate tannins.*	£15.90	MWW, H&H	G
BEAUNE 1ER CRU CENT VIGNES, RENE MONNIER 1990 Burgundy	*A stuctured wine with juicy jammy fruit flavours that bold up for a long, full finish.*	£16.50	ENO	B
BEAUNE, DOMAINE DE LA FEGUINE, DOMAINE PRIEUR 1991 Burgundy	*Asparagus and spice on the nose with herbaceous tones. Full-bodied and warm on palate.*	£16.99	M&S	B
GEVREY-CHAMBERTIN, SERAFIN PERE ET FILS 1989 Burgundy	*Good, lively strawberry nose. Wonderful mix of oak and fruit. Warm balanced finish.*	£17.60	ENO, H&H	B

NUITS-ST-GEORGES 1ER CRU 'LES CHAIGNOTS', ROBERT CHEVILLON 1991 Burgundy	*Aromatic, herbaceous nose, with a stylish concentrated palate of dark cherries and spice. Good now, but will evolve.*	£17.90	WTR, H&H	B
NUITS-ST-GEORGES 1ER CRU 'LES RONCIERES', ROBERT CHEVILLON 1991 Burgundy	*Light red. Sprightly and juicy. Fine, spicy fruit on the nose with ripe plum characters and new oak.*	£17.90	WTR, H&H	S
VOSNE-ROMANEE, DOMAINE JEAN GROS 1989 Burgundy	*Fragrant, complex nose of spice and charred oak, elegant fruit with sappy concentration.*	£18.00	ABY, WR, BU, HEY, DBY	B
POMMARD 1ER CRU, DOMAINE PARENT 1989 Burgundy	*Lots of fruit with toasted oak and caramel. Fruity and woody.*	£18.00	GHL, CAC, F&M	S
MOREY ST-DENIS 'PIERRE VIRANT' LECHENEAUT 1992 Burgundy	*Closed nose; new style, almost macerated fruit bouquet. Ripe tannins, quite strong palate.*	£18.50	ENO	B
VOLNAY SANTENOTS, VALLET FRERES 1990 Burgundy	*Full-bodied style with ripe cherries, spicy wood touches. Dry finish.*	£18.50	DBY	B
NUITS-ST-GEORGES 1ER CRU 'LES CAILLES', ROBERT CHEVILLON 1991 Burgundy	*Deep colour, bright red on the rims. A rich, ripe, jammy, New-World style with subtle oak, soft and sweet.*	£18.80	WTR, H&H	S
LOUIS JADOT NUITS-ST-GEORGES, LOUIS JADOT 1987 Burgundy	*Good, ageing Pinot with a farmyardy nose, ripe fruit, soft vanilla oak.*	£18.85	VW	B
CHAMBOLLE MUSIGNY, LABOURE-ROI 1991 Burgundy	*Clean fruit and firm acidity with slightly aggressive tanins. Would improve in two years.*	£19.50	BAR	B

GEVREY-CHAMBERTIN 'LES CAZETIERS', VALLET FRERES 1990 Burgundy	*Mature nose with some wet wool dankness and fresher ripe fruit flavours on the palate.*	£19.99	DBY, GTR, POR	**G**
VOLNAY CLOS DES CHENES, DOMAINE DU CHATEAU DE MEURSAULT 1992 Burgundy	*Deep ruby, with a ripe, spicy nose. Oaky, juicy fruit with a vibrant ripeness and good length.*	£20.00	HAR, BTH, PAT	**G**
NUITS-ST-GEORGES CLOS DE L'ARLOT, DOMAINE DE L'ARLOT 1991 Burgundy	*Light ruby-red colour. An earthy nose with violets and strawberries.*	£20.00	ABY	**G**
CHAMBOLLE MUSIGNY 'LA COMBE D'ORVEAU', DOMAINE HENRI PERROT-MINOT 1990 Burgundy	*Complex and powerful with a hint of old oak. Soft and creamy with gentle tannins.*	£21.00	WTR	**G**
POMMARD 1ER CRU LES JAROLLIERES, JEAN MARC BOILLOT 1991 Burgundy	*Almost black. Very brambly on the nose. Youthful, fun and very full and sweet.*	£23.00	GH, THP	**S**
NUITS-ST-GEORGES PREMIER CRU CLOS DE L'ARLOT, DOMAINE DE L'ARLOT 1990 Burgundy	*An old-style, oak-aged wine of great depth. Well-balanced with a long, creamy aftertaste.*	£24.00	TH, WR, BU, ABY, BWI	**G**
NUITS-ST-GEORGES 1ER CRU CLOS DES FORETS ST GEORGES, DOMAINE DE L'ARLOT 1991 Burgundy	*Ruby with purple tinges. Well-balanced with low acidity and soft tannins. Huge potential.*	£25.00	ABY	**G**
GEVREY-CHAMBERTIN CLOS ST-JACQUES, DOMAINE G. BARTET 1989 Burgundy	*A vegetal nose and lots of weight in the mouth; mature and meaty with good use of oak.*	£28.00	J&B	**S**

CORTON-POUGETS GRAND CRU DOMAINE LOUIS JADOT 1989 Burgundy	*Warm fruit richness on the palate with new oak flavours. Complex and rewarding.*	£30.49	TH, WR, BU	**B**
VOLNAY CLOS DE LA BOUSSE D'OR, 1989 Burgundy	*Mouth-filling fruit flavours from a light-weight style. Slightly peppery finish.*	£31.50	TH, WR, BU	**B**
CHARMES-CHAMBERTIN, VALLET FRERES 1990 Burgundy	*A clear, ruby-red wine with a rich and warm strawberry nose. Cherries on the palate.*	£32.80	DBY	**S**
CHAMBERTIN CLOS DE BEZE, DOMAINE THOMAS MOILLARD 1988	*Mature wine of length and complexity with farmyardy characters. Ready to drink now.*	£45.00	BBR	**B**
CHAMBERTIN, VALLET FRERES 1990 Burgundy	*Vegetal ageing nose, plenty of lively fruit in evidence despite the presence of wood.*	£45.00	BP	**B**
BONNES-MARES, GRAND CRU, DOMAINE FOUGERAY DE BEAUCLAIR 1992 Burgundy	*Exciting, attractive spicy nose, toasty wood, berry jam flavours and great potential complexity.*	£52.00	RM, B&B	**S**

DRY WHITE

WHITE BURGUNDY, M. MICHELET & FILS 1992 Burgundy	*Spicy, lime nose. Delicious, appley, clean taste. Lively finish.*	£4.99	W	**B**
SOMERFIELD WHITE BURGUNDY, GEORGES DESIRE 1992	*Soft, green appley fruit. Nice spicy lemon/lime finish.*	£4.99	SMF, G,	**G**

VICTORIA WINE CHABLIS, LA CHABLISIENNE 1993 Burgundy	Clean, fresh and lemony with ripe, honeyed, buttery fruit and tangy, limey acid.	£5.99	VW	B
TESCO CHABLIS VAUCHER 1992 Burgundy	A fresh pineappley nose. Honey, apricots and oaky complexity coupled with superb length.	£5.99	TO	B
SOMERFIELD CHABLIS, LA CHABLISIENNE 1993 Burgundy	A stylish lemon/lime nose with biscuity aromas. A characterful wine, crisp and stylish.	£6.19	SMF, G	B
PETIT CHABLIS, ETIENNE BOILEAU 1992 Burgundy	Creamy honeyed fruit. Mouthfilling and rich, crisp and clean.	£6.39	WTR, HLV	B
MACON CHARDONNAY, CUVEE JOSEPH TALMARD 1992 Burgundy	Creamy, rich, exotic and complex with toffeed fruit, subtle nutty oak and limey acid.	£6.50	MOK, SHJ, TAN, ADN, HOT	B
MACON-UCHIZY, DOMAINE TALMARD 1992 Burgundy	A vibrant, peachy nose. Ripe, buttery fruit, smoky oak and zippy, lemony acid.	£6.60	J&B	B
MALT HOUSE VINTNERS CHABLIS, LA CHABLISIENNE 1993 Burgundy	Crisp and buttery with pear-like flavours, good weight, structure, depth and length.	£6.69	MHV	S
MACON CHARDONNAY DOMAINES LES ECUYERS, DUBOEUF 1992 Burgundy	A tropical nose with pineapple fruit on the palate. Ripe, creamy and mouthfilling.	£6.69	JS, BWC	B
CO-OP CHABLIS, LA CHABLISIENNE 1990 Burgundy	Spicy, appley fruit, a rich creamy palate which fades slowly and cleanly.	£6.79	CWS	S

WINEMARK POUILLY FUISSE, PAUL BOUTINOT 1992 Burgundy	*Fruit in abundance coupled with good tangy acid and a faint earthiness. Delicious.*	£6.99	WMK	B
MONTAGNY 1ER CRU, CAVE DES VIGNERONS DE BUXY 1992 Burgundy	*Spicy and tropical, with some intensity and nice honeyed flavours. Dry finish.*	£6.99	M&S, TO	B
CHABLIS PREMIER CRU, LABOURE-ROI 1992 Burgundy	*Nutty and smoky, with sweet buttery fruit, showing leafy greenness and fine skin tannins.*	£7.50	BAR	B
BOURGOGNE CHARDONNAY, DOMAINE ROULOT 1991 Burgundy	*Smoky aroma with light, clean palate. Touch floral with soft juice centre on palate.*	£7.90	JAR, H&H	B
CHABLIS VIEILLES VIGNES, LA CHABLISIENNE 1991 Burgundy	*Grapefruits and cashew nuts precede honeyed, buttery fruit in a wine of good balance.*	£7.99	BU	B
CHABLIS PREMIER CRU FOURCHAUME, PAUL BOUTINOT 1992 Burgundy	*Spicy, honeyed fruit, hints of lemons and butter. Long and clean, a wine of definition.*	£7.99	CEN, SPR, DBY, GAR, BEF, NRW	B
CHABLIS, ALAIN GAUTHERON 1992 Burgundy	*Rich ripe and fruity. An opulent wine which is screamingly good value.*	£7.99	U, NRW	S
CHABLIS VIEILLES VIGNES, LA CHABLISIENNE 1990 Burgundy	*A pebbly and faintly biscuity nose with ripe, and delicate smoky characters.*	£7.99	TH	S
CHABLIS LES JEUNES PRINCES, LABOURE ROI 1992 Burgundy	*Rich and earthy with complex fruit concentration. Well-balanced and clean.*	£8.00	BIN	B

PETIT CHABLIS DOMAINE JEAN GOULLEY ET FILS 1993 Burgundy	*Kiwi fruits on the nose with melony, tropical fruit on the palate, good balance.*	£8.00	VR	**B**
CHABLIS 1ER CRU FOURCHAUME, CHATEAU DE MALIGNY 1992 Burgundy	*The scent of violets is followed by nutty citrus fruit flavours and zippy acid. Very classy.*	£8.00	ABY	**B**
CHABLIS 'VIEILLES VIGNES', GILBERT PICQ ET SES FILS 1992 Burgundy	*Ripe toasty oak, slightly smoky bouquet. Fresh citrus and clean finish to this elegant wine.*	£8.00	LAV, WIN	**S**
AUXEY DURESSES, OLIVIER LEFLAIVE 1992 Burgundy	*Spicy and vegetal character to nose. Rounded fruit and oak balance, with full, rich palate.*	£8.25	JAR, DBY	**B**
CHABLIS, JEAN COLLET 1992 Burgundy	*Honeyed citrus fruit on the nose and palate. Finishes cleanly with tangy acidity.*	£8.95	RES, SAC, PIC, HST, MRF	**B**
CHABLIS 1ER CRU MONTMAINS, CHANSON ET FILS 1992 Burgundy	*Good light nose, with soft crisp fruit palate. Pleasant finish.*	£8.95	MRN	**B**
RULLY VAROT BLANC, ANDRE DELORME 1992 Burgundy	*Beautiful, fragant citric nose. Lemon-lime palate, balance and oaky finish.*	£9.00	FWF	**B**
RULLY 1ER CRU 'RABOURCE', OLIVIER LEFLAIVE FRERES 1992 Burgundy	*Citrus fruit nose with use of toasty oak flavours. Good fruit and oak integration.*	£9.54	C&B, WIA	**B**
MEURSAULT, GEORGES DESIRE 1990 Burgundy	*Light lemon nose. Excellent balance with weighty fruit flavours, slightly sweet mid palate.*	£9.59	SMF, G	**B**

CHABLIS PREMIER CRU FOURCHAUME, LA CHABLISIENNE 1990 Burgundy	*Ripe and powerful fruit concentration with buttery citrus flavours. Fresh and smooth.*	£9.70	ET, WWT, CGW, MIT	S
CHABLIS PREMIER CRU MONT DE MILIEU, ETIENNE BOILEAU 1990 Burgundy	*Rich, complex chardonnay fruit with smoky, buttery citrus flavours. Very stylish.*	£9.89	WTR	B
CHABLIS PREMIER CRU FOURCHAUME, LA CHABLISIENNE 1991 Burgundy	*Delicate and flinty with pear-like fruit. Well-balanced with good structure.*	£9.99	NUR	B
RULLY 1ER CRU LES CLOUS, OLIVIER LEFLAIVE 1992 Burgundy	*Well-balanced, integrated wine, with a good length and nice finish.*	£10.00	L&W, DBY	S
POUILLY FUISSE 'FUTS DE CHENE', DOMAINE DES GERBEAUX 1992 Burgundy	*Deep, ripe, toasty, yeast character on the nose. Delivers a soft, fruit flavour to the palate.*	£10.19	WTR, HLV	G
CHABLIS 1ER CRU VAILLON, DOMAINE VOCORET & FILS 1992 Burgundy	*Young, appley nose, nice fruit and some wood character. Clean.*	£10.50	MWW, H&H	B
CHABLIS 1ER CRU 'GRANDE CUVEE', LA CHABLISIENNE 1990 Burgundy	*This is a lovely, round, complex wine with balanced acid and peppery heat. Bravo!*	£10.85	ET, CGW	S
CHABLIS PREMIER CRU MONTMAINS, JEAN GOULLEY & FILS 1993 Burgundy	*A leafy, lemony, slightly smoky nose followed by tropical fruit flavours and a hint of vanilla.*	£10.99	VR	B
CHABLIS PREMIER CRU VAU DE VEY, DOMAINE DES MALANDES 1992 Burgundy	*Earthy and musky with good fruit concentration, tight structure, complexity and length.*	£11.00	EOR, LWL, WOI, GRT	B

RULLY, JOSEPH DROUHIN 1992 Burgundy	*Tropical, full wine with attractive grapefruit and sweetish vanilla bouquet.*	£11.00	OD, DIO, BEF, MZ, DBY	B
ST-ROMAIN CLOS SOUS LE CHATEAU, JEAN GERMAIN 1991 Burgundy	*Fresh lemon/lime nose with gentle oak flavour and elegant texture. Restrained.*	£11.08	D	B
CHABLIS PREMIER CRU COTES DE LECHET, BERNARD DEFAIX 1989 Burgundy	*Lemony and smoky with great depth and balance, opulent fruit and dry flinty acid.*	£11.60	NIC	B
ST-AUBIN 1ER CRU LA CHATENIERE, DOMAINE GERARD THOMAS 1992 Burgundy	*Smoky, toasty nose with soft round buttery fruit. Clean, rich and well balanced.*	£11.95	CT, HV, M&V	B
MACON CLESSE, DOMAINE DE LA BON GRAN, CUVEE TRADITION 1991 Burgundy	*Ripe, creamy toasty aromas. Full, soft, ripe toast and butter flavours. Honeyed palate.*	£12.00	ADN, B, JFR, NI, GEL	B
CHABLIS, ETIENNE & DANIEL DEFAIX 1990 Burgundy	*Exotic nose with lemon, vanilla and touch of mint. Excellent balance.*	£12.00	L&W, LV	S
POUILLY FUISSE VIEILLES VIGNES, DOMAINE MANCIAT-PONCET 1992 Burgundy	*Deliciously subtle, buttery nose with a hint of vanilla. Lemony fresh with clean flavours and good length.*	£12.50	ENO	S
CHABLIS PREMIER CRU BEAUROY, ALAIN GEOFFROY 1992 Burgundy	*With peardrops on the nose this wine is showing intense ripe fruit character.*	£12.60	TH, WR, BU	B
MEURSAULT 'LES NARVAUX', OLIVIER LEFLAIVE 1992 Burgundy	*Delicate citrus fruit and toast with lime marmalade aromas. Full, soft and ripe.*	£13.50	JAR	B

CHASSAGNE-MONTRACHET 1ER CRU 'LES GRANDES RUCHOTTES', OLIVIER LEFLAIVE 1992 Burgundy	*A complex and subtle wine, light oak but with good clean fruit character. Nice long finish.*	**£13.95**	JAR	S
CHABLIS PREMIER CRU 'LES LYS', DANIEL DEFAIX 1988 Burgundy	*Good structure, gentle green tannins and an excellent finish make this wine hard to fault.*	**£13.99**	L&W	S
PULIGNY-MONTRACHET, MAROSLAVAC-LEGER 1991 Burgundy	*A lovely nose; subtle oak and nice buttery, ripe Chardonnay fruit character.*	**£14.99**	M&S	B
ST-AUBIN 1ER CRU, 'LA CHATENIERE', OLIVIER LEFLAIVE 1992 Burgundy	*Light flavours and subtle oak character. Excellent length, an elegant wine.*	**£15.19**	JAR, DBY	B
CHABLIS GRAND CRU BLANCHOT, VOCORET 1991 Burgundy	*Honeyed, appley nose. Exotic fruits and keen acidic balance.*	**£16.00**	MWW, H&H	B
CHABLIS GRAND CRU VAUDESIR, DOMAINE DES MALANDES 1992 Burgundy	*A lemony, rice-pudding nose preceeds spicy, citrus fruits on the palate. A very classy wine.*	**£17.00**	WSO, WSV, GHL, SAS, FS	B
PULIGNY-MONTRACHET, LABOURE ROI 1992 Burgundy	*Light nose. Touch of pineapple and a slight bitterness to finish.*	**£17.50**	BAR	B
MEURSAULT 1ER CRU 'LES PORUZOTS', OLIVIER LEFLAIVE 1992 Burgundy	*Soft, delicate fruit aromas. Well-balanced fruit, nice length. Ready for drinking now.*	**£17.67**	JAR	B
MEURSAULT 'LES LUCHETS', DOMAINE GUY ROULOT 1991 Burgundy	*Intensely ripe, rich warm nose of honeyed apricot fruit. Buttery, balanced wood flavours.*	**£18.00**	JAR, H&H	B

CHASSAGNE-MONTRACHET, JOSEPH DROUHIN 1990 Burgundy	*Fresh with pineapple flavours and a touch of juniper; lots of richness and vibrancy.*	**£19.99**	VW, CEB	**S**
CHASSAGNE-MONTRACHET 1ER CRU GRANDE MONTAGNE, RENE LAMY 1992 Burgundy	*Crystal clear wine with huge zesty lime juice and tropical fruit flavours. A refreshing style.*	**£20.00**	ABY	**B**
MEURSAULT LES VIREUILS, DOMAINE GUY ROULOT 1991 Burgundy	*Full, firm and bold; an eloquently-structured wine with a good fruity palate.*	**£22.50**	JAR	**S**
PULIGNY-MONTRACHET 1ER CRU 'LES CHAMPS GAINS', HENRI CLERC 1992 Burgundy	*Rich and flavoursome, with lively apricot flavours; excellent fruit and wood integration.*	**£23.00**	ABY	**S**
CHASSAGNE-MONTRACHET, LOUIS JADOT 1989 Burgundy	*Nutty, spicy caramel aromas. Fabulous feel in the mouth. Well-balanced and lasting.*	**£25.29**	TH, WR, BU	**B**
NUITS-ST-GEORGES 1ER CRU BLANC, CLOS DE L'ARLOT 1990 Burgundy	*Big, full oaky flavours. Good medium weight with lowish acidity.*	**£26.00**	BWI, ABY	**B**
MEURSAULT-BLAGNY 1ER CRU, MAISON LOUIS JADOT 1989 Burgundy	*Complex nose of nuts and spices gives this well-oaked Chardonnay a delightful character.*	**£27.99**	TH	**S**
PULIGNY-MONTRACHET 1ER CRU 'LA TRUFFIERE', JEAN-MARC BOILLOT 1991 Burgundy	*Well-structured, with good weight balanced by oak and acid. Stunning, exotic fruit. An exceptional, elegant wine.*	**£30.00**	GH, HEY	**G**

MEURSAULT CLOS DES PERRIERES, ALBERT GRIVAULT 1990 Burgundy	*Golden yellow wine with a warm palate and quite 'hot' finish. Balanced and gentle.*	£35.00	J&B	B

— BEAUJOLAIS —

RED

ST MICHAEL BEAUJOLAIS VILLAGES, GEORGES DUBOEUF 1992 Beaujolais	*Cherry aromas with attractive bitter cherry fruit in mouth. Good tannins on finish.*	£4.99	M&S	B
BEAUJOLAIS VILLAGES, CHATEAU DE LA ROCHE, GERARD DESCOMBES 1992 Beaujolais	*Cherry and soft strawberry fruit with some spiciness. Full in flavour and body.*	£5.29	CVR	B
FLEURIE, CELLIER DES SAMSONS 1993 Beaujolais	*Fragrant raspberry aromas with floral quality. Aromatic scented fruit in the mouth. Good value.*	£5.56	TH, WR, BU, ABY	B
CHENAS, CHATEAU DESVIGNES, PAUL BEAUDET 1993 Beaujolais	*Ripe raspberries and redcurrant jelly nose. Soft textured palate. Good acidity to balance.*	£5.70	ET, ABV	B
MORGON COTE DU PY, DOMAINE JENNY, JEAN-MARC AUJOUX 1992 Beaujolais	*Multifarious fruit-flavours. Rounded, mature with an almond bitterness on the finish.*	£5.79	YW, AUJ	B
JULIENAS, DOMAINES DES MOUILLES, DEPAGNEUX 1993 Beaujolais	*Signs of maturity. Mulberry fruit with hints of spice and strawberries marinated in balsamic vinegar.*	£5.81	NRW, BUT, DBY	B
FLEURIE CLASSIQUE, CELLIER DES SAMSONS 1993 Beaujolais	*Sweet rich cherry fruit balanced by good zingy acidity and a twist of spice on the finish.*	£5.90	ABY	B

JULIENAS, CLAUDE & MICHELLE JOUBERT 1992 Beaujolais	*Excellent berry/bramble fruit nose, slightly meaty with hints of herbs. Fine fresh finish.*	£6.15	MVN	S
CHIROUBLES DOMAINE DU CLOS VERDY, GEORGES BOULON 1992 Beaujolais	*A well-structured wine which shows great complexity. A good example of mature Beaujolais.*	£6.25	PAV	S
MORGON JEAN DESCOMBES, GEORGES DUBOEUF 1993 Beaujolais	*Excellent value and a rich mouthful of flavour, this is a star buy. Great length.*	£6.50	BWC, PAG, TDS, DBY	S
JULIENAS, DOMAINE RENE MONNET, EVENTAIL DES VIGNERONS PRODUCTEURS 1993 Beaujolais	*Fresh juicy blackberry fruit with excellent acidity to give a fine clean finish.*	£6.75	HBV	B
ST AMOUR LES BONNETS, J B PATISSIER, EVENTAIL DE VIGNERONS 1993 Beaujolais	*Intriguing, full of fruity flavour. Ripe and soft strawberry/cherry flavours and good acidity.*	£6.75	THP	B
FLEURIE, DOMAINE MEZIAT, PIERRE DUMONT 1993 Beaujolais	*Attractive bready yeastiness complements rich berry fruits with firm tannins in support.*	£6.99	U	B
ST AMOUR, DOMAINE PIROLLETTE, GEORGES DUBOEUF 1992 Beaujolais	*Vibrant hedgerow fruit, quite soft with hints of spice and almonds. Fresh and lively.*	£6.99	TH, WR, BU	B
MOULIN A VENT, DOMAINE DE LA TOUR DE BIEF, DEPAGNEUX 1993 Beaujolais	*Woody/toasty aromas. Baked plums with a hint of spice and an attractive savouriness.*	£6.99	NRW, DBY	B
MORGON, GERARD BELAID 1991 Beaujolais	*Developing very well. It has a lovely perfumed raspberry aspect.*	£7.25	VR, BN	B

JULIENAS, SYLVAIN FESSY 1993 Beaujolais	*Fresh, racy nose of raspberry and sherbet. Well structured.*	**£7.49**	LAV, WIN	**S**
FLEURIE, GEORGES DUBOEUF 1992 Beaujolais	*Rich, spicy and unusual. Strong tannin with long lasting, deep, rich finish.*	**£7.50**	MRN,	**S**
MOULIN A VENT, GEORGES DUBOEUF 1991 Beaujolais	*Maturing style with spicy oak and hints of liquorice married to soft summer fruit flavours.*	**£7.58**	BWC, AV, D	**B**
FLEURIE DOMAINE DES QUATRE VENTS, GEORGES DUBOEUF 1993 Beaujolais	*Berry fruit nose with gamey quality. Plummy fruit backed by good acidity and some tannins.*	**£7.99**	BWC, PAG, D, WAC, JN, DBY	**B**
ST AMOUR, SYLVAIN FESSY 1993 Beaujolais	*Fresh elegant mulberry fruit aroma with hint of spiciness. Positively overflowing with fruit.*	**£8.54**	LAV, WIN	**S**

— CHAMPAGNE —

SPARKLING

NICOLE D'AURINY RESERVE, UNION AUBOISE Champagne	*Full colour, with a slight pink tone. On the sweeter side of Brut, with a hint of caramel.*	**£8.99**	MRN	**B**
CHAMPAGNE PAUL D'HURVILLE BRUT, CHAMPAGNE Epernay	*Distinctive nose, with a grapey fruit taste that develops; a modern-styled wine.*	**£9.99**	VW	**S**
CHAMPAGNE ST HONORE, DUVAL-LEROY Champagne	*Quite restrained, yeasty and biscuity with a high-dosage taste.*	**£9.99**	SHJ, HOT	**B**

MONTOY BRUT, HOUSE OF BOIZEL Champagne	*Fermentation aromas with a floral note. Quite rich, fruity flavour; large-bubbled mousse.*	£10.49	TH, WR, BU, TDS	B
ANDRE SIMON CHAMPAGNE BRUT, MARNE ET CHAMPAGNE Champagne	*Full flavours with the style of a vintage wine. Biscuit and yeast nose, redolent of Champagne.*	£10.50	WRT	S
CHAMPAGNE DE TELMONT GRANDE RESERVE Champagne	*Savoury nose, even a hint of Marmite. Dry, crisp palate that includes a touch of grass.*	£10.99	MWW	B
CHAMPAGNE DRAPPIER CARTE BLANCHE BRUT Champagne	*Developed, yeasty nose on a wine with a full, long, rich flavour. Will keep and develop.*	£11.71	ABY	B
MEDOT, MEDOT & CIE Champagne	*An intense smell; yeast apparent in a Champagne of complex, and desirable characters.*	£11.89	AUL	B
CHAMPAGNE ALBERT ETIENNE BRUT, MASSE Champagne	*Good, but hard to tell from other good, similarly priced Champagnes.*	£11.95	SAF	B
WM LOW CHAMPAGNE CUVEE SELECTION BRUT, COOPERATIVE BRUN DE NEUVILLE Champagne	*Highly honed, sweet Chardonnay fruit that is hot and exotic in tone. Powerful nose.*	£12.49	WL	S
CHAMPAGNE ALEXANDRE BONNET CUVEE PRESTIGE BRUT Champagne	*Hint of richness and yeast on nose is sweeter than expected. Mousse fades quickly.*	£12.95	PON, FDL, BGW	B
CHAMPAGNE ALBERT ETIENNE BRUT ROSE, MASSE Champagne	*Pale, elegant, well-made. Grand Marque style without the expense.*	£12.95	SAF	B

CHAMPAGNE H BLIN NV BRUT TRADITION Champagne	*Fat, Chardonnay fruit balanced with mid-to-high acidity that lasts well. Will improve with age.*	£12.99	OD	S
CHAMPAGNE CARLIN, J CATTIER 1988 Champagne	*Pleasant mousse, nose and mature flavour that is elegant without great richness.*	£13.43	ABY	B
BARON DE BEAUPRE, ELLNER Champagne	*Sweet, spicy character on nose, rich, fat Chardonnay taste with light acidity. Better as aperitif.*	£13.75	SHJ, HOT, JFR, LS, MCO	B
CHAMPAGNE LE BRUN DE NEUVILLE BLANC DE BLANC Champagne	*Green apples crisp in the mouth, with the right balance of a well-made Champagne.*	£13.99	WAW, PV	B
CHAMPAGNE JACQUART BRUT TRADITION Champagne	*A creamy, Chardonnay nose is the prerequisite to a buttery, rich, fruity style. Quality stuff.*	£14.00	A, SEL, WTP, VTH, PAT	B
CHAMPAGNE LE MESNIL BLANC DE BLANCS BRUT Champagne	*Quite complex with almost all the characteristics looked for in Champagne. Great value.*	£14.35	TH, WR, BU	S
CHAMPAGNE LE BRUN DE NEUVILLE ROSE BRUT Champagne	*Rustic nose with well-sustained fruit and high acidity leading to a sharp finish.*	£14.50	WAW, PV	B
BERRY BROS' UNITED KINGDOM CUVEE BRUT CHAMPAGNE Champagne	*Style of the old school. Cream and biscuit nose, but fruity on palate. Will repay further cellarage.*	£14.95	BBR	B
CHAMPAGNE MASSE BARON EDOUARD VINTAGE 1983 Champagne	*Really rich and firm with a fat style that is enjoyable. Good value for 1983 vintage.*	£14.99	CWW	B

CHAMPAGNE DEVAUX GRANDE RESERVE Champagne	*Rich, creamy, biscuity with lots of fruit and an elegant finish.*	**£15.00**	MAR, WCB	**B**
CHAMPAGNE NICOLAS FEUILLATTE PREMIER CRU BRUT ROSE Champagne	*Good fruit and nut nose. Amber colour, luscious strawberry fruit and good biscuit edge.*	**£15.00**	SSM, HCK, ET	**B**
CHAMPAGNE PHILIPPONNAT NON-VINTAGE Champagne	*Hint of rose and unusual nose. Rich, yeasty palate with some finesse.*	**£15.99**	WW	**B**
JOSEPH PERRIER CUVEE ROYALE BRUT Champagne	*Very aggressive mousse and a taste that promises much. Buy and put away until next year.*	**£15.99**	Widely Available	**B**
CHAMPAGNE FORGET BRIMONT NV BRUT Champagne	*Forget the nose on this, go directly to the mouth and receive rich and fruity flavours.*	**£15.99**	TO	**S**
CHAMPAGNE MERCIER BRUT ROSE Champagne	*Unusual brown-pink colour. Rich biscuit nose. Excellent taste. Full and complex.*	**£15.99**	U, VW, FUL, HAR, P&R, M&C, DBY	**S**
CHAMPAGNE DEVAUX CUVEE ROSE BRUT Champagne	*Pale-pink colour. Delicate and clean aroma with lean and elegant taste. Great balance of style and price.*	**£16.00**	GRP, WRW, MAR, CWL	**S**
CHAMPAGNE HENRIOT SOUVERAIN BRUT Champagne	*Crisp aroma and clean-breaking, taste is well-balanced between fruit and acidity.*	**£16.29**	ABY, NIC	**B**
CHAMPAGNE TRADITION DE MANSARD GRANDE CUVEE BRUT, 1989 Champagne	*Mature-gold colour with a mature, honeyed nose. Well-balanced, light-weight style.*	**£16.49**	COM	**B**

CHAMPAGNE LE BRUN DE NEUVILLE MILLESIME 1986 Champagne	*Mature tasting with a biscuit nose, reminiscent of puddings. Full style. Buy to drink soon.*	£16.50	WAW, PV	B
CHAMPAGNE DELAMOTTE BRUT Champagne	*Spicy, apple-tasting on nose; a flavour that persists with cinnamon tones in mouth.*	£16.69	C&B, WIA	B
CHAMPAGNE CHARTOGNE-TAILLET BRUT Champagne	*An edge to the nose redolent of lemons and gooseberries. For the sweet-toothed.*	£16.99	SAF, VIW, CDE, WTR, EGL	B
CHAMPAGNE CANARD-DUCHENE BRUT ROSE Champagne	*Pale pink. Good fruit and sustained mousse. Lingering sweetness.*	£16.99	MWW, JAG, BYV, CJ, PTR, TBW, DBY	B
CHAMPAGNE GEORGES GARDET ROSE BRUT Champagne	*Good colour and rich, wild-strawberry nose. Long, fruity taste, not lacking finesse.*	£16.99	GH, CNL, CAC, VIW, LV, GRT, DBY	B
CHAMPAGNE POMMERY BRUT ROYAL Champagne	*Lots of gas. A full, rich style remaining clean, light and fresh at finish.*	£16.99	BI, PF, RDW, WAV, TBW, GRT	S
CHAMPAGNE JACQUART BRUT SELECTION Champagne	*Great Champagne characteristics. Vanilla and lemon can be detected in the mouth.*	£17.00	CAG, PAT	B
CHAMPAGNE VILMART & CIE GRAND CELLIER BRUT Champagne	*Great combination of fruit flavours. Slight vegetal character to yeasty nose.*	£17.50	DIR, DUW	B
CHAMPAGNE LE BRUN DE NEUVILLE CUVEE DU ROI CLOVIS Champagne	*Slightly sharp, nutty nose. Nicely balanced fruit. Fine mousse and great length.*	£17.50	WAW, PV	S

CHAMPAGNE GEORGES VESSELLE GRAND CRU BRUT MILLESIME 1986 Champagne	*Light-styled with good yeast and bread nose. Some fruit retained and spread over short finish.*	**£18.25**	JOB	**B**
VICTORIA WINE VINTAGE CHAMPAGNE, MARNE ET CHAMPAGNE 1986 Champagne	*Good, over-burnt fruit and a classic, yeasty Champagne nose. Corn-fizz style. Ages well.*	**£18.59**	VW	**G**
CHAMPAGNE MERCIER VINTAGE BRUT 1988 Champagne	*Mild lemon aroma and a foamy mousse. Lean, flavour and a finish of medium length.*	**£18.99**	FUL, TH, TO, VW, THP, M&C	**B**
CHAMPAGNE MOET & CHANDON BRUT IMPERIAL Champagne	*Mid-gold colour, with a persistent, honey and nut bouquet. Medium-full, dry and fairly soft.*	**£18.99**	Widely Available	**B**
CHAMPAGNE CHARLES HEIDSIECK BRUT RESERVE Champagne	*Good Pinot character to the soft palate with acid-drops and an underly-ing sweetness.*	**£18.99**	TO, U, WIL, L&W, SOH, DBY, TBW	**B**
CHAMPAGNE POMMERY BRUT ROSE Champagne	*Vibrant pink which belies its subtle qualities on nose, palate and finish.*	**£18.99**	BI, PF, RDW, WAV, GRT	**S**
CHAMPAGNE ALFRED GRATIEN BRUT 1985 Champagne	*Tasting very well now with fruit and honey flavours in a beautifully soft palate.*	**£19.50**	WSO	**B**
CHAMPAGNE FRANCOISE DESCOMBES GRAND CRU VINTAGE BRUT, LE MESNIL 1985 Champagne	*Very fine, slow bead to the mousse. Mature Pinot nose, with light colour. Elegant and classy.*	**£19.75**	TH, WR, BU	**B**
CHAMPAGNE VEUVE CLICQUOT YELLOW LABEL BRUT Champagne	*Fine, steady bead. Soft, toasty nose and youthful on palate, good fruit.*	**£19.99**	Widely Available	**B**

CHAMPAGNE DRAPPIER BLANC DE BLANCS Champagne	*Yeast and freshness combine with peach subtlety for flavours that last well.*	£19.99	ABY, DBY	G
CHAMPAGNE LANG BIEMONT CUVEE D'EXCEPTION 1985 Champagne	*A little flowery at first, yet full-bodied and fruity, with a violet mousse that persists.*	£19.99	HOU	B
CHAMPAGNE JOSEPH PERRIER CUVEE ROYALE BRUT ROSE Champagne	*Great, yeasty nose. Pleasing small-bubbled mousse. Dry, clean and well-balanced palate.*	£19.99	ES, H&D, AWV, TBW, GRT	B
CHAMPAGNE POMMERY BRUT VINTAGE 1988 Champagne	*Complex, nutty aromas. Mellow mousse with lots of richness in mouth. Clean finish.*	£20.99	BI, PF, RDW, WAV	S
CHAMPAGNE GOSSET BRUT RESERVE, GOSSET Champagne	*Effervescent with a strong dosage on finish and rounded, fruity taste.*	£21.00	CAR, SOM, TW, SAC, POR, DIO	B
CHAMPAGNE DEVAUX CUVEE DISTINCTION BRUT ROSE MILLESIME 1988 Champagne	*Age has produced a honeyed sweetness, but with a balancing tart, dry edge.*	£21.00	VEX	B
CHAMPAGNE DEVAUX CUVEE DISTINCTION 1988 Champagne	*Gorgeous flavours follow a complex and even confusing nose.*	£21.00	VEX	S
CHAMPAGNE BOLLINGER SPECIAL CUVEE Champagne	*Fine, biscuity taste with excellent balance and weight. Perfect mousse.*	£21.99	Widely Available	B
CHAMPAGNE LANSON BRUT ROSE Champagne	*Pale orangey-pink colour. Creamy and clean with some depth.*	£22.99	SB, VW, TH, CWW, THP, HWA	S
CHAMPAGNE MOET & CHANDON BRUT IMPERIAL VINTAGE 1986 Champagne	*Lovely aromas. Toasty, developed and complex, with great fruit and depth of flavour. Stunning.*	£22.99	Widely Available	G

CHAMPAGNE GOSSET GRANDE ROSE BRUT 1988 Champagne	*Pale-orange colour showing a little age, but still a lively mousse. Toffee and strawberry nose.*	**£23.70**	SEL, CAR, ABE, RE	**G**
CHAMPAGNE MEDOT CLOS DES CHAULINS Champagne	*Individual style that is complex and attractive; very biscuity and with elegant fruit on nose.*	**£24.00**	AUL	**S**
CHAMPAGNE NICOLAS FEUILLATTE CUVEE PALMES D'OR BRUT 1985 Champagne	*Very delicate. Subtle and polished, yet lots of fruit; yeasty with a crisp, fresh edge.*	**£24.00**	HCK	**S**
CHAMPAGNE VEUVE CLICQUOT VINTAGE RESERVE 1988 Champagne	*If you want yeast, this wine has it. Creamy nose, perfect finish, very dry and perfect bubbles.*	**£24.99**	Widely Available	**G**
CHAMPAGNE PHILIPPONNAT LE REFLET BRUT Champagne	*Gutsier than many Champagnes, a good mousse and light citrus aroma and palate.*	**£25.00**	SEL	**S**
CHAMPAGNE CHARLES HEIDSIECK BRUT VINTAGE 1985 Champagne	*A great weight of complexity which has developed into an attractive, long-tasting wine.*	**£25.50**	SEL, BAB, FEN, WCS	**B**
CHAMPAGNE TAITTINGER BRUT VINTAGE 1989 Champagne	*Broad nose with Pinot characters and a long, rich palate. Sweeter than some.*	**£25.95**	PF, SEL, D, DBY	**B**
CHAMPAGNE GOSSET GRANDE MILLESIME 1983 Champagne	*Refined, floral nose. Great chewy palate of luxuriant fruit. Crisp acidity. Fabulous.*	**£25.99**	WIN, SEL, RE	**S**
MOET & CHANDON BRUT IMPERIAL ROSE VINTAGE 1986 Champagne	*Yeast and strawberry nose. Maturity, complexity and weight make a top rosé of the old school.*	**£26.99**	RBS, LV, WAV, CLW, AMA, TBW, ABY	**B**

CHAMPAGNE NICOLAS FEUILLATTE CUVEE SPECIALE BRUT 1ER 1986 Champagne	*Dark on the eye, light on the nose, with slight Chardonnay fruit. Great lift in mid-palate.*	£28.00	SSM, HCK	B
CHAMPAGNE POL ROGER BLANC DE CHARDONNAY 1986 Champagne	*Excellent mousse adds to the clean taste from a lemon-rind tang at the base of the palate.*	£29.99	OD, F&M, MM, WIL, HN, WCS	S
CHAMPAGNE PHILIPPONNAT GRANDE BLANC 1986 Champagne	*Complex yeast characters on nose. Long, rich palate with cleansing acidity. Very interesting.*	£29.99	RAV	G
CHAMPAGNE BOLLINGER GRANDE ANNEE 1985 Champagne	*Strong, classic biscuit tones that announce a heady splash of Pinot. Sheer poetry.*	£31.00	Widely Available	B
CHAMPAGNE POMMERY LOUISE VINTAGE ROSE BRUT 1988 Champagne	*Crisp, dry and fresh taste with good, yeasty nose. Good structure and balance.*	£35.00	BI, RDW	S
CHAMPAGNE JOSEPH PERRIER CUVEE JOSEPHINE BRUT 1985 Champagne	*Glorious mixture on the palate, rich and biscuity, and has good autolytic characters.*	£37.90	FTH, JFR, GRT, FS, GNW	B
CHAMPAGNE CHARLES HEIDSIECK, BLANC DES MILLENAIRES 1983 Champagne	*Great complexity and finesse from a positive flavour and fresh acidity.*	£39.00	REM	G
CHAMPAGNE AYALA, CHATEAU D'AY, GRANDE CUVEE BRUT 1988 Champagne	*Lovely, mousse and yeasty nose, green acids and fresh citrus fruits with a perfumed aftertaste.*	£39.77	LAV, WIN	S
CHAMPAGNE LOUISE POMMERY VINTAGE BRUT 1985 Champagne	*Aromas of Pinot Noir. Rich, toasty and smooth. More fruit than expected from the Old World.*	£45.00	BI, RDW, WAV	S

CHAMPAGNE PHILIPPONNAT CLOS DES GOISSES 1986 Champagne	*Peppery-fruit taste to a lively nose and a hyper-active palate A great finish too.*	**£55.00**	EW	**B**
CHAMPAGNE CUVEE DOM PERIGNON, MOET ET CHANDON 1985 Champagne	*Quite fat, but rich and long in a traditional palate that is a pleasure to receive.*	**£55.00**	Widely Available	**B**
CHAMPAGNE TAITTINGER COMTES DE CHAMPAGNE, BLANC DE BLANCS 1985 Champagne	*Rich, luscious, oak-fermented with a finesse and structure you right-ly expect at the price.*	**£55.00**	HAR, SEL, F&M, DBY	**G**

— ALSACE —

RED

ROUGE DE TURCKHEIM, CAVE VINICOLE DE TURCKHEIM 1990 Alsace	*A rich peppery and spicy nose. Ripe fuit on the palate. Well balanced. long and delightful.*	**£12.00**	DBY	**S**

DRY WHITE

TOKAY PINOT GRIS, BLANCK FRERES 1992 Alsace	*Quite buttery, light and well-balanced. Dry, minerally and oily.*	**£5.25**	W	**B**
GEWURZTRAMINER, COOPERATIVE DE BEBLENHEIM 1992 Alsace	*Rich and well-balanced Excellent fruit perfume. Luscious and ripe with almost waxy texture.*	**£5.89**	WL	**B**
SCHNECKENBERG PINOT BLANC, CVPG PFAFFENHEIM 1993 Alsace	*A steely, aromatic nose, some ripe fruit and ele-gant length.*	**£5.99**	IWS	**B**
PINOT BLANC, ZIND HUMBRECHT 1992 Alsace	*Mature, yeasty and smoky nose, rich with rose petal aroma. Very stylish.*	**£6.32**	ABY	**S**

RIESLING GUEBERSCHWIHR, ZIND HUMBRECHT 1992 Alsace	*Delightful Kiwi fruit nose with crisp zingy palate mark this broadly flavoured off-dry wine.*	**£6.56**	ABY, D	**B**
RIESLING TURCKHEIM, ZIND HUMBRECHT 1989 Alsace	*Complex bouquet of gooseberries, honey and lemon interlaced with a touch of coriander.*	**£6.80**	ABY, WR	**B**
RIESLING TURCKHEIM, ZIND HUMBRECHT 1990 Alsace	*Apricots and raisin fruit and a good oily nose. Quite elegant with a hint of spice. Well made.*	**£6.80**	ABY	**B**
RIESLING TURCKHEIM, ZIND HUMBRECHT 1992 Alsace	*Attractive and elegant fruit. Good acidity and balance. A very enjoyable full flavour.*	**£6.80**	ABY	**B**
RIESLING TURCKHEIM, ZIND HUMBRECHT 1991 Alsace	*Lime flavours with zesty lemony nose. Maturely aromatic, light and balanced. Long citrus finish.*	**£6.80**	ABY	**B**
RIESLING SCHLOSSBERG GRAND CRU, CAVES VINICOLE KAYSERSBERG 1990 Alsace	*A lean and stylish wine, with an elegant stony nose and touches of slate and petrol. Classic.*	**£7.00**	ABY	**B**
GEWURZTRAMINER TURCKHEIM, ZIND HUMBRECHT 1992 Alsace	*A distinctive gold green with a smoky bacon nose. Fat and oily (in the nicest possible way).*	**£7.08**	ABY, D	**B**
GEWURZTRAMINER GRAND RESERVE CUVEE BACCHUS, LES VIGNERONS DE PFAFFENHEIM 1992 Alsace	*Peachy fruit flavours, balanced by good acidity. Full ripe finish. A spice feast with honey on the nose.*	**£7.49**	IWS	**S**
TOKAY PINOT GRIS RESERVE PARTICULIERE, KUEHN 1992 Alsace	*Honeyed, spicy lychee fruit with flowers and almonds. Balanced*	**£7.50**	ASH, LV, VAU, VIW, EVI, SUM	**S**

Wine	Notes	Price	Codes	
RIESLING HERRENWEG, ZIND HUMBRECHT 1990 Alsace	*Lychees, grapefruit, apples and lemons on ripe spicy nose. Delicious length and balance.*	£7.58	ABY, WR	S
MUSCAT, ZIND HUMBRECHT 1992 Alsace	*Rich, complex wine with gorgeous apple and raisin flavours. Classy.*	£7.74	ABY	B
GEWURZTRAMINER HERRENWEG, CAVE DE TURCKHEIM 1992 Alsace	*Restrained and well-coloured with ripe fruit and acidity. Spicy aromas and crisp finish.*	£7.99	U	B
GEWURZTRAMINER, F E TRIMBACH 1991 Alsace	*Spicy, quite pungent with a lingering flavour and good acidity. Big and mouthfilling.*	£8.00	VLW, VTH, BAB, HAR, PTR, DBY, LV	B
TOKAY-PINOT GRIS, CUVEE RABELAIS, CVPG PFAFFENHEIM 1992 Alsace	*Medium-full bodied with adequate acid. Off-dry, with a pleasing quality to the middle palate.*	£8.49	IWS	B
KRITT KLEVNER, MARC KREYDENWEISS 1992 Alsace	*Gentle, flowery bouquet. Sweetly fruity with a grapey, smoky, peachy palate. Elegant.*	£8.50	LV, H&H	S
RIESLING CLOS HAUSERER, ZIND HUMBRECHT 1992 Alsace	*Fine, delicate, nose. Young, quite austere but with brown sugar richness. Touch of class.*	£8.75	ABY	B
RIESLING HERRENWEG VIEILLES VIGNES, ZIND HUMBRECHT 1992 Alsace	*Real style; a rich fresh plum nose. Broad, fleshy palate impeccably balanced with zingy acidity.*	£8.75	ABY	S
GEWURZTRAMINER CLOS ST LANDELIN GRAND CRU VORBOURG 1992 Alsace	*Golden and rich, without being sweet. Fresh lime and zesty lemon with touch of honey.*	£8.75	PAG, BWC	S

GEWURZTRAMINER GRAND CRU HENGST, CAVE DE TURCKHEIM 1990 Alsace	*Fruity nose and clean attack. Ripe grape flavour with spicy mineral and liquorice finish.*	£8.99	MWW, DBY	**B**
RIESLING GUEBERSCHWIHR, ZIND HUMBRECHT 1990 Alsace	*Smoky, spicy and opulent with buttery, honeyed, petrolly and peachy aromas.*	£9.39	ABY, DBY	**S**
RIESLING RESERVE, ROLLY-GASSMANN 1991 Alsace	*Citrus fruits, apricots, melons, mangoes, and plums on nose. Tropical flavours on palate.*	£9.47	TH, WR, BU	**B**
GEWURZTRAMINER GRAND CRU STEINERT, JOSEPH RIEFLE 1988 Alsace	*Richly perfumed floral flavours on palate mingle with grapefruit pith aromas.*	£9.79	WTR	**B**
GEWURZTRAMINER GRAND CRU GOLDERT, ZIND HUMBRECHT 1992 Alsace	*A big and well-balanced wine that could certainly do with being kept for a while.*	£9.87	ABY	**B**
CLOS DU VAL D'ELEON, MARC KREYDENWEISS 1992 Alsace	*Persistent and well-balanced by refreshing acidity. Lemons, limes and a light floral nose.*	£9.95	LV	**B**
PINOT BLANC VIEILLES VIGNES, ZIND HUMBRECHT 1992 Alsace	*Ripe, grapey, spicy fruit nose. Plenty of weight and structure. Shows potential.*	£9.95	ABY, LV	**B**
TOKAY PINOT GRIS CLOS ST LANDELIN GRAND CRU VORBOURG, RENE MURE 1992 Alsace	*Bright, clean, citrus fruit and elegant restrained spice. Traces of lanolin and almonds. Excellent.*	£10.20	PAG, BWC	**B**
GEWURZTRAMINER CLOS WINDSBUHL, ZIND HUMBRECHT 1992 Alsace	*Intense ripe fruit flavours. Long finish, excellent balance, character and elegance.*	£10.27	ABY	**S**

RIESLING GRANDE CRU BRAND, CAVE VINICOLE DE TURCKHEIM 1990 Alsace	*A lovely rice pudding nose emanates from this plump wine. Some grip and a clean finish.*	£11.00	DBY	B
RIESLING GRAND CRU RANGEN DE THANN, ZIND HUMBRECHT 1989 Alsace	*Clean with fruity flavour and balance. A complex and soft palate showing some maturity.*	£11.27	ABY, WR, SEB	B
TOKAY PINOT GRIS GRAND CRU HEIMBOURG, CAVE VINICOLE DE TURCKHEIM 1990 Alsace	*Rich apricot and dried currants; complex, long and creamy with decent length.*	£11.29	DBY	B
RIESLING CLOS WINDSBUHL, ZIND HUMBRECHT 1992 Alsace	*Soft, spicy fruit, good acidity, rich and full. A wine with finesse and power.*	£11.93	ABY	B
GEWURZTRAMINER GRAND CRU GOLDERT, CVPG PFAFFENHEIM 1992 Alsace	*Delicate with a boneyed mango and lychee nose, gentle palate and a nice lemony finish.*	£11.99	IWS	B
GEWURZTRAMINER GRAND CRU CLOS GAENSBROENNEL, WILLM RESERVE EXCEPTIONELLE 1990 Alsace	*Spicy nose, elegant fruit and well-balanced acidity. Long citrussy finish. Hints of spices and cloves.*	£11.99	SEL, ROD	B
RIESLING CLOS ST URBAIN, ZIND HUMBRECHT 1992 Alsace	*Full, soft and rich. Lychee and peach flavours. Apple blossom and elderflower scents.*	£12.28	ABY	B
GEWURZTRAMINER GRAND CRU PFINGSTBERG, MATERNE HAEGELIN ET FILS 1991 Alsace	*Strong, dry, spicy palate with fruit - varietal character - complete with good depth of flavour.*	£12.28	ABY	B

GEWURZTRAMINER CLOS WINDSBUHL, ZIND HUMBRECHT 1990 Alsace	*Peachy and guava-like on nose and ripe on palate. Sweet, rich with honey and spice tones.*	**£12.28**	ABY	**B**
RIESLING BRAND, ZIND HUMBRECHT 1992 Alsace	*Rich brown sugar and butter. Tremendously long with creamy, sweet limes. Big, rich and ripe.*	**£12.28**	ABY	**S**
GEWURZTRAMINER GRAND CRU GOLDERT, ZIND HUMBRECHT 1991 Alsace	*Ripe fruit and weight with a herbal, spicy, soft, rich nose. Exuberant perfumed flavour.*	**£12.28**	ABY	**S**
TOKAY PINOT GRIS HEIMBOURG, ZIND HUMBRECHT 1992 Alsace	*Huge ripe fruit on this Alsatian wine. Could use more time to evolve further. Classy.*	**£12.36**	ABY	**B**
GEWURZTRAMINER GRAND CRU STEINERT, CVPG PFAFFENHEIM 1992 Alsace	*Subtle, elegant - nicely understated. Rich melon fruit, excellent length. Acidity lifts it beautifully.*	**£12.49**	IWS	**B**
HATSCHBOURG TOKAY-PINOT GRIS, CVPG PFAFFENHEIM 1990 Alsace	*Medium fullness with fresh acidity; off-dry. Quite stylish honey and apple flavours .*	**£12.49**	IWS	**B**
STEINERT TOKAY-PINOT GRIS, CVPG PFAFFENHEIM 1992 Alsace	*Peaches and spice on the nose. A good, crisp, appley palate. Youngish, with good depth.*	**£12.49**	IWS	**B**
STEINERT RIESLING, CVPG PFAFFENHEIM 1992 Alsace	*A lovely dry, but ripe, wine. Splendid limey, fruit and flower characters. Well made.*	**£12.49**	IWS	**S**
TOKAY PINOT GRIS CLOS WINDSBUHL, ZIND HUMBRECHT 1992 Alsace	*Full, well-balanced oily fruit and a rich, pungent nose. Excellent length. Not for the faint hearted.*	**£13.44**	ABY	**S**

TOKAY PINOT GRIS GRAND CRU MOENCHBERG VENDANGES TARDIVES 1992 Alsace	*Richly spicy fruit has depth with notes of orange peel and honey coming through.*	**£13.50**	LV, H&H	**B**
RIESLING CUVEE FREDERIC EMILE, F E TRIMBACH 1988 Alsace	*Spicy, assertive and rich. Lemon and lime aromas with petrolly touches.*	**£14.00**	OD, JEH, AMP, DBY, HAR, LV	**S**
GEWURZTRAMINER GRAND CRU KESSLER, DOMAINES SCHLUMBERGER 1989 Alsace	*Powerful melon and banana nose with palate of ginger, cinnamon, grapefruit. Massive!*	**£14.00**	JN, DBY, L&W, LV	**G**
RIESLING CLOS HAUSERER VENDANGE TARDIVE, ZIND HUMBRECHT 1990 Alsace	*Full, rich pleasing flavour. Honeyed character, balanced sweetness. Good finish, very nice.*	**£14.91**	ABY	**S**
GEWURZTRAMINER GRAND CRU HENGST VENDANGE TARDIVE, 1990 Alsace	*Ripe on the nose with a rich flavour - concentrated and spicy with a zesty zing. Great finish.*	**£15.09**	ABY, DBY	**G**
TOKAY PINOT GRIS CLOS SAINT URBAIN GRAND CRU RANGE 1992 Alsace	*Gorgeously aromatic nose. Smoky, rich, appley fruit with a lovely silken texture.*	**£15.13**	ABY	**B**
GEWURZTRAMINER HEIMBOURG, ZIND HUMBRECHT 1992 Alsace	*Elegant. Good structure. Rich well-balanced fruit with lemon, mangoes, lychees and apricots.*	**£15.50**	ABY	**G**
TOKAY PINOT GRIS, VIEILLES VIGNES, ZIND HUMBRECHT 1992 Alsace	*Full bodied and fairly firm with good concentration; Spicy aromas. on mid palate and finish.*	**£15.95**	ABY, LV	**B**
GEWURZTRAMINER GRAND CRU GOLDERT VENDAGE TARDIVE, 1990 Alsace	*Full and ripe on palate with honey and ripe apricot aromas; zesty with a good finish.*	**£16.30**	ABY	**B**

TOKAY PINOT GRIS GRAND CRU GLOECKELBERG VENDANGES TARDIVES, CHARLES KOEHLY 1989 Alsace	*Peaches, apricots and a touch of residual sugar all combine in this nutty wine to give a lovely finish.*	£17.82	BWI	B
RIESLING CLOS HAUSERER VENDANGE TARDIVE, ZIND HUMBRECHT 1989 Alsace	*Rich, fruity and spicey. Touch of botrytis.*	£17.94	ABY	B
GEWURZTRAMINER VENDANGE TARDIVE, DOMAINE JOSEPH RIEFLE 1990 Alsace	*Golden yellow with pineapple and guava aromas. Good sweetness and acidity balance.*	£18.99	WTR	B
TOKAY-PINOT GRIS VENDANGES TARDIVES, CVPG PFAFFENHEIM 1990 Alsace	*Full-bodied, alcoholic and fairly soft, medium-dry. Spicey flavour with good length.*	£21.95	IWS	B
SWEET WHITE				
GEWURZTRAMINER VENDANGE TARDIVE, BEBLENHEIM 1990 Alsace	*Good green colour with light, fragrant bouquet. Excellent. Young but with great elegance.*	£9.99	MWW	B
RIESLING VENDANGE TARDIVE MUENCHBERG, ANDRE OSTERTAG 1990 Alsace	*Peachy/apricot bouquet; light but rich palate, quite zappy. Good acidity with clean, crisp finish*	£25.00	HC, M&V, LV	B
GEWURZTRAMINER SELECTION DES GRAINS NOBLES, CVPG PFAFFENHEIM 1989 Alsace	*Honeyed bouquet of light intensity. Sweet raisins, honey and fruit. Good length and freshness.*	£29.95	IWS	B

GEWURZTRAMINER KRITT SELECTION DES GRAINS NOBLES, 1992 Alsace	*Honey, pineapple nose. Rich fruit palate. Intensely sweet, unctuous flavours with buttery, salty overtones which last.*	**£30.00**	LV, H&H	**S**
TOKAY CLOS JEBSAL VENDAGE TARDIVE, ZIND HUMBRECHT 1990 Alsace	*Rich, complex, spicey wine with lovely peary flavours.*	**£32.50**	ABY, LV	**S**
TOKAY ROTENBURG SELECTION DE GRAIN NOBLES, ZIND HUMBRECHT 1991 Alsace	*Mid-golden colour of medium intensity. Fresh, spicy nose, honeyed fruit, almost syrupy palate.*	**£41.94**	ABY	**S**

SPARKLING

MAYERLING CREMANT D'ALSACE, CAVE VINICOLE DE TURCKHEIM Alsace	*Desirable small bubbles, light-nosed and has a gentle hint of fruit that steals silently away.*	**£8.99**	DBY	**B**
CREMANT D'ALSACE BRUT ROSE, DOMAINE JUX Alsace	*Deep salmon-pink. A big, appeal in mouth and nose. Crisp, balanced with strong finish.*	**£11.01**	LAV, WIN	**B**

— LOIRE —

RED

BOURGUEIL CLOS DE GAUCHERIE, CASLOT-GALBRUN 1990 Loire	*Lovely intriguing nose of stewed apple, strawberry jam and raspberries. Delicate soft ripe red fruit.*	**£6.35**	ET, ABV	**B**
CHINON, CHATEAU DE LA GRILLE, ALBERT GOSSET 1989 Loire	*Still young. Good acidity and tannin, already displays ripe peppery fruit.*	**£8.65**	GI, SEL, WIN	**B**

SANCERRE ROUGE 'LES CAILLERIES', DOMAINE VACHERON 1991 Loire	*Attractive but simple with good fruit, tannin and acidity; a tarry finish.*	**£9.99**	ET, ABV, BEN, FDL, GSJ, THP, LV	**B**

DRY WHITE

SAUVIGNON DE TOURAINE, DOMAINE GIBAULT 1993 Loire	*Soft ripe fruity aroma with good gooseberry intensity.*	**£4.50**	W	**B**
MUSCADET DE SEVRE ET MAINE SUR LIE, DOMAINE DE LA FURONNIERE, CELLIERS DU PRIEURE 1993 Loire	*Light, fresh and perfumed. Buttery, honeyed fruit and crisp flinty acid. Very stylish.*	**£4.75**	LCC	**B**
SAUVIGNON BLANC, VIN DE PAYS DU JARDIN DE LA FRANC DOMAINE PIERRE BLANCHE 1993 Loire	*Fragrant, light dandelion nose. Palate is crisp and dry, with good level of zippy gooseberry fruit.*	**£4.99**	ENO	**B**
MUSCADET DE SEVRE ET MAINE SUR LIE, DOMAINE DES DEUX-RIVES, D HARDY & C LUNEAU 1992 Loire	*Gooseberries on the nose and quinces on the palate. Has some complexity. Clean with flinty acid.*	**£4.99**	LES	**B**
MUSCADET DE SEVRE ET MAINE SUR LIE, DOMAINE DE L'ECU, GUY BOSSARD 1993 Loire	*Floral nose, palate is a rich mixture of green apples and blue cheese. Crisp and appealing.*	**£5.00**	SAF, ORG	**B**
MUSCADET DE SEVRE ET MAINE SUR LIE 'PREMIERE', DOMAINE JEAN DOUILLARD 1992 Loire	*Big and fruity, rich and full with crisp lemony acidity giving a dry finish.*	**£5.45**	JS	**B**
MUSCADET DE SEVRE ET MAINE SUR LIE CLOS DE BEAUREGARD, PIERRE LEROUX 1990 Loire	*Raisiny sweetness on nose and honeyed fruit on the palate. Opulent wine and good value.*	**£5.67**	JAR	**S**

MUSCADET DE SEVRE & MAINE SUR LIE, CHATEAU DE GOULAINE, MARQUIS DE GOULAINE 1993 Loire	*Classic food wine that screams to be consumed with a large bowl of mussels.*	**£5.99**	LOL	**B**
SANCERRE, SERGE LALOUE 1993 Loire	*Spicy lemon nose with ripe gooseberry and passion fruit.*	**£6.15**	ABY	**B**
SANCERRE DOMAINE CROIX SAINT URSIN, SYLVAIN BAILLY 1992 Loire	*Flinty, stony tones and leafy lemon fruit with hints of asparagus. The palate is rich.*	**£6.99**	CAC, H&H	**B**
SANCERRE, GUY SAGET 1993 Loire	*Pungent bouquet of grassy meadow flowers. Crisp and fresh.*	**£6.99**	GI, WMK, MRN, BEF, HAL	**B**
SANCERRE LA COTE DOMAINE DES P'TITS PERRIERS, ANDRE VATAN 1993 Loire	*Rounded and ripe goose-berry nose - very tart fruit, racy and mouth-watering*	**£7.50**	SAF, H&H	**B**
POUILLY FUME, MASSON-BLONDELET 1993 Loire	*Strong Sauvignon aroma of grass and net-tles. Slightly spritzy.*	**£7.80**	W, GRT	**B**
AUGUSTE COUILLAUD CHARDONNAY, VIN DE PAYS DU JARDIN DE LA FRANCE 1991 Loire	*Floral notes to bouquet with nice fruit style to palate. Quite elegant, lean and fresh.*	**£7.99**	FUL	**B**
VOUVRAY, CUVEE DES FONDRAUX, DIDIER CHAMPALOU 1992 Loire	*Crisp and fresh with con-centrated fruit. Well-bal-anced,clean and bright.*	**£7.99**	H&H, DBY, BU	**B**
MENETOU SALON BLANC MOROGUES, HENRY PELLE 1993 Loire	*Fresh sherbet aromas and gooseberry fruit. Plenty of depth. Good long finish.*	**£7.99**	TH, H&H, NRW, DBY	**B**
SANCERRE 'LE CHENE', LUCIEN CROCHET 1992 Loire	*A balance of rich tropi-cal fruit and grassy herbaceous notes.*	**£7.99**	ABY	**B**

POUILLY FUMÉ, DOMAINE JEAN CLAUDE CHATELAIN 1993 Loire	*Classic catty varietal nose with hints of pears and apples. Well balanced.*	**£8.00**	CT, HV, WCE, H&H, D, HEY	**B**
VOUVRAY MARC BREDIF VOUVRAY 1989 Loire	*Quite herbaceous, clean and fruity with pears and apricots on palate and great depth.*	**£8.75**	MWW, MHW, PTR, P&R, N&P, DBY, DIO	**B**
SANCERRE 'LA CHATELLENIE', JOSEPH MELLOT 1993 Loire	*Pale straw in colour with a nice rich nose. The palate is light, elegant and easy.*	**£8.80**	LAV, WIN	**B**
SANCERRE LES ROCHES, JEAN LOUIS VACHERON 1993 Loire	*Good, intense gooseberry nose. WOnderful full fruit palate. Soft balance finish.*	**£8.99**	ET, ABV, U, MWW, JAV, THP, AON	**B**
FORTNUM & MASON SANCERRE, VACHERON 1993 Loire	*Good elderflower nose. Clean and crisp and tasting strongly of fresh gooseberries.*	**£9.65**	F&M	**B**
POUILLY FUMÉ, LA ROCHE DU MOINE, PIERRE ARCHAMBAULT 1993 Loire	*Gooseberry and fruit salad aroma; rich tropical fruit in mouth. Soft and easy with bags of flavour.*	**£9.70**	FFR	**B**
SANCERRE CUVEE EDMOND, DOMAINE LA MOUSSIERE, ALPHONSE MELLOT 1992 Loire	*A rich and obvious oak character well integrated with some warm, soft fruit.*	**£9.99**	AV, CEB	**B**
POUILLY FUMÉ, CHATEAU DE TRACY 1992 Loire	*Fragrant bouquet of apples and pears overlying a restrained palate of soft attractive fruit.*	**£10.00**	L&W, ADN, GRT, DBY	**B**
POUILLY FUMÉ DOMAINE BUISSON MENARD, DIDIER DAGUEN 1992 Loire	*Delicate tropical aromas showing elegance, depth and finesse. Well integrated fruit on palate.*	**£11.99**	TH, WR, BU, ABY	**B**

POUILLY FUME PUR SANG, DIDIER DAGUENEAU 1992 Loire	*Plenty of oak, ripe well developed and mouthfilling with plenty of rich Sauvignon flavour.*	£14.63	ABY	**S**
POUILLY FUME SILEX, DIDIER DAGUENEAU 1992 Loire	*Lots of rich toasted oak barrels give this an excellent flavour with crisp acidity.*	£20.33	ABY	**B**

MEDIUM WHITE

VOUVRAY DEMI-SEC, DOMAINE DE LA MABILLIERE 1992 Loire	*Earthy and honeyed showing nice developed characters. Peaches and apricots on the palate.*	£4.99	TH, WR, BU, TDS, BUT, WES, NRW	**B**
VOUVRAY DEMI-SEC, CHATEAU MONCONTOUR 1992 Loire	*Earthy with floral overtones, appealing citrus fruit and clean but gentle acidity.*	£6.59	ET, ABV, BH, MIT, JN	**B**
VOUVRAY, VITICULTEURS DU VOUVRAY 1976 Loire	*Lifted lemony nose with chewy honeyed fruit. Faintly spicy with great depth. Well-crafted.*	£9.99	U	**S**
VOUVRAY AIGLE BLANC VIN DE TRIS, PRINCE PHILIPPE PONIATOWSKI 1989 Loire	*Complex and concentrated, showing rich, buttery, limey fruit. Luscious.*	£16.95	LV, ADN, AK, DBP, WAC	**B**

ROSE

CHINON, CHATEAU DE LA GRILLE, ANTOINE GOSSET 1992 Loire	*Medium salmon garnet; finishes strongly with flavours of raspberries, cherries and plums.*	£9.99	GI, SEL, WIN	**B**

SPARKLING

SAUMUR, VIGNERONS DE SAUMUR Loire	*Fresh, clean and fruity; bursts forth, great mouth-filling taste.*	£6.49	CWS, TO	**B**

| **Vouvray Brut Blanc de Blanc, Chateau Moncontour 1992** Loire | *Light nose, pale gold with toasty taste that lasts well. Hint of sweetness adding to palate.* | £7.95 | ET, ABV, BH, MIT, JN | B |

— RHONE —

RED				
Domaine Bouche Vin de Pays de Vaucluse 1990 Rhone	*Sweet red fruit nose, soft leathery palate with fresh strawberry flavours.*	£2.95	ETV	S
Cotes du Rhone, Chateau Saint Maurice, A Valat 1991 Rhone	*Easy-drinking style of delicate fruit flavours with light tannins and hints of leaf tobacco.*	£3.95	W	B
Chateau Pesquie, Coteaux des Valerianes, Vin de Pay de Vaucluse 1993 Rhone	*Vibrant bramble and rhubarb aroma with berry fruit. Good dose of black pepper and spice in mouth.*	£3.99	TH	B
Cellier Des Dauphins Cotes du Rhone Prestige Rouge 1992 Rhone	*Confected, lollipop nose, with peppery spice and a fruity palate. Good, clean fun.*	£3.99	HOT, MRN, MA, BTM	B
Vacqueyras, Vieux Clocher, Arnoux et Fils 1990 Rhone	*Spicy musky nose with concentrated berry and stone fruit flavours.*	£4.59	SMF, G, FG	S
Vacqueyras, Vieux Clocher, Arnoux et Fils 1991 Rhone	*Attractive earthy nose of leather, tar and pepper. Berry fruit flavours. Enjoyable and good value.*	£4.59		G
Crozes-Hermitage Domaine Barret 1992 Rhone	*Open style with bright raspberry fruit and spicy Syrah characteristics.*	£4.90	TH, WR, BU, CEB	S

VACQUEYRAS CUVEE DU MARQUIS DE FONSEGUILLE, CAVES DE VACQUEYRAS 1991 Rhone	Cedarwood cigar-box nose, black olives, dark cherry fruit and old Virginia tobacco. Enjoyable to drink.	£4.95	CWS	B
COTES DU RHONE, VIGNOBLE DE LA JASSE, DANIEL COMBE 1992 Rhone	Light, but rich, fruit style with cherries and black-berries and good alcohol/fruit balance.	£4.99	VER, OD, WHO, PEP, CEN	B
ST-JOSEPH LA PILATTE, MICHEL MOURIER 1991 Rhone	Vegetal, composty aromas and jammy, strawberry flavours.	£4.99	TO	B
COTES DU RHONE RESERVE LA VIEILLE FERME, J P & F PERRIN 1992 Rhone	Rich, well-balanced wine of some complexity with bags of plummy fruit and firm acidity.	£4.99	TO	S
COTE DU VENTOUX LA CIBOISE, M CHAPOUTIER 1993 Rhone	Lovely, open strawberry nose, light spicy pleasant fruit and full tannic finish. Drink, don't wait!	£5.00	MW, DBY, MZ	B
COTES DU RHONE 'GOLD LABEL RESERVE', LA VIEILLE FERME 1990 Rhone	Stableyard aromas of worked leather, straw and wood, excellent fresh fruit balance .	£5.19	SEB	B
MHV CROZES HERMITAGE ROUGE, CAVE DE TAIN L'HERMITAGE 1991 Rhone	Ripe cherry fruit with fresh herb spiciness balanced by keen and attentive tannins.	£5.49	MHV	B
RASTEAU COTES DU RHONE VILLAGES, CHATEAU DU TRIGNON 1989 Rhone	Pronounced floral and tobacco nose. Plump and delicious with good structure and acidity.	£5.50	WL, DBY	B
SABLET LA RAMILLADE, COTES DU RHONE VILLAGES, CHATEAU DU TRIGNON 1991 Rhone	Classic nose of ripe fruit and white pepper with spicy raspberry flavours and light oak touches.	£5.79	TH, WR, BU	B

COTES DU RHONE, E GUIGAL 1991 Rhone	*A wine of great potential,soft oak influence, berry fruit richness and structured tannins.*	**£6.00**	WR, IRV, PAG, SEL, AMD, ABY, CEB,OD	**B**
CROZES HERMITAGE ROUGE, DOMAINE DES ENTREFAUX 1990 Rhone	*Richly textured wine with toffee and butterscotch flavours.Ideal with spicy winter foods.*	**£6.00**	ABY, BGC	**S**
CROZES HERMITAGE ROUGE, DOMAINE DES ENTREFAUX 1992 Rhone	*Lovely, spicy Syrah flavours with stalky, green tannins make a richly textured wine.*	**£6.00**	ABY, SUM	**S**
VACQUEYRAS, CUVEE DES TEMPLIERS, DOMAINE LE CLOS DES CAZAUX 1990 Rhone	*Hot, tarry nose with olive and blackberry flavours on palate. Not for the faint-hearted!*	**£6.60**	J&B	**B**
SABLET COTES DU RHONE VILLAGES, CHATEAU DU TRIGNON 1991 Rhone	*Showing well with spicy, peppery elements, clean fresh acidity and a ripe fruit finish.*	**£6.95**	ALL, GRT	**B**
CROZES HERMITAGE, BERNARD CHAVE 1992 Rhone	*Pronounced peppery nose, good rounded fruit palate and spicy herb flavours.*	**£6.99**	H&H, NY, FUL	**B**
ST-JOSEPH, A OGIER ET FILS 1990 Rhone	*Seductive, Syrah nose with tarry depth and liquorice lightness.*	**£6.99**	LAV, WIN, MWW	**B**
VACQUEYRAS CUVEE DES TEMPLIERS, DOMAINE LE CLOS DES CAZAUX 1991 Rhone	*Concentrated damson fruit and minty freshness on nose, wild cherry palate. Quite a mouthful.*	**£6.99**	TAN	**B**
CROZES HERMITAGE LES LAUNES, DELAS FERRES 1990 Rhone	*Mature, gamey nose, plenty of young fruit, meaty richness and supople tannins.*	**£7.00**	LAY, VTH, BEF, GRTY, DBY	**B**

CHATEAUNEUF DU PAPE LA SOURCE AUX NYMPHES, LES FILS D'ETIENNE GONNET 1991 Rhone	*Delicate strawberry nose with richer cooked fruit flavours. Well-balanced with good length.*	£7.69	SAF	B
LIRAC ROUGE, CHATEAU D'AQUERIA 1990 Rhone	*Fully structured with open gamey flavours and leathery texture.*	£7.79	MWW	B
ST-JOSEPH, CAVES DE SAINT DESIRAT 1989 Rhone	*Bitter, tarry nose, raw crisp fruit with toasty oak flavours.*	£7.85	SMF, G, FG	B
ST-JOSEPH CUVEE MEDAILLE D'ARGENT, CAVE DE ST DESIRAT 1990 Rhone	*Youthful oaky nose, powerful tannic palate and cooked fruit sweetness. Good length finish.*	£7.85	SMF, GMN, WHC	B
COTEAUX DU TRICASTIN, DOMAINE DE ST LUC 1991 Rhone	*Dark, almost opaque colour, ripe jammy nose and balanced fruit flavours.*	£7.99	THP	B
CHATEAUNEUF DU PAPE, CELLIER DES PRINCES 1991 Rhone	*Aromatic, spicy vanilla nose, luscious red fruit palate and spicy, peppery finish.*	£7.99	CWS	B
ST-JOSEPH, LES LARMES DU PERE, ALAIN PARET 1991 Rhone	*Crushed, red fruit sweetness balanced by dry, peppery tannins.*	£7.99	PHI, CRL, EE, POR, SAN	B
CHATEAUNEUF DU PAPE LES ARNEVELS, VIGNOBLES JEROME QUIOT 1992 Rhone	*Ripe, spicy nose with Provençal herb flavours and red fruit concentration.*	£7.99	TO	B
ST-JOSEPH, CUVEE COTE DIANE, LES PRODUCTEURS DE ST-DESIRAT 1989 Rhone	*A wine that leads from the front - gunpowder nose, spicy fruit and rich tannins. Massive!*	£7.99	TH, WR, BU	B

CROZES HERMITAGE LA PETITE RUCHE, M CHAPOUTIER 1992 Rhone	*Outstanding wine with classic stature, young generous fruit and old wood tannins.*	**£7.99**	VW, M, FUL, MZ, DBY, CEB	**G**
CROZES HERMITAGE, DOMAINE POCHON 1992 Rhone	*Tangy acidity and medium strength tannins ensure balance to the fruit flvours.*	**£8.16**	J&B	**S**
GIGONDAS, DOMAINE RASPAIL AY, DOMINIQUE AY 1990 Rhone	*Youthful with excellent potential - strapping tannins and underlying fruit flavours.*	**£8.55**	HVW, TOJ	**B**
CHATEAUNEUF DU PAPE RESERVE DES SEIGNEURS EVEQUES, DOMAINE DE FARGUEROL 1991 Rhone	*Warm, earthy flavours and white pepper spice with good fruit, acid and tannin balance.*	**£8.85**	CNL, GH	**B**
LIRAC CUVEE PRESTIGE LA FERMADE, DOMAINE MABY 1989 Rhone	*Complex nose of fruit and spice with weighty blackcurrant flavours.*	**£8.95**	RES, SAC, PIC, HST, MRF	**S**
CORNAS, A OGIER ET FILS 1989 Rhone	*Spicy, rich and tannic with ripe peppery fruit flavours. Great potential.*	**£8.99**	LAV, WIN, MWW	**B**
ST-JOSEPH, PIERRE COURSODON 1991 Rhone	*Ripe mulberry jam aromas with minty fruit, and spicy bell peppers.*	**£8.99**	WR, BU	**B**
CORNAS, CAVE DE TAIN L'HERMITAGE 1990 Rhone	*Soft spicy aromas of cloves and oranges. Ripe red fruit flavours with good acidity. Delicious.*	**£9.99**	NRW, DBY	**S**
DOMAINE FONT DE MICHELLE, CHATEAUNEUF DU PAPE, LES FILS D'ETIENNE GONNET FRERES 1990 Rhone	*Scented pepper and thyme aromas, fruit flavours with good oak base. Long finish. A real character.*	**£10.00**	D	**S**

ST-JOSEPH DESCHANTS, M CHAPOUTIER 1991 Rhone	*Initially closed nose opens up well, with good tannins and a ripe finish.*	£10.99	DBY, WR, BU	B
CHATEAUNEUF DU PAPE, CHANTE-CIGALE 1990 Rhone	*Excellent structure, supple tannins and good length make this a wine of some pedigree.*	£10.99	PON, BH, LUV, NRW, DBY	S
DOMAINE FONT DE MICHELLE CHATEAUNEUF DU PAPE 1992 Rhone	*Fresh and elegant nose of perfumed fruit, with raspberry richness on the palate.*	£11.00	TH, D	S
ST-JOSEPH L'OLIVAIE, P COURSODON 1992 Rhone	*Good colour and bouquet. Excellent concentration of fruit flavours and well balanced.*	£11.29	WR, BU	B
ST-JOSEPH L'OLIVAIE, P COURSODON 1991 Rhone	*Elegantly structured wine with cooked fruit and butterscotch flavours. Smooth finish.*	£11.29	WR, BU	G
CORNAS CUVEE 'C', MARCEL JUGE 1991 Rhone	*Animal nose followed by peppery spice and clean fruit. Will develop.*	£11.50	WTR, H&H	S
CHATEAUNEUF DU PAPE LA BERNADINE, M CHAPOUTIER 1990 Rhone	*Light minty and vanilla richness on nose, plummy fruit and spicy, white pepper flavours.*	£12.00	OD, MZ, DBY	B
CHATEAUNEUF DU PAPE, DOMAINE DU PERE CABOCHE, JEAN-PIERRE BOISSON 1985 Southern Rhone	*Good balanced style with classy berry fruit ripeness, tarry texture, and far-reaching*	tannins. £12.50	R, S&J, AV, BUT	B
CORNAS, RENE BALTHAZAR 1991 Rhone	*Deeply intense ruby/ garnet colour with mature nose of spicy fruit. Smoothly textured finish.*	£13.00	HC	S

COTE ROTIE, J VIDAL-FLEURY 1990 Rhone	*Full nose of cedarwood spice and fruit, ripe plum and mulberry flavours on palate.*	**£13.55**	WWT, DBY	S
CORNAS CUVEE 'SC', MARCEL JUGE 1991 Rhone	*Cleanly made with an open style and good fruit concentration. Balanced, complex and delicate.*	**£14.00**	WTR, H&H	G
CORNAS COTEAU, R MICHEL 1991 Rhone	*Minty spice and full berry-fruit flavours that hint at good pedigree.*	**£14.99**	TH, WR, BU	B
COTE ROTIE, COTES BRUNE ET BLONDE, E GUIGAL 1989 Rhone	*Soft fleshy voluptuous nose, well developed damson flavours and piquant spice.*	**£14.99**	ABY, WR, BU	S
HERMITAGE CUVEE MARQUISE DE LA TOURETTE, DELAS FRERES 1990 Rhone	*Bramble fruit flavours that develop srongly in glass and soft tannin finish. Quite delicious.*	**£16.00**	LAY, PST, DBY, GRT	G
COTE ROTIE, EUIGAL 1990 Rhone	*Aromatic Syrah nose with ripe fruit flavours that really follow through.*	**£17.00**	WR, OD, L&W, AMD, PAG	S
CHATEAU DE BEAUCASTEL, CHATEAUNEUF-DU-PAPE, J P & F PERRIN 1990 Rhone	*Slightly vegetal, spicy nose giving way to rich fruit and liquorice tannins. Wonderful stuff.*	**£17.00**	FAR, TAN, SK, BBR, J&B, SEB, BWI, DBY	G
COTE ROTIE LE CRET, B LEVET 1990 Rhone	*Earthy, vegetal nose with rich stone fruit flavours and firm acidity.*	**£18.29**	LAV, WIN	B
COTE ROTIE CHAMPIN LE SEIGNEUR, JEAN-MICHEL GERIN 1991 Rhone	*Stylish and elegant, capitalises on full fleshy fruit for both flavour and texture.*	**£18.75**	WTR	G

HERMITAGE ROUGE, E GUIGAL 1990 Rhone	*Fresh youthful wine with juicy dark berry fruit and peppery spice.*	**£20.00**	OD, IRV, L&W, AMD, S&J	**G**
COTE ROTIE LES GRANDES PLACES, JEAN-MICHEL GERIN 1991 Rhone	*Sweet plums and peppery spice on nose, biting cherry fruit with good natural acidity.*	**£21.99**	WTR	**B**

DRY WHITE

CHATEAU DE LA TUILERIE, CARTE BLANCHE BLANC 1992 Rhone	*Vibrant bouquet of mangoes and fresh English strawberries. Very summery nose.*	**£5.40**	AV, MJW, IRV	**S**
VIOGNIER, VIN DE PAYS DE L'ARDECHE, GEORGES DUBOEUF 1993 Rhone	*A delicately perfumed nose with hints of cassis and soft fruit on the palate.*	**£5.50**	BWC, PAY	**B**
VIOGNIER, COTES DU RHONE, FRANCOIS PELLE 1993 Rhone	*Lemon-coloured with a light, clean nose. Full-bodied, some ripe fruit, not much acidity.*	**£6.99**	BWC, BU	**B**
HERMITAGE BLANC, GUIGAL 1991 Rhone	*Toasty and rich on the palate, nice balance and length. Good acid and a pleasant finish.*	**£14.99**	TH, WR, BU, ABY	**B**
CONDRIEU DOMAINE DU CHENE 1992 Rhone	*Rich aromas, a hint of baked bread on the nose. Fair body and fruit.*	**£15.29**	TH, WR, BU	**B**
CONDRIEU COTEAUX DE CHERY, ANDRE PERRET 1992 Rhone	*Richly coloured with plenty of ripe fruit on the nose. Firm and full-bodied.*	**£16.99**	ADN	**B**
CONDRIEU LA COTE CHERY, CAVES DES PAPES, A OGIER 1992 Rhone	*Solid and sound, with good fruit and body and a faint spritz on the palate.*	**£22.75**	LAV, WIN	**B**

CHATEAUNEUF-DU-PAPE BLANC, CHATEAU DE BEAUCASTEL, J P & F PERRIN 1991 Rhone	Plenty of new French oak lends a creamy, toasty character to this smooth rounded wine.	£23.50	FAR, HAR	B

SPARKLING

COMTESSE DE DIE CLAIRETTE DE DIE TRADITION, CAVE COOPERATIVE DE DIE 1992 Rhone	Fresh and clean with a light, Muscat-style aroma and a taste of peaches and pears. Lingers pleasantly.	£5.95	W	B

— PROVENCE —

RED

MAS DE GOURGONNIER RESERVE DU MAS 1990 Provence	Savoury nose, red fruit flavours and white pepper spice. Bring on the winter casserole.	£7.00	ADN, CHF, UBC, SAN, HPD, ORG	B
CHATEAU PIBARNON, BANDOL 1990 Provence	Raisiny richness with a complex range of plum, fig and chocolate flavours.	£9.79	ABY	B
CHATEAU PIBARNON, BANDOL 1989 Provence	The peppery capsicum nose gives way to a full fruit softness.	£9.97	ABY	B

DRY WHITE

CHATEAU LA VERRERIE, BLANC DE BLANCS, COTES DU LUBERON 1992	Aromatic and spicy on the nose, yet bone-dry. Full-bodied wine with interesting character.	£8.38	RTW	B

Pinpoint who sells the wine you wish to buy by turning to the stockist codes. If you know the name of the wine you want to buy, use the alphabetical index. If price is your motivation, refer to the invaluable price guide index; red and white wines under £5 and sparkling wines under £10. Good hunting!

SOUTHWEST

RED				
BUZET, DOMAINE DE LA CROIX, TESCO LES DOMAINES, VIGNERONS DE BUZET 1989 Southwest	*A clean and fruity, carbonic-maceration style which displays spicy, plummy fruit and great concentration and length.*	£3.99	TO	B
CHATEAU LES OLLIEUX, SURBEZY-CARTIER 1991 Southwest	*The reserved, floral, violet aroma with tones of raspberries was followed by a plummy palate.*	£4.80	AUL	B
MADIRAN DOMAINE DE IANESTOUSSE, ROBILLARD 1989 Southwest	*This rich, meaty wine contains flavours of ripe currants and tones of cloves and coriander.*	£5.50	TO	B
IROULEGUY, DOMAINE MIGNABERRY 1992 Southwest	*A nice, elegant, leathery nose. Keep for one to three years.*	£6.42	ABY	B
CAHORS, CLOS LA COUTALE 1990 Southwest	*Despite its rather backward, coconut nose, this has a nice, soft balance of fruit flavours.*	£6.90	NIC	B
CHATEAU LAROCHE VIELLA, MADIRAN, VIGNOBLE DE GASCOGNE 1988 Southwest	*A full, well-made wine, rich and opulent, with a hot, spicy bouquet.*	£6.90	SAF	S
MADIRAN BOUSCASSE, ALAIN BRUMONT 1991 Southwest	*Delicious full flavour, plummy fruit with a good backbone of soft tannin.*	£8.00	BU, LV, NY, HN, H&H	G
MADIRAN, CHATEAU MONTUS, FUTS DE CHENE, ALAIN BRUMONT 1990 Southwest	*A wine that is light in the mouth, full of peppery, spicy, plum fruit and firm tannins.*	£9.99	TH, WR, BU, H&H, LV	B

MADIRAN, MONTUS, ALAIN BRUMONT 1991 Southwest	*Almost black. Rich, oaky nose. Gutsy liquorice and cherry character with oaky superstucture.*	**£11.00**	WR, HN, RD, LV, BEL, H&H	**S**
	DRY WHITE
VIN DU PAYS DU GERS BLANC 1993, PRODUCTEURS PLAIMONT 1993 Southwest	*Pale, clean and bright with a spicy, lemony nose. Ripe, soft, cooked apple fruit on the palate.*	**£2.99**	W, SPR	**B**
BELLEFONTAINE TERRET, VIN DE PAYS DES COTES DE THAU, PAUL BOUTINOT 1993 Southwest	*Interestingly herby wine with a slight liquorice flavour.*	**£3.30**	S&W, NRW, WES, DBY, BUT	**B**
DOMAINE DU BIAU, VIN DE PAYS DES COTES DE GASCOGNE 1993 Southwest	*Lemon sherbet on the nose of this clean wine. Some grassiness and grapefruit flavours.*	**£3.69**	VW	**B**
DOMAINE LE PUTS, VIN DE PAYS DES COTES DE GASCOGNE, HUGH RYMAN 1993 Southwest	*Very pale with green highlights. Layers of ripe fruit zinging with citrus acidity. Medium-bodied.*	**£3.69**	MWW, WAV, WL	**S**
DOMAINE DE LA ROCHE, COTES DE DURAS, HUGH RYMAN 1993 Southwest	*Lovely vanilla oak and herbaceous grassy fruit with a hint of mangoes and pineapples.*	**£3.99**	WL, AB, VW, G, SMF	**B**
DOMAINE DE PETITOT, COTES DE DURAS, HUGH RYMAN 1993 Southwest	*Very floral with masses of fruit on the nose. Lots of clean lemony fruit. Well balanced finish.*	**£3.99**	MWW	**B**
DOMAINE D'AUGERON, VIN DE PAYS DE TERROIRS LANDAIS BLANC, BUBOLA 1992 Southwest	*Intensely lemony nose, some nice fruit on the palate. Good acidity and balance.*	**£4.24**	RES, SAC, PIC, HST, MRF	**B**

DOMAINE DE LABALLE, VIN DE PAYS DES TERROIRS LANDAIS BLANC, NOEL LAUDET 1993 Southwest	*A fresh, young, fruity nose with good acidity and fruit in the mouth. Generally fresh, grapey and very quaffable.*	**£4.29**	PTR	**B**
CUVEE DES FLEURS, JACQUES LURTON 1992 Southwest	*Fresh with limey, buttery fruit on the nose. Good appley, peachy fruit in the mouth. Good length.*	**£4.33**	JAR	**B**
MAUZAC VIN DE PAYS DE L'AUDE, LA BATTEUSE, BERNARD DELMAS 1993 Southwest	*Pale gold. Bouquet of peach, Victoria plum and dried fruit. Full, rounded, herby palate. Good balance.*	**£4.55**	VR, BUM, BN, RAV	**S**
DOMAINE DE RIVOYRE CHARDONNAY HUGH RYMAN 1993	*A well made modern wine, with a hint of pineapple.*	**£4.99**	SAF	**B**
COTES DE DURAS SAUVIGNON VIEILLES VIGNES, BERTICOT 1993 Southwest	*A fresh aromatic wine with plenty of ripe gooseberry fruit. Crisp and balanced. Lots of Sauvignon character.*	**£4.99**	GI	**B**
CHATEAU DE LA JAUBERTIE BERGERAC BLANC, HUGH RYMAN 1992 Southwest	*Excellent nose, fresh and grassy, with flavours of peach and tropical fruit. Very drinkable.*	**£4.99**	JN	**B**
DOMAINE DU PETIT PARIS, BERGERAC SEC, JEAN GENESTE 1993 Southwest	*Good potential. Well-developed fruit on a perfumed nose, with honeyed fruit in the mouth and a dry finish.*	**£4.99**	GWI, PIM	**B**
CHATEAU DE LA JAUBERTIE BERGERAC SEC, HENRY RYMAN 1993 Southwest	*Pale straw in colour with a shy nose and a fruity palate. Quite delicate and elegant.*	**£4.99**	VW	**B**

CHATEAU GRAND MOULIN, CORBIERES BLANC, JEAN-NOEL BOUSQUET 1993 Southwest	*A striking, flavoursome wine. Grassy, peardrop aroma with crisp acidity and peachy fruit. Toasty, yeasty notes.*	**£4.99**	JS	**B**
PIERRE VIDAL CHARDONNAY, JAMES HERRICK 1992 Southwest	*A classic Chardonnay with a spicy nose hinting cloves and pepper. Creamy and long.*	**£5.83**	JAR	**B**
DOMAINE DE GRANDCHAMP BERGERAC SEC SAUVIGNON BLANC, NICK RYMAN 1993 Southwest	*A soft and gentle wine with a little spritzy edge of clean lemon fruit; elegant with good length.*	**£5.99**	Widely Available	**B**
CHATEAU DE LA JAUBERTIE BERGERAC SAUVIGNON, NICK RYMAN 1993 Southwest	*A fat and ripe style, full of soft tropical fruit flavours of gooseberries, grass and grapefruits.*	**£5.99**	JS	**B**
JURANCON SEC GRAIN SAUVAGE, CAVE DES PRODUCTEURS DE JURANCON 1993 Southwest	*Fresh lemon sorbet and ripe gooseberry on the nose. Sweet attack of fat, pineapple fruit, fleshy and attractive.*	**£6.50**	NIC	**S**
BLANCHE DE BOSREDON BERGERAC SEC, TÎTE DE CUVEE 1992 Southwest	*Creamy toasted lemon oak adds a richness and structure to the clean Sauvignon fruit.*	**£6.99**	BAR	**B**

SWEET WHITE

DOMAINE DU HAUT RAULY MONBAZILLAC 1990 Monbazillac	*Pale-straw colour. Fruity aromas of lemon, nuts, honey, luscious grapefruit and pineapple.*	**£3.49**	CWS	**S**
CHATEAU LA PASSONE, LOUPIAC 1992 Loupiac	*A soft, honeyed nose and a spot of botrytis. Citric and weighty.*	**£6.29**	BP	**B**

CHATEAU LA GIRONIE, MONBAZILLAC 1990 Southwest	Full-bodied, with a rich flavour of fruit. Well-balanced, but a slight bitterness on the finish.	£7.75	ADN	S
CLOS D'YVIGNE, SAUSSIGNAC, JAMES ATKINSON 1990 Southwest	Honeyed, quite delicate. Well made wine with an attractive floral style.	£10.90	J&B	B
DOMAINE DU PETIT PARIS CUVEE EXCEPTIONELLE, MONBAZILLAC 1990 Southwest	New oak on the nose with hints of coconuts. Unusual, well-balanced, creamy and lingering.	£13.99	GWI, IVY	S

FORTIFIED

CHATEAU DE BEAULON, 10-YEAR-OLD PINEAU DES CHARENTES Southwest	Mid-brown with red lights. Spirited and fruity, with a sweet, nutty finish on the palate.	£15.00	PAG, BWC	B

— LANGUEDOC-ROUSSILLON—

RED

ASDA CORBIERES, VAL D'ORBIEU Midi	Lovely nose of raspberry and blackberry, followed by fresh, berry acidity and gentle tannins.	£2.75	A	B
ASDA ST CHINIAN, VAL D'ORBIEU Midi	Attractive, redcurrant fruit. Soft, easy-drinking wine with gentle tannins.	£2.85	A	B
ASDA MERLOT VIN DE PAYS D'OC, SKALLI Midi	A wine which is peppery and complex, with smoky oak and blackberry characteristics.	£2.89	A	B
ST-CHINIAN, JEAN D'ALMON, RMDI 1992 Languedoc	Deep plum coloured wine with a full, ripe banana nose.	£2.95	SMF, G, FG	B

SAINSBURY'S FAUGERES, DOMAINES VIRGINIE Midi	*A delicious, spicy plum-skin nose precedes a palate full of fat, ripe, plummy fruit.*	**£2.99**	JS	**B**
VAL DU TORGAN, TUCHAN Midi	*A wine of excellent character, nice and chocolaty with excellent fresh, peppery fruit.*	**£3.00**	TH, WR, BU, TDS	**B**
SYRAH VIN DE PAYS D'OC, MAISON JEAN JEAN 1991 Midi	*Purplish colour, and a nose bursting with lean liquorice and sweet, ripe, blackberry fruit.*	**£3.19**	SMF, G, FG	**B**
VIN DE PAYS DES CEVENNES, VIN DE PAYS DE L'HERAULT, CAVES COOP DE L'UZEGE Midi	*Good, ripe, clean fruit boasting a hint of strawberry, with spicy yet subtle gamey flavours.*	**£3.29**	VW	**B**
DOMAINE ST PIERRE MERLOT, VIN DE PAYS D'OC, LES CHAIS BEAUCAIROIS Midi	*A bouquet of violets, damsons and bramble precedes blackcurrant fruit in the mouth.*	**£3.29**	U	**B**
CO-OP COSTIERES DE NIMES, RMDI Midi	*Great, peppery Syrah nose full of attractive, ripe berry fruit and subtle tones of earth.*	**£3.35**	CWS	**B**
ST MICHAEL FITOU, CAVES DU MONT TAUCH 1991 Midi	*Appealing cherry-and-ginger palate, which has gentle tannins and excellent length.*	**£3.49**	M&S	**B**
DOMAINE DU SOLEIL VEGETARIAN SYRAH, VIN DE PAYS DE L'AUDE 1993 Midi	*A great bramble nose which is lifted by soft spices and rich, plummy fruit.*	**£3.49**	VER	**B**
SPAR FITOU, VAL D'ORBIEU Midi	*Lovely, maturing, mildly singed raspberry fruit; tannins softening nicely - extremely well-made.*	**£3.49**	SPR	**B**

Wine	Description	Price	Stockist	
ST MICHAEL DOMAINE ROCHE BLANCHE, VIN DE PAYS D'OC, DOMAINES VIRGINIE Midi	*With flavours of black-berries and cedar. Makes simple and quaffable drinking.*	**£3.49**	M&S	**B**
CHATEAU DE BELESTA COTES DU ROUSSILLON VILLAGES, LES VIGNERONS CATALANS 1992 Midi	*Strong Syrah palate with plenty of attractive, soft fruit and a rich, spicy, tannic finish.*	**£3.49**	SAF	**S**
DOMAINE DES SALICES MERLOT, VIN DE PAYS D'OC, J & F LURTON 1993 Midi	*Good fruit bouquet; lightweight and easy. Wll balanced ripe juicy fruit flavours.*	**£3.50**	TH, WR, BU	**B**
SYRAH ROUGE, VIN DE PAYS D'OC, GEORGES DUBOEUF 1993 Midi	*Delicious cross between Beaujolais and the Rhone. Juicy and spicy.*	**£3.50**	BWC, PAY, NRW	**B**
GEMINIAN CABERNET SAUVIGNON, VIN DE PAYS D'OC, CAVE DE CUXAC 1993 Midi	*The verdict: balanced and full of sappy, juicy fruit.*	**£3.59**	BUD, WHC	**B**
BESTVIN FITOU, LES CHAIS BEAUCAIROIS Midi	*A mature, creamy, cakey nose with tones of tar and jam on the palate. Soft, and very mellow.*	**£3.59**	BES	**B**
FITOU TERROIR DE TUCHAN, TUCHAN 1991 Midi	*Rich, powerful Grenache/ Syrah fruit and open berry flavours. Creamy, rich and balanced stuff.*	**£3.69**	TH, WR, BU	**B**
DOMAINE GRANGE DU PIN, JEAN JEAN 1993 Languedoc	*Intense, smoky nose, good peppery fruit extract. Firm balance.*	**£3.69**	SAF	**B**
COTES DU ROUSSILLON ROUGE, ARNAUD DE VILLENEUVE, LES VIGNERONS DE RIVESALTES 1990 Midi	*A sweet, almost Port-like nose. Tannic, but with huge potential for devel-opment.*	**£3.75**	LAV, WIN	**B**

Minervois Abbaye de Tholomies, Jeanjean 1991 Minervois	*Chalky, dusty, cherry fruit makes this a massive, earthy and concentrated wine.*	£3.75	SAF	B
Berloup Prestige St-Chinian, Coop de Berloup 1992 Midi	*Elegant with excellent concentration, weight and traditional-style nose.*	£3.79	TH, WR, BU	B
Fortant de France Cabernet Sauvignon, Skalli 1993 Midi	*Good deep colour and plummy nose, in a soft, minty style. Nice ripe fruit structure.*	£3.89	SAF, CEL, BKW	B
Domaine de Thelin Vin de Pays d'Oc Syrah 1991 Midi	*Purple-red and packed with whiffs of earth and pepper.*	£3.90	DN	B
Phillippe De Baudin Cabernet Sauvignon, Vin de Pays d'Oc, Domaine de la Baume 1992 Midi	*Here is a very clean, meaty nose. The wine itself is full of nice, light fruit and excellent structural tannins.*	£3.99	SG, LKL, CSW, FVW, WHC, CVW, CWS	B
Domaine Fouletiere, Coteaux du Languedoc 1991 Midi	*Muted nose of beetroots and earth. Palate is rounded and soft.*	£3.99	MWW	B
Domaine des Henrys, Vin de Pays des Cotes de Thongue, Clos Ferdinand, H F Bouchard 1993 Midi	*Deep crimson in colour with masses of juicy raspberry fruit. Perfumed and spicy, with good length.*	£3.99	NRW, DBY	B
St Michael Domaine Mont Rose Syrah-Cabernet, Vin de Pays d'Oc, Domaines Virginie Midi	*Gentle berry fruit shows a touch of spiciness. Rich and full, with an excellent tannic structure.*	£3.99	M&S	B
Figaro Rouge, Vin de Pays de l'Herault 1993 Midi	*A vivid purple colour, raisiny nose and a youthful fruit palate.*	£3.99	TDS	B

FORTANT DE FRANCE MERLOT, SKALLI 1993 Midi	*Deep ruby-red colour. Slightly closed, but with berry fruit aromas and some oak on the nose.*	£3.99	CEL, BKW	S
COTES DU ROUSSILLON ROUGE, ARNAUD DE VILLENEUVE, LES VINS FINS DU RIVESALTES 1993 Midi	*Spicy plum nose, hot, full, peppery fruit. Warm long finish*	£3.99	LAV, WIN	S
MONASTERE DE TRIGNAN, COTEAUX DU LANGUEDOC 1992 Midi	*Full-bodied, gutsy wine, full of smooth, rounded tannins.*	£3.99	MWW	S
DOMAINE DES COMBELLES, MINERVOIS 1991 Midi	*An inviting bouquet of smoke, mushroom, sand and hazelnuts.*	£4.29	NRW, DBY	G
CUVEE DU CEPAGE CABERNET SAUVIGNON, VIN DE PAYS D'OC, DOMAINE ST HILAIRE 1992 Midi	*Rich and well-structured. A ripe, fruity Cabernet, supported by firm but soft tannins.*	£4.40	BEN, DVI, GRT	G
PHILIPPE DE BAUDIN MERLOT, VIN DE PAYS D'OC, DOMAINE DE LA BAUME 1992 Midi	*Light, simple and clean, with a touch of chocolate. A wine with good palate structure.*	£4.45	LKN, WHC, GPW, CVR	B
CHATEAU DE CARAGUILHES CORBIERES 1990 Midi	*Simple and spicy. Full of lovely, savoury tannins and rounded fruit.*	£4.50	SMF, G, FG, ORG, TO	B
MINERVOIS DOMAINE SAINTE EULALIE, M BLANC 1991 Midi	*Spicy, soft tannins and Cabernet-tinged fruit. A pleasantly balanced and agreeable wine.*	£4.55	TH, WR, BU, D	B
MINERVOIS, CHATEAU DE VIOLET CUVEE CLOVIS 1992 Midi	*A ruby-red wine, hosting fresh raspberries and peppery, cherry fruit. Soft and slightly sweet.*	£4.79	TH, WR, BU	B

CORBIERES CHATEAU GRAND MOULIN 1991 Midi	*Brightly coloured wine containing lots of spicy flavour and light, easy-drinking tannins.*	£4.79	ENO	B
CHAIS BAUMIERE CABERNET SAUVIGNON, VIN DE PAYS D'OC, DOMAINE DE LA BAUME 1992 Midi	*Attractive, supple red fruit with a hint of oak, hosting warm, rich flavours and soft tannins on the palate.*	£4.95	JS	B
CORBIERES, CHATEAU DE LUC, ELEVE EN FUTS DE CHENE 1991 Midi	*Deep, rich, summer fruit on the palate and gorgeous, smooth tannins.*	£4.99	MWW	B
CHAIS BAUMIERE CUVEE PROPRIETAIRE, VIN DE PAYS D'OC. DOMAINE DE LA BAUME 1990 Midi	*Great crushed, redberry fruit and lovely tones of balancing, spicy vanilla-oak.*	£4.99	WHC	B
CHATEAU LES PINS, COTES DE ROUSSILLON VILLAGES 1991 Midi	*A broad, earthy wine, with plenty of vanilla oak and smooth tannins.*	£4.99	VER	B
CORBIERES, CHATEAU DE LASTOURS, CUVEE SIMONES DESCAMPS 1991 Midi	*Soft-boiled sweet fruit may be found on the nose. A pleasing, rounded palate.*	£4.99	DBY	B
DOMAINE DE LA BAUME, VIN DE PAYS D'OC, CHAIS BAUMIERE, CUVEE 1991 ProprietaireMidi	*Deep ruby-red colour. Ripe aroma of new oak and minty blackberry.*	£4.99	WHC	S
MINERVOIS, CARIGNANISSIME DE CENTEILLES, BOYER-DOMERGUE 1992 Midi	*Peppery, Grenache style. Clean, fruity nose, almost floral. Fresh, juicy, spicy cherries.*	£4.99	ADN, CHF, SOM, OD	S
FAUGERES, CHATEAU LA LIQUIERE, CUVEE AMANDIERS, VIDAL 1992 Midi	*Rich, young, southern French wine with pepper, smoke and ripe cabenet flavours.*	£5.60	TH, WR, BU	B

LES CHEMINS DE BASSAC VIN DE PAYS D'OC ROUGE, ISABELLE & REMI DUCELLIER 1992 Languedoc	*Spice, white pepper and leather, earth and sweet cherry fruit are all evident on the nose of this juicy wine.*	**£5.89**	WTR	**B**
DOMAINE DE LUNARD, VIN DE PAYS DES BOUCHES DU RHONE 1990 Midi	*Mature, sweet, oxidative style underpinned by good fruit and tones of liquorice and herbs.*	**£5.95**	MK	**B**
DOMAINE DE TRIENNES, LES AVRELIENS, VIN DE PAYS DU VAR 1991 Midi	*Intense fruit, elegance and maturity make this a wine with depth and traditional values.*	**£5.99**	JAR	**S**
LIMBARDIE TRADITION, COTEAUX DE MURVIEL, HENRI BOUKANDOURA 1991 Herault, Midi	*Dark purple-black colour. Rich and full in the mouth, with lots of sweet Cabernet fruit.*	**£5.99**	ACH, M&V	**G**
LES CHEMINS DE BASSAC, VIN DE PAYS D'OC, CUVEE PIERRE ELIE, ISABELLE & REMI DUCELLIER 1992 Midi	*Intense, vegetal, spicy nose lifted by tones of white pepper, mulberries and plums. A balanced wine.*	**£6.49**	WTR	**B**
CORBIERES, CHATEAU CASCADAIS 1992 Languedoc	*Good, green-cherry fruit and a well-balanced palate of quality oak.*	**£6.50**	BI	**B**
CHATEAU DE LASTOURS CORBIERES, FUTS DE CHINE 1989 Midi	*Light, mature red. Full, rich, sweet and fruity on the palate. Drink now.*	**£6.50**	WES, DBY, BUT	**S**
CORBIERES, CHATEAU GRAND MOULIN, FUT DE CHINE, J N BOUSQUE 1990 Midi	*Good, soft, ripe fruit and mature tannins make up a wine with a delightful smoothness.*	**£6.60**	OZQ	**B**
MINERVOIS, CAMPAGNE DE CENTEILLES, P BOYER-DOMERGUE 1990 Midi	*Spicy, peppery and full of good, clean fruit that is gently sweet on the palate.*	**£6.95**	HPD	**B**

CHATEAU HELENE, CORBIERES, CUVEE HELENE DE TROIE 1989 Midi	*Big, smoky, oaky nose and a mass of rich, ripe fruit on the palate. Should mature well.*	£6.95	WAW, PV, FUL	S
MINERVOIS CHATEAU VILLERAMBERT JULIEN, CUVEE TRIAN 1990 Midi	*Sporting a rich, garnet colour, a delicious, sweet, fruity palate and a wonderful light body.*	£7.45	TAN	B
DOMAINE RICHEAUME CABERNET SAUVIGNON, COTES DE PROVENCE 1992 Midi	*Lovely, deep-purple with a dusty, farmyard character and lots of jammy, greengage aromas.*	£7.99	SAF, DBY	B
COTES DU ROUSSILLON VILLAGES, DOMAINE GAUBY 1990 Midi	*Rich, spicy, with hints of blackcurrant and violets. Full, ripe tannins with an earthy grip.*	£8.55	THP	B

PERSONAL TASTING NOTES

SIGHT	Clear Bright Hazy Cloudy Colour
SMELL	Fresh Musty Floral Fruit Vegetal Animal Wood/Oak Others
TASTE	Weight Sweetness Dryness Acidity Fruit Vegetal Wood/Oak Balance
SUMMARY	Age Maturity Location Vintage

MAS DE DAUMAS GASSAC, VIN DE PAYS DE L'HERAULT 1992 Midi	*Slightly stalky nose, followed by vanilla and cherry flavours. Some style and complexity.*	**£10.50**	TOS, ADN, LV	**B**
TERRES BLANCHES AURELIA, COTES DE PROVENCE, NOEL MICHELIN 1990 Midi	*Woody and peppery with great berry flavours and a hint of fresh, raspberry fruit.*	**£10.75**	ABY, ORG	**B**
FAUGERES CUVEE SYRAH, CHATEAU DES ESTANILLES, MICHEL LOUISON 1992 Midi	*Deep, youthful purple, with delicious rich fruit on the nose. Lots of style. Keep for four to six years.*	**£10.99**	ADN, NI, LWE, BEN	**S**

DRY WHITE

MUSCAT, VIN DE PAYS COLLINES DE LA MAURE, HUGH RYMAN 1993 Midi	*Lively Muscat fruit bouquet. Sweet, luscious palate with good acidity and depth.*	**£2.99**	TDS, TH, WR, BU, MWW, HHR	**B**
TESCO DOMAINE SAINT ALAIN, VIN DE PAYS DE COTES DE TARN BLANC, ALAIN GAYREL 1993 Midi	*Refreshing, with some tropical fruit and apple flavours. Medium to high acidity and an excellent finish.*	**£3.29**	TO	**B**
DOMAINE BRIAL MUSCAT DE RIVESALTES, VIGNERONS DE BAIXAS 1993 Midi	*Bright and breezy. Excellent appley palate with strong acid finish*	**£3.49**	SAF	**B**
LE PIAT D'OR DRY WHITE, PIAT PERE ET FILS	*Medium body, zingy acidity and a lovely fresh finish.*	**£3.69**	Widely Available	**S**
DULONG CHARDONNAY, VIN DE PAYS D'OC 1993 Midi	*A tropical fruit nose and spicy, melon flavours give a summery feel.*	**£3.80**	VEX, EOO	**B**
RESPLANDY VIOGNIER, VIN DE PAYS D'OC 1993 Midi	*Delicate, flowery, fruity nose with light flavours. Fair acidity on the palate.*	**£3.90**	CWS	**B**

VENDANGE BLANC, VIN DE PAYS DES COTES CATALANES, LES VIGNERONS DU ROUSSILLON 1993 Midi	*Pale lemon colour. Lovely fragrant nose of honeysuckle and peaches. Mouthfilling fruitiness.*	£3.95	SK, RAE, UBC, HAR	S
DOMAINE DE LA TUILERIE CHARDONNAY, VINS DE PAYS D'OC, HUGH RYMAN 1993 Midi	*A rich, smoky wine with apricots and peaches on the nose and palate. Great value at this price.*	£3.99	SMF, G, HHR	B
ST MICHAEL DOMAINE MANDEVILLE CHARDONNAY, VIN DE PAYS D'OC 1993 Midi	*Apples and peaches on the nose, buttery citrus fruit on the palate, good balance.*	£3.99	M&S	B
DOMAINE DES SALICES SAUVIGNON VIN DE PAYS D'OC, J & F LURTON 1993 Midi	*Green and grassy with a crispy aftertaste, this is well-balanced and very palatable.*	£3.99	TH, WR, BU, TDS, FUL	B
SPAR VIOGNIER CUXAC, VAL D'ORBIEU 0 OC	*A sound wine with a delicate nose and some soft, ripe fruit.*	£3.99	SPR	B
LA SERRE SAUVIGNON BLANC, VIN DE PAYS D'OC 1993 Midi	*Pale gold in colour, showing all the hall-marks of a really classy, elegant wine.*	£3.99	BI, VW, FUL, NRW	G
FORTANT DE FRANCE SAUVIGNON BLANC, SKALLI 1993 Midi	*A rather grassy nose, crispy acidity, packed with crunchy green fruit.*	£4.00	FUL, WL, A, BKW, CEL	B
LA SERRE CHARDONNAY, VIN DE PAYS D'OC 1993 Midi	*A subtle lemon citrus nose with hints of lano-lin and apple skins on the palate.*	£4.25	BI, FUL, VW	B
OZIDOC CHARDONNAY, VIN DE PAYS D'OC, DOMAINE VIRGINIE 1993 Midi	*Bread and walnuts on the nose preceed fresh, lemon fruit. Good fruit and acid balance.*	£4.75	ADN	B

OZIDOC SAUVIGNON, DOMAINE VIRGINIE 1993 Midi	*Gooseberries on the nose, full-flavoured sweet Sauvignon fruit on the palate.*	**£4.75**	ADN	**B**
PHILLIPPE DE BAUDIN SAUVIGNON BLANC, DOMAINE DE LA BAUME 1993 Midi	*A delicate fragrant wine with a slightly grassy aroma, full of soft clean fruit flavour.*	**£4.80**	WHC, CVR, DBY	**S**
CHAIS BAUMIERE SAUVIGNON BLANC VIN DE PAYS D'OC, DOMAINE DE LA BAUME 1993 Midi	*A lovely young and fresh aroma. A fat and juicy wine with grassy nettley flavour and a hint of soft ripe peaches.*	**£4.95**	JS	**S**
DOMAINE 'VIRGINIE' CHARDONNAY, VIN DE PAYS D'OC 1992 Midi	*Lemon jelly on the nose with tropical pineapple and mango flavours. Potent yet silky.*	**£4.99**	JFR, SHJ, ADN, BLS, LTW, CWS	**B**
JAMES HERRICK CHARDONNAY, VIN DE PAYS D'OC 1993 Midi	*Medium wood character and light fruit style; crisp finish and length.*	**£4.99**	OD, D, VW, JS, SAF, FUL, DBY	**B**
DOMAINE DE RIVOYRE CHARDONNAY, VIN DE PAYS D'OC, HUGH RYMAN 1992 Midi	*Generous, soft, ripe fruit flavours. Complex but balanced. A super, pleasing wine.*	**£4.99**	SAF, HHR	**B**
CHATEAU GRAND MOULIN, CORBIERES BLANC, J N BOUSQUE 1992 Midi	*Attractive golden-green, with a good blend of fruit and acid and a delicate, flowery nose.*	**£4.99**	OZQ	**B**
CHARDONNAY VIN DE PAYS D'OC, HUGH RYMAN 1993 Midi	*Nicely-styled wine of subtle tropical fruit aromas; a good balance of fruit and oak flavours.*	**£4.99**	JS, HHR, FUL	**S**
FORTANT DE FRANCE COLLECTION SAUVIGNON BLANC, SKALLI 1992 Midi	*Rich and spicy, showing hints of honey, grapefruit and elderflower. Refreshing.*	**£5.95**	SKA	**B**

LA PORCII CHARDONNAY, VIN DE PAYS D'OC, NEGOCIANTS INTERNATIONAL 1992 Midi	*Clean, fruity fresh style, quite mellow. Soft middle with nice balance of fruit and oak.*	**£5.99**	OD, FIN	**B**
JACQUES FRELIN COSTIERES DE NIMES VIOGNIER, JACQUES FRELIN 1993 Midi	*A pleasant, medium-bodied wine with a good, lemon-grapefruit sherbet nose.*	**£5.99**	VER, HDR	**B**
DOMAINE DES SALICES VIOGNIER, VIN DE PAYS D'OC, J & F LURTON 1993 Midi	*A blockbuster! Good grassiness and gooseberry fruit on the nose, well-balanced and firm.*	**£5.99**	OD, FUL	**B**
VIOGNIER, VIN DE PAYS DE L'ARDECHE, CEVENNE 1992 Midi	*Rich nose and good, ripe, acidity on palate. Very pleasant and stylish.*	**£5.99**	WL	**B**
DOMAINE LA COMBE BLANCHE, VIOGNIER, VIN DE PAYS D'OC, GUY VANLANCKER 1993 Midi	*A full, soft, almost unctuous, plummy nose. A full wine with fair fruit.*	**£6.35**	WES, DBY	**B**
PYRAMUS, CHATEAU ROUTAS, COTEAUX VAROIS BLANC 1992 Midi	*Deep, heavy buttery wine. Very strong memorabl aftertaste.*	**£6.40**	HC, M&V	**B**
VIOGNIER, VIN DE PAYS D'OC, FORTANT DE FRANCE COLLECTION, SKALLI 1992 Midi	*Full-lemon colour. Good strong floral nose, aromatic and slightly honeyed.*	**£6.95**	TH, WR, BU	**S**
TOQUES ET CLOCHES CHARDONNAY ELEVE EN FUTS DE CHENE, VIN DE PAYS DE L'AUDE 1992 Midi	*Light and agreeable wine, fresh and buttery. Good backbone and length with lemony fruit character.*	**£7.60**	NIC	**B**
MAS JULLIEN LES VIGNES OUBLIEES, COTEAUX DE LANGUEDOC BLANC, OLIVIER JULIEN 1992 Midi	*Full, gold colour, earthy and buttery on the nose. This is a gently spicy, full, blousy wine.*	**£8.95**	LV	**G**

MUSCAT DE RIVESALTES, DOMAINE CAZES 1992 Midi	*Floral and lemony bouquet; and slightly spicy flavour, . Soft acidity with good complexity*	£9.99	HN, PON, LV	B
MAS DE DAUMAS GASSAC BLANC, VIN DE PAYS DE L'HERAULT 1993 Midi	*A clean and delicately perfumed nose with ripe floral tones and a hint of spice.*	£15.50	POP, PAV, ADN, LV	B

ROSE

ROSE D'SYRAH, VIN DE PAYS D'OC, VAL D'ORBIEU Midi	*An elegant and delicate wine: pale in colour, quite light with gentle soft fruit.*	£2.99	SPR	B
FORTANT DE FRANCE CABERNET ROSE, VIN DE PAYS D'OC, SKALLI FORTANT DE FRANCE 1993 Midi	*A full soft fruity nose precedes quite a light but ripe palate showing just a hint of sweetness. Clean and well made.*	£3.89	SKA	B
DOMAINE DE TUILERIE, VIN DE PAYS D'OC, MERLOT ROSE 1993 Midi	*Well made and nicely rounded. Gently aromatic with soft, slightly sweet, ripe fruit.*	£3.99	JS,	B
DOMAINE DE L'HORTUS, COTEAUX DU LANGUEDOC, J ORLIAC 1993 Midi	*A weighty wine with very likeable fresh fruit flavours ranging from herbs to blackcurrants.*	£4.99	TH, WR, BU, TDS	B
TERRES BLANCHES ROSE, NOEL MICHELIN 1993 Midi	*Good fruit. Good length. Appley aromas precede a clean fresh palate of candied fruits.*	£7.00	ABY	B

FORTIFIED

NOILLY PRAT, NOILLY PRAT Midi	*Fresh herbs, lemons, wormwood and hints of orange blossom on the nose. Dry and complex.*	£5.99	JS, SAF, TO, W, OD, THP, TBW, DBY	B

| MAS AMIEL 15 ANS D'AGE, CHARLES DUPUY Midi | *Tawny red, with an interesting nose of raisins, bitter chocolate, and hints of tobacco.* | **£13.95** | LV | **B** |

— OTHER REGIONS —

BLENDS

ST. MICHAEL DUBOEUF SELECTION ROUGE, GEORGES DUBOEUF	*Soft warm damson nose with a wonderful clean fruity followthrough. Delicious.*	**£3.29**	M&S	**B**
CHARDONNAY BLANC DE BLANCS, CAVES DES MOINES, VARICHON ET CLERC Savoie	*Refreshing and vibrant. Rich honeyed caramel and toffee over a good length.*	**£4.99**	A	**B**
VARICHON ET CLERC CARTE BLANCHE BLANC DE BLANCS Savoie	*A buttery palate, combined with clean fruit, giving a ripe-tasting wine.*	**£6.50**	SHJ, HOT, TAN, BLS, MOK	**B**
REBELLE CUVEE NO.4, DULONG	*Fascinatingly complex wine with pepper, smoke and ripe Cabernet flavours.*	**£8.00**	WWI, HBV, VEX	**B**
REISLING CUVEE PARTICULIERE, ANDREE TOMAS 1990	*A perfumed nose, ripe peach fruit and golden-green colour mark this off-dry number.*	**£10.50**	VT	**B**

PERSONAL TASTING NOTES

SIGHT	
	Clear Bright Hazy Cloudy Colour
SMELL	
	Fresh Musty Floral Fruit Vegetal Animal Wood/Oak Others
TASTE	
	Weight Sweetness Dryness Acidity Fruit Vegetal Wood/Oak Balance
SUMMARY	
	Age Maturity Location Vintage

Pinpoint who sells the wine you wish to buy by turning to the stockist codes. If you know the name of the wine you want to buy, use the alphabetical index. If price is your motivation, refer to the invaluable price guide index; red and white wines under £5 and sparkling wines under £10. Good hunting!

GERMANY

GERMANY IS THE SOURCE of some of the world's greatest white wines, made in styles unparalleled elsewhere. Sadly, many producers are chasing the rainbow of dry wine while some of the biggest names are letting themselves down with shoddy winemaking. All of which helps to explain the presence of new-wave winemakers as medal winners, who are often more quality-conscious than many of their forebears.

——THE MOSEL——

DRY/MEDIUM WHITE

SCHARZHOFBERGER RIESLING KABINETT, RUDOLF MÜLLER 1990 Mosel-Saar-Ruwer	*Ripe, raisiny aroma. Well-made with good balance and delicate sweetness.*	**£4.59**	SMF, G	**B**
WILTINGER KLOSTERBERG RIESLING KABINETT, VAN VOLXEM 1989 Mosel-Saar-Ruwer	*Nice, petrolly, intense nose with smell of roses. Full with great fruit on palate. Quite sweet but good balancing acidity.*	**£4.99**	WL	**S**
TRITTENHEIMER APOTHEKE RIESLING AUSLESE, GRANS-FASSIAN 1983 Mosel-Saar-Ruwer	*Elegant elderflower and petrol nose. Nice citrus fruit complexity, sweetness and lowish alcohol with fresh fruit acidity on finish.*	**£5.49**	MMW, TO	**S**
TRITTENHEIMER APOTHEKE RIESLING KABINETT, FRIEDERICH-WILHELM GYMNASIUM 1991 Mosel-Saar-Ruwer	*Subtle Riesling nose, floral and petrolly. Quite rich and fat in mouth, floral and limey. Medium dry and very pleasant.*	**£5.49**	TO	**S**
DR LOOSEN RIESLING 1992 Mosel-Saar-Ruwer	*A drier style, with good fruit and acidity. Grapey and well made.*	**£5.99**	TH, BAL, HAM, SHJ, CHH, H&H	**B**

GRAACHER HIMMELREICH RIESLING KABINETT, REICHSGRAF VON KESSELSTATT 1993 Mosel-Saar-Ruwer	*Good, aromatic nose; clean, spicy and light. On palate good sweetness and fruit. Nice rich wine with good acidity.*	**£5.99**	A	**B**
PIESPORTER GOLDTRÖPFCHEN RIESLING QbA, GRANS-FASSIAN 1992 Mosel-Saar-Ruwer	*Pear aromas and a silky, clean palate. Squeaky clean flavours precede a lemon/lime finish.*	**£5.99**	OD	**S**
SERRIGER HEILIGENBORN RIESLING SPÄTLESE 1983 Mosel-Saar-Ruwer	*Good, strong, positive aromas. Sweet with good acidity and Riesling flavour. All in all a nice wine.*	**£6.39**	VW	**B**
KRÖVER KIRCHLAY RIESLING SPÄTLESE, WEINGUT RÖMERHOF 1992 Mosel-Saar-Ruwer	*Crisp, clean, honeyed bouquet with a very clean palate. Honey flavours and a touch of grapefruit.*	**£6.75**	RH	**B**
TRITTENHEIMER ALTÄRCHEN RIESLING KABINETT, GRANS-FASSIAN 1991 Mosel-Saar-Ruwer	*Attractive, petrolly, Riesling aroma. Quite sweet, oily with delicious lemony flavour. Good structure and acidity.*	**£7.99**	MWW	**S**
WEHLENER SONNENUHR RIESLING AUSLESE, DR F. WEINS-PRÜM ERBEN 1983 Mosel-Saar-Ruwer	*Complex, rich, caramel bouquet with fresh, clean, full, fruit flavours. Nice balance of fruit and acidity. Long and flavoursome.*	**£8.65**	THP	**B**
PIESPORTER GOLDTRÖPFCHEN RIESLING KABINETT, KESSELSTATT 1992 Mosel-Sarr-Ruwer	*Full, flowery nose with hints of peaches, and citrus. Spritzy feel, pleasant fruit and good balance. Attractive drinking.*	**£8.95**	BBR	**B**

GRAACHER HIMMELREICH RIESLING SPÄTLESE, FRIEDRICH-WILHELM GYMNASIUM 1992 Mosel-Saar Ruwer	*Attractive nose with good weight and high acidity followed by a well-balanced palate.*	£8.95	MVN	B
BERNKASTELER BADSTUBE RIESLING SPÄTLESE, DR THANISCH 1989 Mosel-Saar-Ruwer	*Classy, oily Riesling. Good grapefruit nose and plenty of fresh, zingy lime and grapefruit. Fine crisp acidity.*	£9.80	J&B	S
BRAUNEBERGER JUFFER-SONNENUHR RIESLING SPÄTLESE, MAX-FERD RICHTER 1990 Mosel-Saar-Ruwer	*Good backbone to flavours found here of fruit and hints of honey. A rich, persistent finish. Strong and well-made.*	£9.90	UM	S
TRITTENHEIMER APOTHEKE RIESLING AUSLESE, FRIEDRICH-WILHELM GYMNASIUM 1988 Mosel-Saar-Ruwer	*A fresh, acidic, flowery, fruit bouquet characterises this attractive, light flowery style. It ends with a fresh, limey finish.*	£10.19	VW	B
DR LOOSEN WEHLENER SONNENUHR RIESLING SPÄTLESE 1992 Mosel-Saar-Ruwer	*Despite understated nose, this has good fruit on palate, with length and acidity. Good quality.*	£10.99	WSG, HAM, HC, H&H	B
PIESPORTER GOLDTRÖPFCHEN RIESLING AUSLESE, REICHSGRAF VON KESSELSTATT 1990 Mosel-Saar-Ruwer	*Clean, fresh and with good fruit, this is a weighty white which has depth and some length.*	£11.20	MWW, DBY	S
MAXIMIN GRÜNHÄUSER 'ABTSBERG', VON SCHUBERT 1992 Mosel-Saar-Ruwer	*The excellent nose is spicy and complex; the palate has lovely, piercing, citric acidity. There is also good balance.*	£12.75	ADN	B

TRITTENHEIMER APOTHEKE RIESLING-AUSLESE, GRANS-FASSIAN 1990 Mosel-Saar-Ruwer	*Lovely, complex pineapple, petrol and lime aroma. Spicy, with superb sugar/acid balance and sherbert, lemon finish.*	£20.00 UW	S

—THE RHINE—

DRY/MEDIUM WHITE

KWIK-SAVE MORIO MUSKAT, ST. URSULA 1993 Pfalz	*Spicy nose and hints of violets and apricots. Tropical fruits and pleasant finish.*	£2.29 KS	B
BEREICH NIERSTEIN, ST GERTRUDIS-KELLEREI GMBH 1992 Rheinhessen	*Peachy, aromatic nose; soft fruit with nice freshness. Clean stuff. Very good value at the price.*	£2.39 CRG	B
ST URSULA MORIO MUSKAT QbA 1993 Pfalz	*Floral with good aromatic nose and tasty citrus spicy fruit. Medium-sweet. A bargain.*	£2.79 SAF, G, SMF	B
CO-OP SPÄTLESE RHEINPFALZ, GWG RIETBURG 1990 Pfalz	*Golden yellow; clear and bright. Well made with good depth; vanilla character. Good length.*	£3.49 CWS	B
ST URSULA GALERIE, PINOT BLANC DRY 1993 Pfalz	*Aromatic, grapey nose and flavour of raisins on palate. Clean and fresh with a little spritz.*	£3.79 OD, W, CWS	B
WESTHOFENER BERGKLOSTER AUSLESE, ST. URSULA 1992 Rheinhessen	*Attractive wine with subdued nose. Good, clean ripe fruit on medium-sweet palate.*	£3.99 W, CWS	B
SAFEWAY RHEINPFALZ AUSLESE, ST. URSULA 1992 Pfalz	*Rich, pineapple-and-honey bouquet. Sweet and spicy palate.*	£3.99 SAF	B

TESCO GOLDEN HARVEST, ZIMMERMANN GRAEFF 1992 Pfalz	*Grapey nose with touch of spice, and good balance. Nice fruit complexity with dry finish.*	**£4.49**	TO	**B**
SCHEUREBE DIENHEIMER TAFELSTEIN KABINETT, BRÜDER DR BECKER 1993 Pfalz	*Pleasant, grassy, fruit bouquet and full palate with good finish. Attractive with crisp acidity.*	**£4.99**	SAF	**B**
OPPENHEIMER KREUZ RIESLING KABINETT, GUSTAV ADOLF SCHMITT'SCHES 1991 Rheinhessen	*Light, fruity nose with lemon/lime, citrus character. Clean stuff with an individual flavour.*	**£5.29**	BP	**B**
DEINHARD PINOT BLANC 1991 Pfalz	*Sumptuous fruit on nose; followed by delicious grapiness on palate.*	**£5.49**	TDS	**B**
UNGSTEINER HERRENBERG RIESLING SPÄTLESE, KURT DARTING 1992 Pfalz	*Some citrus fruit, which has nice, sweet mid-palate and good acid level. Attractive drinking with some sweetness.*	**£5.99**	OD	**B**
NIERSTEINER PETTENTHAL RIESLING SPÄTLESE, BALBACH 1988 Rheinhessen	*Clean, good fruit. Nice balance of acidity and sweetness. Full, mature, peachy character.*	**£6.69**	VW	**B**
NIERSTEINER REHBACH KABINETT, BALBACH 1988 Rheinhessen	*Honey aromas, oily and rich. Fullish fruit on palate. Well balanced.*	**£6.69**	VW	**B**
NIERSTEINER PETTENTHAL RIESLING AUSLESE, GRAF WOLFF METERNICH 1992 Rheinhessen	*Tasters noted a lychee and lime bouquet, with some apricot tones. Try this one for a young, wild and exotic wine.*	**£6.99**	A	**B**

HOCHHEIM, DEINHARD HERITAGE COLLECTION 1988 Rheingau	*A food wine. Golden yellow with appley fruit on nose and excellent weight in mouth. A goody.*	**£7.99**	TDS, CNL, DBY	**S**
RIESLING SPÄTLESE DIENHEIMER KREUZ, BRÜDER DR BECKER 1991 Rheinhessen	*Full, ripe bouquet; pink grapefruit, flowery and sherbert. Medium sweetness.*	**£7.99**	WMK	**B**
MÜLLER CATOIR RIESLING TROCKEN 1991 Rheinhessen	*Great colour. Fruity nose and a character- ful and lively palate.*	**£8.49**	WMK	**B**
HAARDTER MANDELRING SCHEUREBE KABINETT, MÜLLER CATOIR 1991 Pfalz	*Delicate, perfumed nose and pronounced botrytis character. Mix of fruit flavours. Lovely long fin- ish. Very well made.*	**£8.59**	WMK	**G**
KREUZNACHER BRÜCKES RIESLING AUSLESE, SCHLOSS VON PLETTENBERG 1989 Nahe	*Stylish wine with peaty flavours on the palate. This is well-balanced with nice acidity. Poise and class here.*	**£8.99**	TH, WR, BU	**S**
RIESLING AUSLESE TROCKEN SCHALES, WEINGUT SCHALES 1989 Rheinhessen	*Elegant, soft, honeyed with petrolly nose and touch of lemon. Good balance and excellent length.*	**£8.99**	TAN	**B**
RÜDESHEIMER KIRCHENPFAD RIESLING SPÄTLESE, JOSEF LEITZ 1992 Rheingau	*Peaches and honeyed fruit with good balance and clean finish. Excellent.*	**£10.95**	WSG, HC, LWE	**B**
RIESLANER MUSSBACHER ESELSHAUT AUSLESE, MÜLLER-CATOIR 1992 Pfalz	*Attractive aromatic lemon nose. Clean, flo- ral and honeyed. Full ripe fruit and clean fin- ish. Well made.*	**£11.99**	OD	**S**

SCHLOSS JOHANNISBERGER RIESLING AUSLESE, FÜRST VON METTERNICH 1993 Rheingau	*Slight, flowery, peardrops bouquet. Nice, simple fruit flavours. Quite sweet wine, with surprisingly complex, fruity finish.*	**£15.49**	DBY	**S**

SWEET WHITE

FORSTER SCHNEPFENFLUG HUXELREBE TROCKENBEERENAUSLESE, KURT DARTING 1992 Pfalz	*Luminous orangey-gold. Luscious, honeyed, aromatic nose. Complex, zingy, tropical fruit flavour. Long, rich peel finish. Well-balanced.*	**£13.99**	OD	**G**
NIERSTEINER OELBERG RIESLING & SILVANER EISWEIN, GUSTAV ADOLF SCHMITT'SCHES 1985 Rheinhessen	*Strong nose of ripe grapes and honeyed toffee-apples. Palate is well concentrated with rich, candied fruit. A big wine.*	**£17.99**	BP	**S**
MUSSBACHER ESELSHAUT RIESLANER TROCKENBEERENAUSLESE, MÜLLER-CATOIR 1992 Pfalz	*Rich gold. Light, fresh and subtle nose with honeyed flavours of citrus fruits, grapes and lychees. Good acidity. Well balanced.*	**£29.00**	OD	**G**
KIEDRICHER GRÄFENBERG RIESLING BEERENAUSLESE, ROBERT WEIL 1992 Rheingau	*Amber colour, with a luscious, apricot nose. Firm, complex and well-balanced with a crisp acidity giving a real lift.*	**£70.00**	BAR	**G**
KIEDRICHER WASSEROS RIESLING EISWEIN, ROBERT WEIL 1992 Rheingau	*Luscious, perfumed bouquet with delicious fruit palate of citrus peel, apricots and lychees.*	**£75.00**	BAR	**G**

— OTHER REGIONS —

RED

AFFENTALER SPÄTBURGUNDER ROTWEIN BADEN-AUSLESE 1990 Buhl Baden	*Beetroot aroma, savoury palate with some sweeter tinges of vanilla, and a quietly assertive finish.*	**£24.26**	WSC	**B**

PERSONAL TASTING NOTES

SIGHT	
	Clear Bright Hazy Cloudy Colour
SMELL	
	Fresh Musty Floral Fruit Vegetal Animal Wood/Oak Others
TASTE	
	Weight Sweetness Dryness Acidity Fruit Vegetal Wood/Oak Balance
SUMMARY	
	Age Maturity Location Vintage

ITALY

N OT SO MUCH A COUNTRY as a loosely attached collection of regions, Italy defies vinous description. There is everything to be found, here: from reds produced using methods almost as ancient as the grape varieties from which they are made, to ultra-modern Bordeaux and Burgundy lookalikes and inventive vini da tavola unlike wines produced anywhere else in the world.

— NORTH WEST —

RED				
BARBERA DEL PIEMONTE SAN ORSOLA, FRATELLI MARTINI SECONDO LUIGI 1993 Piedmont	*A vibrant ruby, full of lively, juicy cherry fruit. A youthful modern-style wine.*	£3.00	BP	**B**
BARBERA DEL PIEMONTE, GIORDANO 1992 Piedmont	*A light bouquet of raspberries and currants, followed by a hint of cherries.*	£4.00	U	**B**
FRANCIACORTA ROSSO VILLA PADULE, VILLA PADULE 1992 Lombardy	*Its classic nose shows a combination of rich, plummy fruit, hints of mint, and stylish oak.*	£4.99	CTL	**B**
DOLCETTO D'ALBA, AURELIO SETTIMO 1992 Piedmont	*Vibrant red in colour, this is a juicy, earthy wine with leather overtones.*	£5.55	WAW, PV	**B**
BARBERA D'ASTI GEMMA 1990 Piedmont	*Massively coloured and rather closed. It should open out wonderfully in three to five years.*	£5.99	A	**B**

DOLCETTO D'ALBA PIANROMUALDO, MASCARELLO 1993 Piedmont	*A tremendous purple colour, with masses of bramble and black-currant aromas.*	£6.95	WCE	B
BAROLO, TERRE DEL BAROLO 1989 Piedmont	*A mature scent, redolent of almonds and liquorice, with rich fruit and chewy tannins.*	£6.99	VW, SAF, BC, CWS	B
BARBERA D'ALBA VIGNOTA, CONTERNO FANTINO 1992 Piedmont	*Smoky, spicy oak layered over some really rich, plummy fruit. Plenty of depth.*	£7.54	OD, WIN	B
BARBERA D'ALBA SUPERIORE, FRATELLI DE NICOLA 1989 Piedmont	*Rather backward now, but with enough softness to make it excellent in two to three years.*	£7.70	WCF.	B
BAROLO, AURELIO SETTIMO 1989 Piedmont	*A big and youthful wine, loaded with tannin that needs time to mellow.*	£7.75	WAW, PV	B
FRANCIACORTA ROSSO FANTECOLO, IL MOSNEL 1990 Lombardy	*Lovely, oaky, blackcurrant fruit. Good balance of fruit with soft tannins .*	£8.00	MON	B
BAROLO, FONTANAFREDDA 1989 Piedmont	*Dank, vegetal nose, reminiscent of truffles and raisined grapes with hint of smoke.*	£8.99	PTR, CEL, MRN, JN, TH, D	B
BAROLO DI SERRALUNGA, FONTANAFREDDA 1988 Piedmont	*Rather elegant, and full of cedary wood aromas and mellow, gentle fruit.*	£8.99	BKT, EWG, UBC, VOL, CEL	B
BRIC MILEUI, ASCHERI 1992 Piedmont	*Christmas-pudding aromas along with some spice, herbs and toasty, new American oak.*	£8.99	OD, WCE, D	B

BAROLO RISERVA, GIACOMO BORGOGNO & FIGLI 1988 Piedmont	*Brick-red colour. Ripe berry fruit, sweet and fragrant. Ripe tannins and complex finish.*	**£9.25**	A, RIB, RBS, THP	**S**
CABERNET SAUVIGNON' IL FALCONE', LA PRENDINA 1990 Lombardy	*Dark purple colour with spicy nose. Coffee and fruit flavours.*	**£9.95**	WTR	**B**
RE NOIR, VILLA LANATA 1991 Piedmont	*Smoky, lead-pencil oak nose with tones of violets. Soft in the mouth with nutty, rich fruit.*	**£9.99**	M&S	**B**
BARBERA D'ASTI 'POMOROSSO' COPPO 1989 Piedmont	*Strong, spicy oak with tones of tar and ripe, dark fruit. Promises great depth.*	**£12.79**	HLV, WTR	**B**
BARBARESCO, AZIENDA AGRICOLA GUISEPPE CORTESE 1988 Piedmont	*Mid-red centre with browning rim suggests maturity. Leathery and spicy, with intense fruit.*	**£13.75**	GI, LAY	**G**
VALTELLINA SFURSAT, NINO NEGRI 1989 Valtellina	*A good, ripe-fruit character shows through on this wine.*	**£14.50**	V&C, LV	**B**
BAROLO VIGNA DEL GRIS, CANTINA CONTERNO FANTINO 1989 Piedmont	*Ripe fruit flavour, this is a mid-cherry red with pink edges to delight the eye.*	**£14.67**	LAV, WIN	**B**
TAJARDINO, CAVALLERI 1989 Lombardy	*Youthful pinkish colour; a restrained vegetal nose and a palate that is full of fat, fresh fruit.*	**£15.00**	ENO	**G**
BAROLO SORI GINESTRA, CANTINA CONTERNO FANTINO 1989 Piedmont	*A rather earthy nose full of morello cherry, wrapped up in a lovely peppery, spicy style.*	**£15.54**	LAV, WIN	**B**

BAROLO VIGNETO BOSCARETO, BATASIOLO 1988 Piedmont	*Palate is classic and firm, but the hard, chunky tannins will need time to soften.*	**£16.00**	MON	B
BAROLO CRU RISERVA VIGNA D'LA ROUL, ROCCHE DEI MANZONI 1988 Piedmont	*Fans of classic Italian cherry fruit with a great deal of concentration will have a field-day.*	**£17.45**	LU	B
BAROLO VIGNETO LA CORDA DELLA BRICCOLINA, BATASIOLO 1988 Piedmont	*Rich and full, a classic cocktail of leather, tar, bitter-cherry fruit and lovely new oak.*	**£18.00**	MON	S
BAROLO CRU RISERVA VIGNA BIG, ROCCHE DEI MANZONI 1988 Piedmont	*The deep tobacco nose shows lots of tar, prunes and tomato. This is a very full, tannic wine.*	**£18.75**	LU	B
BAROLO BUSSIA, PARUSSO 1989 Piedmont	*Plenty of firm tannins make for a real block-buster with a long life ahead of it.*	**£21.95**	LV	B

DRY WHITE

ST MICHAEL ITALIAN CHARDONAY, FRATELLI MARTINI 1993 Piedmont	*Youthful and vibrant with limey, appley fruit and tangy, lemony acid.*	**£3.29**	M&S	S
LE MONFERINNE CHARDONNAY, ARALDICA 1993 Piedmont	*Pineappley, modern and refreshing. An interesting wine.*	**£3.75**	SAF	B
ST MICHAEL CHARDON-NAY DEL PIEMONTE VINO DA TAVOLA, 1993 Piedmont	*Clean, quite creamy, light and refreshing wine.*	**£3.99**	M&S	S

CHARDONNAY DEL PIEMONTE, ARALDICA 1993 Piedmont	*Limes and pineapple on the nose with buttery and faintly coconut flavours.*	**£4.00**	WCE, GRT, SEB, NRW	**B**
MOSCATO D'ASTI, BAVA 1993 Piedmont	*Muscat and honey aromas; sweet palate. Spicy, orangey style, good and fresh.*	**£7.85**	DEL	**B**
CHARDONNAY DEL PIEMONTE 'MONTERIOLO', COPPO 1991 Piedmont	*Good upfront, fresh fruit palate. Plenty of oak character.*	**£12.79**	HLV, WTR	**B**
CHARDONNAY VIGNETO MORINO, BATASIOLO 1990 Piedmont	*Creamy vanilla and floral bouquet; nice fruit character, with good acidity. Well-balanced.*	**£14.00**	MON	**B**
FORTETO DELLA LUJA, SCAGLIONE 1990 Piedmont	*Sherbet, lemony bouquet; light and fragrant with a hint of peaches. Rounded and smooth.*	**£18.00**	PST, HLV, GNW, WTR	**B**

SPARKLING

MORRISONS ASTI SPUMANTE, GIANNI, IVI SpA Piedmont	*Perfumed fruit balanced with enough acidity for a non-cloying wine.*	**£4.59**	MRN	**S**
ASTI SPUMANTE, ARALDICA Piedmont	*Dry, light mousse with an obvious floral and Muscat aroma.*	**£5.99**	WCE, SEB	**B**

LOW ALCOHOL

PIEMONTELLO LIGHT, SANTERO Piedmont	*A nice floral and Muscat nose. Good grapey flavour, soft with zingy acidity. Lemony.*	**£2.29**	TO, WL, KS, CWS	**B**

— NORTH EAST —

RED				
MALT HOUSE VINTNERS VALPOLICELLA, SARTORI 1993 Veneto	*Ruby red, with morello cherry and apple fruit. A delicious light wine full of soft, ripe fruit.*	£2.89	MHV	B
ROCCA SUENA, AMARONE RECIOTO DELLA VALPOLICELLA, PRODUTTORI ASSOCIATI SOAVE 1986 Veneto	*Soft, gamey fruit, and ripe cherries and cedar in what proved to be a very palatable wine.*	£3.69	U	B
CA'VIT MERLOT DEL TRENTINO, I MASTRI VERNACOLI 1991 Trentino	*Deep damson coloured. Earth and mushroom aromas complemented by smoky oak.*	£3.69	BP	B
TEROLDEGO ROTALIANO I MESI, CASA GIRELLI 1991 Trentino	*Deep, almost opaque, ruby colour. Bitter cherry flavour backed up by soft old oak.*	£3.99	KEL, C&A	B
TEROLDEGO ROTALIANO, CA'VIT 1992 Teroldego Rotaliano	*This has a young, macerated fruit style with an aroma of bananas and cherries.*	£4.49	BP	S
FIORI D'INVERNO, CA'VIT 1992 Trentino	*Attractive soft strawberry fruit with complexity of mature gamey character.*	£4.95		B
CAPITEL SAN ROCCO ROSSO, VINO DI RIPASSO, FLLI TEDESCHI 1990 Veneto	*A big, animal nose, with some lovely fruit, rich American oak and thick, chewy tannins.*	£6.35	LAV, WIN	B
VALPOLICELLA CLASSICO SUPERIORE CAPITEL NICALO, AZIENDA AGRICOLA FRATELLI TEDESCHI 1990 Veneto	*A rich wine, packed with good cherry fruit flavours. Give it three to five years.*	£6.50	LAV, WIN	B

Santo Stefano de le Cane, P Boscaini 1990 Veneto	*Sniff here for a rich, slightly Porty nose.*	**£6.50**	MWW	**B**
Collio Cabernet Franc, Conte Attems 1991 Friuli	*A dusty and earthy wine, with dark, cherry aromas offset by a little oak complexity.*	**£7.45**	LU, V&C	**B**
La Grola Valpolicella, Allegrini 1990 Veneto	*A slightly casky character, while on the palate, a blend of fruit and wood.*	**£9.00**	WCE, SEB	**B**
Palazzo Della Torre, Allegrini 1990 Veneto	*Big brute of a wine with very dry tannins, accompanied by rich baked fruit.*	**£9.00**	WCE	**B**
Recioto Della Valpolicella, Flli Tedeschi 1988 Veneto	*A very dark wine, brimming with raspberries and morello cherries. Delicious.*	**£9.50**	MWW	**B**
Malbech Del Veneto Orientale, Santa Margherita 1987 Veneto	*A powerful nose full of rich, meaty, leathery spice and gamey cherry fruit. Full-bodied.*	**£9.95**	LU, RBS, V&C	**S**
Recioto Amarone della Valpolicella Classico, Zenato 1986 Veneto	*A very big wine, purple-coloured, with a high level of alcohol. A lot of ripe cherry flavour.*	**£9.99**	TH, WR, BU	**B**
Amarone Della Valpolicella, Tedeschi 1988 Veneto	*This is a young, full-bodied example with a good deal of concentration and length.*	**£10.00**	MWW	**B**
Amarone Classico, Recioto Del Valpolicella, Brigaldara 1988 Veneto	*Black-cherry colour. This very young heavyweight retains highly astringent tannins.*	**£11.69**	WTR	**B**

AMARONE DELLA VALPOLICELLA CLASSICO, BOLLA 1986 Veneto	*A rich, deep-red colour. Loads of fruit in a well-structured wine which is full of soft tannins.*	£12.00	HAR, V&C, HTW	**B**
AMARONE RECIOTO CLASSICO DELLA VAL-POLICELLA, ALLEGRINI 1985 Veneto	*Deep damson colour. Old oak, cherry, damson and blackberry on the nose. Dry, but fruity.*	£12.00	WCE	**S**
CRESO ROSSO, BOLLA 1989 Veneto	*The mildly cheesy nose is full of vibrant, juicy fruit.*	£12.95	DID, LU	**S**
AMARONE CAPITEL MONTE OLMI, AZIENDA AGRICOLA FRATELLI TEDESCHI 1988 Veneto	*Deep Morello-cherry colour. Nose both earthy and perfumed, with spice and violets.*	£14.95	ADN	**G**
AMARONE, LE RAGOSE 1985 Veneto	*Deep ruby-garnet. Dusty, spicy raisin and blackberry aroma. A very long finish.*	£17.00	HAR, UBC, LV	**S**
CABERNET 'LOWENGANG', ALOIS LAGEDER 1990 Alto Adige	*Good colour; cassis and cedar nose. Balanced tannins, medium good length.*	£17.99	ENO	**S**
DRY WHITE				
ST MICHAEL CHARDONNAY DEL VENETO, GIRELLI Veneto	*Fresh varietal nose, punctuated with apple and lychee fruit aromas. Well-balanced.*	£2.99	M&S,	**B**
SAINSBURY'S BIANCO DI CUSTOZA, GEOFF MERRILL / GIV 1993 Veneto	*Buttery and fresh with a hint of spice. Crisp, with good balance between fruit and acid.*	£3.19	JS	**B**
SAINSBURY'S PINOT GRIGIO, ATESINO, GIV 1993 Veneto	*A light, well-made wine with a fresh, grassy nose and fair fruit.*	£3.29	JS	**B**

CHARDONNAY TERESA RIZZI, GRUPPO ITALIANO VINI 1993 Veneto	*Refreshing and clean. Well made with good finish.*	£3.79	WL, MRN	B
CHARDONNAY LE VERITIERE, GRUPPO ITALIANO VINI 1993 Veneto	*Light appley nose, slight effervescence. Soft, smooth rounded style. Good austere finish.*	£4.50	V&C, HAR, BBR, HN, C&B	B
PINOT GRIGIO, TORRE DI LUNA, GAIERHOF 1993 Trentino	*Ripe and spicy on the nose with clean, peachy fruit on the finish. This is refreshing.*	£4.99	CTL	B
CHARDONNAY ALTO ADIGE, E VAN KELLER 1993 Trentino/ Alto Adige	*Refreshing and clean. Fruity, rich flavours.*	£5.02	TO	B
COLLIO SAUVIGNON, ENOFRIULIA 1993 Friuli	*Elegant with a touch of fresh zingy grassiness and a crisply balanced palate.*	£5.99	WCE	B
PINOT GRIGIO ëBENEFIZIUM PORERÍ, ALOIS LAGEDER 1992 Alto Adige	*A bright and fruity nose on a complex wine with good depth and concentration.*	£7.10	HAR, EWG	B
PINOT BIANCO 'HABERLEHOF', ALOIS LAGEDER 1992 Alto Adige	*Bright and clear with good lychee and citrus flavours. Quite full, with good acidity.*	£8.99	ENO	B
CAPITEL CROCE, ANSELMI 1991 Veneto	*Light greeny-gold colour. Soft, lemony, buttery character on nose. Very fruity, but quite oaky.*	£9.99	PON, V&C	S

PINOT BIANCO, JERMANN 1992 Friuli	*Grapiness on the nose and some warm, spicy, cooked fruit flavours in the mouth.*	**£9.99**	LUV, HAR, HN, PON, V&C	**B**
VINNAE, JERMANN 1992 Friuli	*Good, lush, clean fruit, ripe, citrus palate with a zesty finish. Well made, intense style.*	**£11.99**	LUV, BWS, V&C, LV, VLW	**S**
CHARDONNAY, VINO DA TAVOLA, JERMANN 1992 Friuli Venezia Giulia	*Spicy with a lemon-grass nose and pineapple and guava flavours. A soft spicy finish.*	**£12.95**	F&M, HN, V&C, LV	**B**
CHARDONNAY 'LOWENGANG', ALOIS LAGEDER 1991 Alto Adige	*Light, clean fresh bouquet. Lovely under-tone of wood balanced by good fruit. Fine, steady palate.*	**£16.50**	PON	**B**
SWEET WHITE				
VINO SANTO TRENTINO, COLLEZIONE DI CA'VIT, CANTINA 1985 Trentino	*Rich sherry-like, intense and complex. Nutty, raisiny flavours.*	**£8.00**	TH	**S**
TORCOLATO VINO DOLCE NATURALE, MACULAN 1991 Veneto	*Light, elegant and subtle but warm on the nose. Hot, spicy palate and full, sweet and clean.*	**£22.89**	CC, GAR, GER, WB	**B**

— TUSCANY —

RED				
TESCO CHIANTI CLASSICO, AMPELOS, SAN CASCIANO 1991 Tuscany	*Hints of liquorice, violets and currants, as well as rich tannins and soft, subtle fruit.*	**£3.99**	TO	**S**

CHIANTI RUFINA, VILLA DI VETRICE 1991 Tuscany	*Creamy damson flavours and soft, sweet, cherry fruit may be found.Soft and easy.*	£4.00	TH, WCE, NRW	**B**
SAINSBURY'S CHIANTI CLASSICO, CECCHI 1991 Tuscany	*A deep-cherry colour; a perfumed, plummy bouquet with a suggestion of green capsicum.*	£4.49	JS	**B**
CHIANTI CLASSICO, CONTI SERRISTORI 1990 Tuscany	*An aromatic nose, crammed with truffles, flowers and mushrooms.*	£4.85	SMF, G	**S**
CHIANTI RUFINA RISERVA, VILLA DI VETRICE 1990 Tuscany	*Brambly fruit on the nose, followed by a juicy, earthy palate full of round, warm fruit. Warm aftertaste.*	£4.99	TH, WCE, H&H,	**B**
CHIANTI CLASSICO CLEMENTE VII, CASTELLI DEL GREVEPESA 1990 Tuscany	*Here is a wine full of spicy, cherry fruit, opulent damson and black-cherry flavours. Good value.*	£5.00	CTL	**B**
BARCO REALE, TENUTA DI CAPEZZANA 1993 Tuscany	*Intense, berryish, herby Tuscan wine.*	£6.00	TH, WCE	**B**
CHIANTI CLASSICO CONTESSA DI RADDA, GEOGRAFICO 1990 Tuscany	*A highly fruity nose goes before a palate bursting with delightful fruit and light tannin.*	£6.00	CC, LU, SMV	**B**
ALTE D'ALTESI ROSSO, ALTESINO 1988 Tuscany	*Opaque, deep rich bitter chocolate, berry palate warm medium finish.*	£6.09	PF	**B**
CHIANTI CLASSICO RISERVA MONTEGIACHI, GEOGRAFICO 1990 Tuscany	*Earthy, Sangiovese bouquet, with tones of mint and cherries, sweet fruit and firm tannins.*	£6.66	CC, LU, SMV	**B**

CHIANTI CLASSICO RISERVA, BADIA A PASSIGNANO, ANTI 1990 Tuscany	*Great concentration of flavour, and the palate is nicely oaked, powerful, long and excellent.*	£6.79	SV, LRW	**B**
ROSSO DELLE MINIERE, SORBAIANO 1990 Tuscany	*Delicious, Cabernet-style blackcurrant fruit and lots of warm and welcoming spicy oak.*	£6.99	A	**B**
CHIANTI RUFINA, CASTELLO DI NIPOZZANO RISERVA, FRESCOBALDI 1990 Tuscany	*On the nose, a stylish, mature bouquet of redcurrant jelly and rather austere wood.*	£6.99	OD, AB	**B**
CHIANTI CLASSICO, FELSINA BERARDENGA 1991 Tuscany	*Well made, quite full bodied, rich traditional Chianti.*	£6.99	OD, WCE	**B**
CHIANTI CLASSICO RISERVA, RICASOLI 1988 Tuscany	*Elegant and quite young but beginning to show signs of maturing.*	£6.99	BP	**B**
CHIANTI CLASSICO, CASTELLO DI VOLPAIA 1988 Tuscany	*A lovely bouquet of soft, ripe, berry fruit should make really attractive drinking.*	£6.99	L&W, ADN, SHJ	**B**
PARRINA ROSSO RISERVA, LA PARRINA 1990 Tuscany	*A stylish aroma of gamey, ripe fruit, cigars and cherries.*	£6.99	WCE, NRW	**G**
CHIANTI CLASSICO RISERVA, VILLA ANTINORI 1989 Tuscany	*Soft and rounded, showing some maturity, tones of vanilla and attractive, juicy fruit.*	£7.35	TH, WR, BU	**B**
ROSSO DI MONTALCINO LA CADUTA, TENUTA CAPARZO 1991 Tuscany	*A deep, ruby-red colour. An earthy, tarry wine with excellent, creamy fruit on the palate.*	£7.72	ROB	**B**

CHIANTI CLASSICO RISERVA DI FIZZANO, ROCCA DELLE MACIE 1988 Tuscany	*Definite signs of maturity from the distinct browning colour to the sweet fruit aromas.*	£8.00	BKT, F&M, VW, V&C, LV	B
LE VOLTE, TENUTA DELL'ORNELLAIA 1992 Tuscany	*A rich aroma of manure and blackberry fruit, with notes of earth and spice.*	£8.00	TH, WCE	B
CHIANTI CLASSICO, POGGERINO GINORI CONTI 1991 Chianti	*A big, rich, damson nose, loaded with vanilla oak. Extremely full, tannic wine.*	£8.25	MYS, DBY	B
SER GIOVETO, ROCCA DELLE MACIE 1989 Tuscany	*A superb production, with leather, tobacco and Mediterranean black olive.*	£8.75	WL, UBC, V&C, VTH	B
CHIANTI CLASSICO, QUERCIABELLA 1990 Tuscany	*Big, ripe and juicy with loads of mature bramble fruit and elegant cigar-box oak.*	£8.95	LEA	B
CHIANTI CLASSICO, ISOLE E OLENA 1990 Tuscany	*Tasters found a very modern, fresh and youthful style with hints of earthy complexity.*	£8.99	WCE, SGB	B
CHIANTI CLASSICO RISERVA DUCALE ORO, RUFFINO 1988 Tuscany	*Spicy, old-fashioned, long wood-aged, traditional style. Warm, ripe, plummy, spicy fruit.*	£9.79	V&C	S
BRUNELLO DI MONTALCINO CASTELLOGIOCONDO RISERVA, MARCHESI DE FRESCOBALDI 1986 Tuscany	*The palate is almost impossibly full of velvety blackcurrant and bramble fruit.*	£11.00	W, LAV, WIN	S
CAMPACCIO, TERRABIANCA 1988 Chianti	*Young, ripe and chewy. Full of earthy, minty fruit and cherries. A long life ahead.*	£11.67	JAR	B

COLTASSALA, CASTELLO DI VOLPAIA 1988 Tuscany	*Light in colour and light on the nose, this showed hints of liquorice and dusty wood.*	£12.50	ADN	S
PALAZZO ALTESI ROSSO, ALTESINO 1990 Tuscany	*Mishmash of liquorice, coffee, figs, prunes and raisins show it at its best right now.*	£12.99	POR	B
BRUNELLO DI MONTALCINO, COL D'ORCIA 1988 Tuscany	*Brick-red in colour with a fruity nose. Lively, blackcurrant and new-oak palate.*	£13.05	CD	B
BRUNELLO DI MONTALCINO, LA MAGIA 1988 Tuscany	*Beginning to show signs of maturity, this wine is a powerful mouthful of ripe, spicy fruit.*	£13.75	LWE, HOL, CTH	S
CHIANTI RUFINA RISERVA VIGNETO BUCERCHIALE, FATTORIA SELVAPIANA 1988 Tuscany	*A subtle, elegant nose, some grassy herbaceous-ness precedes lots of extracted flavour.*	£14.25	WCE	B
BRUNELLO DI MONTALCINO 'VIGNA DEL FIORE', FATTORIA DI BARBI 1988 Tuscany	*Exciting aromas of dried prunes and figs with a hint of resin characterise this wine.*	£14.50	LUV	B
CHIANTI CLASSICO RISERVA LA PRIMA, CASTELLO VICCHIOMAGGIO 1988 Tuscany	*Coloured a deep plum tone, this is a savoury wine with an excellent, flavoursome palate full of rich fruit.*	£15.10	MHC, NIC, SEL	B
I SODI DI SAN NICCOLO, PODERI CASTELLARE DI CASTELLINA 1990 Tuscany	*Good Cabernet nose. Nice concentration and length supported firm wood tannins.*	£15.50	ADN, SHB	S

Cabreo Il Borgo Capitolare di Biturica, Ruffino 1988 Tuscany	*Dusty wood and cassis are softly integrated with vanilla, cherries and plums.*	£15.75	LU, V&C, CD	G
Brunello di Montalcino, Banfi 1989 Tuscany	*Rich and balanced, with chewy, dry tannins and oodles of blackberry fruit. This wine is powerful.*	£16.00	PST, HLV	S
Brunello di Montalcino Riserva, Arfiano 1988 Tuscany	*Palate rich and earthy, full of the flavours of cherry and plum. Masses of character.*	£16.00	WCE	S
Mormoreto Capitolare Di Biturica, Marchesi de'Frescobaldi 1990 Tuscany	*Delicate nose of new oak and raspberry, firm raspberry on palate, rich and chocolatey.*	£16.01	ADN, BH, AFI	B
Coniale - Cabernet In Purezza - Poderi Castellare di Castellina 1990 Tuscany	*Victoria plums again, this time in combination with figs and subtle oak.*	£16.84	LAV	B
Flaccianello, Tenuta Fontodi 1990 Tuscany	*Vibrant colour. Lovely finish, lots of tannin but good fruit too. Huge potential.*	£16.89	WR, WCE, SEB	S
Vintage Tunina, Jermann 1992 Friuli	*Guavas on the nose and clean, ripe fruit on the palate. Delicious!*	£18.99	V&C, RD, MYS	B
Where The Dreams Have No End, Jermann 1989 Friuli	*Soft balance of wood and fruit flavours, with a good ripe fruit concentration.*	£29.95	PON, SEL, V&C	S

TIGNANELLO, ANTINORI 1990 Tuscany	*Young cherry-red colour. Lots of ripe, fragrant fruit on the nose and more on the palate.*	£20.00	SV, HAR, WR, C&B, GSJ, SEB	S
SUMMUS, BANFI 1988 Tuscany	*A deep ruby/garnet colour, loads of soft and juicy cherry fruit and an elegant long finish.*	£21.00	PST	B
CAMARTINA, AGRICOLA QUERCIABELLA 1988 Tuscany	*One sniff revealed a deep, dark nose. Plenty of underlying richness and concentration.*	£22.95	LEA	S
BRUNELLO DI MONTALCINO RISERVA, POGGIO AL VENTO, COL D' ORCIA 1985 Tuscany	*Deep red in colour, elegant, black-cherry flavours and soft, integrated wood.*	£23.00	LU	B
BRUNELLO DI MONTALCINO RISERVA, POGGIO ALL'ORO, BANFI 1986 Tuscany	*Extremely complex and concentrated, stuff, and needs time to come into its own.*	£25.00	PST	B
SASSICAIA, INCISA DELLA ROCHETTA 1990 Tuscany	*New oak and tight underlying fruit, firm, well-knitted tannins. Needs three years.*	£40.00	TH, HAR, F&M, RBS, V&C, TBW, SEB	G
SOLAIA, ANTINORI 1990 Tuscany	*Deeply coloured, intense minty nose, needs time to open up. Rich, ripe cherry fruit.*	£42.00	SV, HAR, BAL, WC, V&C, SEB	G

DRY WHITE

LIBAIO, TENUTA DI CASTELVECCHIO, RUFFINO 1993 Tuscany	*Good, fresh and lemony with some light, clean fruit in the mouth and a soft finish.*	£5.69	LU, CD	B

AVIGNONESI BIANCO, AVIGNONESI 1993 Tuscany	*Excellent summer wine, with spicy, lavender nose and appley fruit on palate.*	**£6.69**	RD, C&B, LEA, CC, WIM, D	**B**
ISOLE E OLENA CHARDONNAY 1992 Tuscany	*Light golden wine with soft creamy rich nose. Full, soft, clean palate, slightly woody.*	**£11.50**	WCE	**B**

SWEET WHITE				
BROLIO VIN SANTO, BARONE RICASOLI 1985 Tuscany	*Amber coloured wine with a clean, developed, dry nose. Good depth of flavours.*	**£8.99**	BP	**S**

—OTHER REGIONS—

RED				
SQUINZANO, MOTTURA Puglia	*Ruby red. Spicy classic Italian with bitter cherries and dark chocolate.*	**£2.59**	VW	**S**
MONTEPULCIANO D'ABRUZZO, CORTENOVA 1992 Abruzzi	*A youthful, juicy wine, light ruby in colour and quite full on the palate.*	**£2.74**	MRN	**B**
SOMERFIELD MONTEREALE ROSSO, CALATRASI Sicily	*A brightly coloured wine with a light, plummy nose and green, herbaceous flavours.*	**£2.99**	SMF, G	**B**
MONTEPULCIANO D'ABRUZZO, CANTINA TOLLO 1992 Abruzzi	*Easy-going cherry fruit makes this vibrant, juicy and very drinkable.*	**£3.49**	A, SPR	**B**
LAZIO MERLOT/SANGIOVESE, CASALE DEL GIGLIO 1993 Latium	*A medium-weight wine with soft, cakey fruit, mild tannins and gentle oak.*	**£3.49**	TO, G	**B**

COPERTINO, CANTINE SOCIALE COPERTINO 1990 Puglia	*Light and packed with cherry fruit, with a touch of vegetal development on the nose.*	£3.59	SAF, SEB, DBY	B
SAINSBURY'S COPERTINO RISERVA, CANTINA SOCIALE CO-OP COPERTINO 1991 Puglia	*A deep garnet colour with tinges of brown heralds a mature wine redolent of fruitcake.*	£3.59	JS	B
CIRO ROSSO CLASSICO, LIBRANDI 1990 Calabria	*Fresh, ripe raspberry and bramble fruit flavours, make this tangy and almost sweet. Full bodied and rich.*	£3.99	SMF, G, FUL	B
GUTTURNIO ROSSI, COLLI PIACENTINI, CANTINE 4 VALLI Emilia Romagna	*Juicy, tangy and youthful, with characterful and attractive fresh-fruit style.*	£3.99	CTL	B
ROSSO CONERO, UMANI RONCHI 1992 Marches	*This rich, ruby-red wine has flavours of bitter cherries, tobacco and smoky oak.*	£4.00	W, CEL, V&C, WL, LUV	B
LAMBRUSCO GRASPAROSSA DI MODENA SECCO, TENUTA GENERALE CIALDINI, CHIARLI 1993 Emilia Romagna	*A Light and frothy wine, with a pinky red colour and some delicious strawberry fruit. Excellent zip.*	£4.19	SAF, DBY	B
CIRO ROSSO CLASSICO, LIBRANDI 1992 Calabria	*A smoky, pungent, almost burnt character, full of sharp and juicy fruit flavours.*	£4.67	G, A, V&C, NET, L&W	B
SALICE SALENTINO, CANDIDO 1989 Puglia	*Smoky with hints of burnt currants, a herby wine with tones of toffee, coffee and berry fruit.*	£4.99	WCE, SEB, NRW	B

CARIGNANO DEL SULCIS, C S SANTADI 1991 Sardinia	*A wine at its peak, with warm aromas of coffee and spice and a hint of mint and almonds.*	**£4.99**	WCE, NRW	**B**
NOTARPANARO ROSSO DEL SALENTO, AZ AG TAURINO 1985 Puglia	*A nicely balanced combination of rich, raisiny fruit and soft, old-oak characters.*	**£4.99**	MWW	**B**
MONTEPULCIANO D'ABRUZZO, CONTE DI BORDINO 1990 Abruzzi	*Style, drinkability, colour and attraction are all here. Concentrated and long.*	**£4.99**	CTL	**B**
AMARONE VIGNETI CASTERNA, FRATELLI PASQUA 1988 Veneto	*A shy, rather elegant nose and a soft, rich palate with bags of oak flavour.*	**£5.99**	MRN	**B**
CIRO CLASSICO RISERVA, DUCA SANFELICE, LIBRANDI 1987 Calabria	*A bright, clarety colour and intense, vanilla-and-ripe-fruit nose precede almondy flavours.*	**£6.99**	LEA	**B**
DUCA D'ARAGONA, CANDIDO 1988 Salento	*A well-balanced wine, which is full of ripe, stewed fruit and a great depth of flavour.*	**£6.99**	WCE	**S**
CARBIO, COLLI AMERINI 1991 Umbria	*A tarry nose followed by lots of gentle, cherry fruit backed up by soft, chewable tannins.*	**£7.49**	IT	**S**
PETROSO MERLOT, VIGNETO DELLE TERRE ROSSE 1990 Emilia Romagna	*Deep coloured. Ripe plums, blackberries and strawberries with a firm tannic structure.*	**£8.49**	WTR	**B**
AGLIANICO DEL VULTURE RISERVA, D'ANGELO 1988 Basilicata	*Fragrant, smoky, raspberry-jam nose. With its oaky overtones, this is pleasant drinking.*	**£8.65**	LU, RBS, V&C	**B**

SAGRANTINO MONTEFALCO, CAPRAI 1988 Umbria	*Spicy and ripe with subtle mint and eucalyptus, and some lovely, chewy tannins.*	**£10.00**	WCE	**S**
TURRIGA, VINO DA TAVOLA DI SARDEGNA 1988 Sardinia	*Warm, smoky red fruits with hints of eucalyptus and chocolate. This a big, developed wine.*	**£12.33**	RD, V&C, CC, WIM, RWW	**B**
SAN GIORGIO, ROSSO DELL'UMBRIA LUNGAROTTI 1985 Umbria	*A blood-red wine with brown tinges, full of excellent fruit. Serious stuff.*	**£14.85**	V&C, RBS	**B**
MARCHESE DI VILLAMARINA, SELLA & MOSCA 1989 Sardinia	*Combines vanilla oak and candied blackcurrant with a veneer of soft, wood tannins.*	**£17.05**	LU	**G**
DRY WHITE				
SAINSBURY'S CHARDONNAY DELLE TRE' VENEZIE, GEOFF MERRILL Veneto	*Herbs, gooseberrys and fresh tropical fruits on the nose. Fresh clean and long.*	**£3.59**	JS	**B**
CA' MADUNINA PINOT GRIGIO FRIULI, BIDOLI/ GAETANA 1993 Friuli	*Fruity wine with some hints of spicy, cooked apples and a bit of spritz.*	**£3.79**	SAF	**B**
SAUVIGNON BLANC VINO DA TAVOLA, GEOFF MERRILL/GIV 1993 Veneto	*Apple, asparagus and floral aromas of lavender and heather, give bags of character.*	**£3.95**	JS	**B**
SAINSBURY'S ITALIAN GRECHETTO, GEOFF MERRILL/GIV 1993 Veneto	*Light, easy-drinking. Clean, refreshing with some good appley fruit.*	**£3.95**	JS	**B**
CHARDONNAY DEL SALENTO, CANTELE/K MILNE 1993 Puglia	*Ripe fruit, new oak nose; soft balance of acidity. Good fruit length.*	**£3.99**	TO, VW, SAF, TH, OD	**B**

SAINSBURY'S FRASCATI SECCO SUPERIORE, GEOFF MERRILL 1993 Latium	*A zippy, clean wine with a slightly yeasty nose and some good fruit flavours.*	**£3.99**	JS	**B**
CHARDONNAY DEL SALENTO, CANTELE 1993	*Tropical fruit characters, good weight, balance and length with fresh, limey acidity.*	**£3.99**	SAF	**S**
SAINSBURY'S CHARDONNAY, VINO DA TAVOLA, GEOFF MERRILL/GIV 1993	*Sweet, clean and spicy oaked nose; sweet vanilla character on palate. Good balance.*	**£4.75**	JS	**B**
NURAGUS, DOLIANOVA 1993 Sardinia	*A fruity wine with a slight spritz and an appley finish.*	**£5.45**	TO, W, C&B, CC, V&C, D	**B**
LA PRENDINA BIANCO, VINO DA TAVOLA 1993	*Complex, rich and full, with the taste of apples and peardrops. Dry, clean and well-bodied.*	**£5.99**	MWW	**B**
LE ARENARIE, SELLA AND MOSCA 1992 Sardinia	*Fresh herbaceous nose of grassy fruit and nettles. A fresh and lively wine.*	**£7.45**	LU, DID, CD	**B**
PASSITO DI PANTELLERIA, CARLO PELLEGRINO & C SPA 1993 Sicily	*Developed bouquet of hot caramel and spice. Rich luscious style with clean fruit character.*	**£8.50**	LAV, WIN	**S**
CERVARO DELLA SALA, ANTINORI 1992 Umbria	*Rounded and buttery aromas give a complex, subtle bouquet. Rich, vibrant and elegant.*	**£18.00**	HAR, GNW	**S**

SWEET WHITE

MORSI DI LUCE, MOSCATO DE PANTELLERIA, FLORIO 1990 Pantelleria	*Rich, lovely ripe and curranty. Super and full of honey.*	**£14.95**	JN, BWS, P&R, V&C, TAN	**B**

NEW ZEALAND

FOR TOO LONG IN THE SHADOW of its Antipodean neighbour, New Zealand produces wines which are unlike those made anywhere else in the world. Here is a combination of pure, often tropical, fruit flavours with the freshness only found in grapes grown in quite cool climate conditions. Sauvignon is already an international success, but Chardonnays, sparkling wines and reds are all developing.

RED				
MONTANA CABERNET SAUVIGNON 1991 MARLBOROUGH	*Slightly spicy and green fruit nose; good fruit palate. Development potential.*	**£4.99**	BKW	**B**
ESK VALLEY MERLOT/CABERNET FRANK DRY ROSE, HAWKE'S BAY 1979	*Excellent fruit, impeccable balance and a long finish. Clean, fresh, and well-made.*	**£6.95**	TH, WR, BU, GRT	**S**
CHURCH ROAD CABERNET SAUVIGNON, MONTANA 1991 Hawkes Bay	*Warm, slightly jammy bouquet. Deep peppery fruit; solid and ripe, good texture and nice oak.*	**£7.00**	CD, TH, VW, ABY	**B**
CORBANS PRIVATE BIN CABERNET SAUVIGNON/ MERLOT, MARLBOROUGH 1991 Marlborough	*Full deep-ruby wine. Blackcurranty nose with some maturity. Loads of fruit in mouth.*	**£7.99**	JS, CAX	**S**
CABERNET MERLOT, COOPERS CREEK 1991 Huapai	*Fullish colour with good closed nose. Toffee /caramel flavours and light fruit.*	**£8.00**	MWW, CFT, ES	**B**
ESK VALLEY RESERVE MERLOT/CABERNET SAUVIGNON 1991 Hawkes Bay	*Deep plum colour with full ripe palate and luscious soft fruit. Clean elegant and well-balanced.*	**£8.69**	WR, BU	**B**

C J PASK CABERNET/MERLOT 1992 Hawkes Bay	*Youthful, cherry red colour. Light, sweetish blackcurrant/cherry nose. Good balance.*	£8.99	L&W, SHJ, LS, HOT	B
CORBANS PRIVATE BIN MERLOT 1992 Marlborough	*Cassis, cedar, mint, spice and oak on nose. Rich berry and fresh cassis flavours. Fruity palate.*	£8.99	VW, CAX	G
MORTON ESTATE BLACK LABEL CABERNET/MERLOT 1991 Hawkes Bay	*Deep-coloured and full cedar-scented with spicy fruit and excellent finish. Nice bottle in two years.*	£9.50	PAG, ROB	B
ST NESBIT CABERNET SAUVIGNON/CABERNET FRANC/MERLOT 1988 South Auckland	*Pale intensity, auburn coloured wine. Minty aroma with medium tannins.*	£9.50	KF, RBS, GI, HAR, KF	B
VIDAL HAWKES BAY RESERVE CABERNET SAUVIGNON/MERLOT 1992 Hawkes Bay	*Good fruit character, minty soft fruit and hard young tannins. Well balanced.*	£9.59	KF	S
VAVASOUR PINOT NOIR 1992 Marlborough	*Light and soft, with a nice toasty nose. Mature, sweet fruit on palate. Very drinkable.*	£9.99	PO	B
C J PASK CABERNET SAUVIGNON 1991 Hawkes Bay	*Medium intensity, with soft aromas, mint and sweet fruit.*	£10.00	L&W, SHJ	B
VAVASOUR RESERVE CABERNET SAUVIGNON 1991 Marlborough	*Rich, mature, ripe flavours. Plenty of oak on the finish.*	£10.50	OD, DBY, EOR, MRF, BNK, H&H	B
NEUDORF VINEYARD MOUTERE PINOT NOIR 1992 Nelson	*Attractive nose with echoes of dry seaweed. Fruity. Plenty of depth; ages well.*	£11.95	ADN, HN	G

VILLA MARIA CABERNET SAUVIGNON/MERLOT RESERVE 1991 Hawkes Bay	*Ripe fruit character, cherries and plums and good tannins. Will be excellent.*	£12.25	TH	G
GOLDWATER CABERNET SAUVIGNON/MERLOT 1990 Waiheke Island	*Smoky oaked nose. Young blackberry and bramble jelly fruit character. Will be very good.*	£15.99	GWM, IVY, POR, CC	S
ESK VALLEY RESERVE MERLOT/MALBEC/CABERNET FRANC 1992 Hawkes Bay	*Aromatic with cherry fruits. Elegant, juicy, jammy and mouthfilling. Good depth.*	£17.68	BBR, AV	S

DRY WHITE

COOKS DISCOVERY SAUVIGNON BLANC, COOKS NZ WINES 1993 Gisborne	*Grassy Sauvignon nose, attractive medium weighted wine. Well-balanced appley fruit flavours.*	£4.99	TO, TH, WR, SPR, D, CAX, NRW	B
MONTANA SAUVIGNON BLANC 1993 Marlborough	*Aromatic grassy bouquet with floral tones. Fresh and spritzy with lots of soft fruit flavour.*	£5.00	BKW, THP, KF, TBW, ABY, D	S
VILLA MARIA ESTATE, PRIVATE BIN MARLBOROUGH RIESLING 1993 Marlborough	*Classic Riesling aromas – pineapple, grapefruit, grapes and peaches. Rich, dryish and full-flavoured.*	£5.49	TH	B
NOBILO MARLBOROUGH SAUVIGNON BLANC 1993 Marlborough	*Lots of leafy, asparagus aromas and plenty of gooseberry fruit. Crisp and full., will improve.*	£5.50	AV, TO, FUL, OD, GRT, TBW, TH	B
ROTHBURY ESTATE RHINE RIESLING 1993 Marlborough	*Botrytis on nose. Creamy acidity and flavours of apples, peaches and honey.*	£5.50	LAV	S
VILLA MARIA PRIVATE BIN SAUVIGNON BLANC 1993 Marlborough	*Lemon and lime fruit. Aroma of cut grass. Crisp, well balanced and stylish.*	£5.75	TH, VW, TO, W	B

CHENIN BLANC, HAWKES BAY, COLLARD BROTHERS 1993 Hawkes Bay	*Attractive tropical fruit nose, with some residual sugar on the palate. A good, clean finish.*	**£5.75**	BI, TH	**B**
JACKSON ESTATE MARLBOROUGH DRY RIESLING 1993 Marlborough	*Rich, ripe and long - a good modern style . Highly gluggable. Lemon and pineapple nose.*	**£5.99**	F&M, DBY, TAN, SV	**B**
ROTHBURY ESTATE MARLBOROUGH SAUVIGNON BLANC 1993 Marlborough	*Herbaceous and vegetal, full of ripe New World fruit and richness.*	**£5.99**	LAV	**B**
COOPERS CREEK GISBORNE SAUVIGNON BLANC 1993 Gisborne	*Ripe fruit with distinct asparagus and lemon nose. Rich flavour with touch of peachy warmth.*	**£5.99**	VW, MWW, ES	**B**
COOPERS CREEK GISBORNE CHARDONNAY 1992 Gisborne	*Fine perfumed character, good open fruit. Balanced with length. Zingy acid.*	**£6.00**	MWW	**B**
THE BROTHERS VINEYARD MARLBOROUGH SAUVIGNON BLANC-SEMILLON 1992 Marlborough	*Rich aromas of nettles and gooseberries. Depth of fruit flavour that lasts all the way to the next sip.*	**£6.49**	OD, POM, PIM	**S**
LINCOLN VINEYARDS BARREL FERMENTED CHENIN BLANC 1993 Waikato	*Faintly cedary nose, appley fruit, great length and complexity and a clean finish.*	**£6.75**	BP	**B**
VILLA MARIA PRIVATE BIN CHARDONNAY 1993 Gisborne	*Clean bouquet - lemon and apple. Good marriage of fruit and wood.*	**£6.99**	VW, WL, G	**B**
ROTHESAY VINEYARD CHARDONNAY, COLLARD BROTHERS 1991 Henderson	*Quite powerful , with masses of fruit, vanilla and wood. Very rich and ripe.*	**£6.99**	BI	**B**

CHURCH ROAD CHARDONNAY, MONTANA 1992 Hawkes Bay	*Very smooth, full flavoured and complex. Strong peel character and quite long finish.*	**£6.99**	JS, ABY	**B**
COOKS WINEMAKERS RESERVE CHARDONNAY 1989 Marlborough	*Beautiful colour, with a powerful flavour and long finish; a big, ripe, rich mouthful.*	**£6.99**	GSH, BWS, AUC, PEA, JCK, CAX	**S**
CORBANS PRIVATE BIN MARLBOROUGH FUME BLANC 1991 Marlborough	*Plenty of resiny oak, but well integrated with the dry, boneyed fruit flavour.*	**£7.49**	PEA, EGL, JCK, WTR, CEN	**B**
MORTON ESTATE WHITE LABEL CHARDONNAY 1991 Hawkes Bay	*Rich melon fruit, quite buttery oaky nose. Good acidity with a touch of pineapple on the palate.*	**£7.50**	PAG, TDS, ROB	**B**
JACKSON ESTATE SAUVIGNON BLANC 1993 Marlborough	*Lean asparagus style on nose, softer on palate showing lots of crisp, ripe fruit in perfect balance.*	**£7.50**	WR, C&A, L&W, ADN, TAN, H&H, D	**B**
CORBANS PRIVATE BIN CHARDONNAY 1991 Marlborough	*Well-defined character on the nose, with good fruit flavours on the palate.*	**£7.50**	GSH, PEA, WTR, CDE, EGL, CAX	**S**
NAUTILUS CHARDONNAY, MARLBOROUGH 1993 Marlborough	*Complex caramel and ripe fruit bouquet. Lean style with good balance. Long oak and peel finish.*	**£7.60**	EWG, WOC, CAC	**B**
JACKSON ESTATE CHARDONNAY, MARLBOROUGH 1992 Marlborough	*Smooth and complex lemon, orange and lime peel fragrance. Buttery and rich.*	**£7.99**	TAN, CHH, HN, W, WR, H&H NY	**B**
C J PASK CHARDONNAY 1992 Hawkes Bay	*Citrus fruit palate with good body and depth. Nicely integrated wood flavours.*	**£7.99**	L&W, SH	**B**

MARTINBOROUGH VINEYARD RIESLING 1993 Martinborough	*Zippy wine with some citrussy, spicy fruit character. Good length and depth.*	£7.99	ADN, NI	B
COOPERS CREEK MARLBOROUGH SAUVIGNON BLANC 1993 Marlborough	*A classic wine in the New World style with warm, ripe fruit flavour and touch of sweetness.*	£7.99	MWW, CAX	S
THE BROTHERS VINEYARD CHARDONNAY, MARLBOROUGH 1992 Marlborough	*Touch of honey and buttery oak. Lemony, tropical style. Good intensity. Well balanced.*	£8.00	POM, PIM	B
MORTON ESTATE RESERVE BLACK LABEL CHARDONNAY 1991 Hawkes Bay	*Nice, full-flavoured, with excellent palate and touch of spice. Stylish, elegant and clean.*	£8.20	PAG, ROB	S
MILLTON VINEYARD CHARDONNAY 1992 Gisborne	*Ripe, intense, well-structured and packed with fruity character; lovely oak handling.*	£8.29	SAF, ORG	G
MORTON ESTATE BLACK LABEL CHARDONNAY 1992 Hawkes Bay	*Full-styled, oaky Chardonnay, attractive, ripe fruit character and clean, lemony finish.*	£8.75	BWC	S
MATUA VALLEY JUDD ESTATE CHARDONNAY 1993	*Fresh fruity tropical wine with rounded, rich flavours. Aromatic and forthcoming.*	£8.99	TH, BU, GRT, MZ	B
PALLISER ESTATE CHARDONNAY, MARTINBOROUGH 1992 Martinborough	*Rounded flavour; peachy character to nose and slight sweetness on palate.*	£8.99	WR, BU, J&B, HHC, PON, ABY, SEB	B
GOLDWATER CHARDONNAY 1993 Marlborough	*Fine elegant nose; nice, full young flavour. Discrete palate with a clean fresh flavour.*	£8.99	IVY, POR, CC, FUL, MWW	S

HUNTER'S SAUVIGNON BLANC 1993 Marlborough	*Classy and stylish. Clean, elegant balance. Lovely, racy, lemony acidity. Lots of concentration.*	£8.99	HCK, WR, MJW, DUW, BSE, H&H	**S**
PALLISER ESTATE SAUVIGNON BLANC 1993 Martinborough	*Full-flvoured superbly balanced, and loaded with wonderful ripe, honeyed exotic fruit.*	£8.99	J&B, WR, BU, HOU, DBY, H&H, ABY, SEB	**G**
WAIRAU RIVER CHARDONNAY, MARLBOROUGH 1992 Marlborough	*Fruity, new oak, well intergrated. Restrained and very well made with excellent balance.*	£9.95	WR, SOM, ALV, CEB, H&H	**B**
HUNTER'S CHARDONNAY, MARLBOROUGH 1991 Marlborough	*Oaky, toffee nose and lemon character. Nice tropical fruit up front, rich and exotic on palate.*	£9.95	OPW, WR, MJW, DUW, BSE, H&H	**B**
GIBBSTON VALLEY SOUTHERN SELECTION CHARDONNAY, MARLBOROUGH 1993 Central Otago	*Full, ripe nose with a lovely tropical fruit palate.*	£9.95	ADN	**S**
NEUDORF VINEYARD SAUVIGNON BLANC 1993 Nelson	*Powerful leafy aroma with tons of asparagus, over lovely tart lemon acidity. Refreshing.*	£9.95	ADN, TDS, MRT, JN, NRW	**S**
HUNTER'S OAK-AGED MARLBOROUGH SAUVIGNON BLANC 1992 Marlborough	*Crisp and light with intense asparagus bouquet and a hint of oak. Well weighted. Good length*	£9.99	BBR, WR, WSO, CPW, BSE	**B**
VAVASOUR OAK-AGED MARLBOROUGH SAUVIGNON BLANC 1993 Marlborough	*Rich herbaceous nose of nettles, peapod and asparagus. Light, fresh and zingy fruit flavours.*	£9.99	OD, WR, BNK, BU, ABY	**B**
BABICH IRONGATE CHARDONNAY 1991 Hawkes Bay	*Intensely fruity nose; apples and citrus and very full fruit palate.*	£10.00	JS, SEL, WTL, EVI, MRT, ABY	**B**

MARTINBOROUGH VINEYARD CHARDONNAY 1992 Martinborough	*Fresh gooseberry nose; full wood and fruit palate. Zingy, fresh style with good finish.*	£10.00	TDS, OD, WL, ADN, SOM	B
COOPERS CREEK SWAMP RESERVE CHARDONNAY 1992 Hawkes Bay	*Flavoursome with intense, tropical aromas. Powerful, but not too heavy or serious.*	£10.00	WMP	S
WAIPARA SPRINGS CHARDONNAY 1992 Waipara	*Mango and lychee nose; rich and full with a ripe citrussy fruit flavour.*	£10.50	WAW, FNZ, PV, FSW	S
VAVASOUR RESERVE CHARDONNAY, MARLBOROUGH 1993 Marlborough	*Lemon green, and soft, leafy, fruit freshness making this big-nosed wine lean and elegant.*	£10.99	DBY, OD, FUL, H&H	G
VILLA MARIA CELLAR SELECTION SAUVIGNON BLANC 1992 Marlborough	*Mature, rich nose with earthy and herby tones. On the palate plenty of rich herbaceous fruit.*	£11.58	TH	B
VILLA MARIA CELLAR SELECTION SAUVIGNON BLANC 1993 Marlborough	*Refined, youthful goose-berry flavour with hint of melon and blackcur-rant. Lovely stuff.*	£11.58	TH	B
VILLA MARIA CHARDONNAY, MARLBOROUGH 1993 Marlborough	*Fresh, cool-fermented aromas, with fine acidi-ty and good underlying oak flavours.*	£11.58	TH	S
VILLA MARIA RESERVE BARRIQUE-FERMENTED CHARDONNAY 1993 Auckland	*Good chardonnay nose with some maturity; soft well-balanced palate with freshness and zing.*	£12.20	DBY	S
VILLA MARIA RESERVE BARRIQUE-FERMENTED CHARDONNAY 1989 Gisborne	*Ripe, honeyed bouquet; Grapefruit and toasty character. Austere but still quite buttery.*	£12.20	DBY	B

NEUDORF VINEYARD MOUTERE CHARDONNAY 1992 Nelson	Bright, exotic peach aromas. Intense fruit and oak. Honey and honeysuckle palate.	**£14.95**	ADN, MRT, TDS	**B**
VILLA MARIA BARRIQUE-FERMENTED RESERVE CHARDONNAY 1991 Gisborne	A very correct wine; good acidity and not over oaked. Well-balanced finish.	**£17.68**	DBY	**B**
VILLA MARIA BARRIQUE-FERMENTED RESERVE CHARDONNAY 1992 Gisborne	Good quality ripe nose; lots of oak and good length. Full and mouthfilling.	**£17.68**	DBY	**B**

ROSE

ESK VALLEY MERLOT/CABERNET FRANC DRY ROSE 1992 Hawkes Bay	Excellent fruit, impeccable balance and a long finish. Clean and fresh. Has real presence.	**£6.95**	TH, WR, BU, GRT	**S**
VIDAL PRIVATE BIN HAWKES BAY MERLOT ROSE 1993 Hawkes Bay	Complex nose: blackcurrants, smoked ham, strawberries and touch of smoke. Long and deep.	**£6.99**	TH	**B**

SPARKLING

DEUTZ MARLBOROUGH CUVEE, MONTANA Marlborough	Nose of lemon and yeast. Fresh, clean palate with lime acidity.	**£9.99**	CD, TH, TO, VW, KF	**B**
DANIEL LE BRUN BRUT NV, CELLIER LE BRUN Marlborough	Unusual red-brown hue with a buttery, fat nose and almost a sweet character. Very fizzy.	**£10.99**	HAR, VW, F&M, EWD, CWS	**B**
DANIEL LE BRUN VINTAGE, CELLIER LE BRUN 1990 Marlborough	Good gold colour and mousse. Fine nose that is soft and elegant with toasty tones. Full bodied.	**£15.00**	SV, HW	**G**

DANIEL LE BRUN BLANC DE BLANC, CELLIER LE BRUN 1990 Marlborough	*Biscuit everywhere! Noticeable maturity with spicy tone on fat, rich palate.*	£22.00	SV, HW	B

PERSONAL TASTING NOTES

SIGHT	
	Clear Bright Hazy Cloudy Colour
SMELL	
	Fresh Musty Floral Fruit Vegetal Animal Wood/Oak Others
TASTE	
	Weight Sweetness Dryness Acidity Fruit Vegetal Wood/Oak Balance
SUMMARY	
	Age Maturity Location Vintage

NORTH AMERICA

Northing America is a far more diverse source of wine than is generally recognised. Washington State and Oregon both make wines sufficiently distinctive to be considered in their own right, while, within California, there are a growing number of up-and-coming regions which challenge the notion of Napa Valley supremacy.

— CALIFORNIA —

RED				
TESCO CALIFORNIAN ZINFANDEL, STRATFORD WINERY California	*Chunky, chocolatey wine with soft blackberry and cherry fruit. Will benefit from ageing.*	**£3.99**	TO	**B**
ROBERT MONDAVI ZINFANDEL 1991 Napa Valley	*Classic Pinotage style. Full blackberry flavours and carefully blended oak. Clean and crisp.*	**£5.25**	JN	**B**
FETZER ZINFANDEL 1991	*Lovely rich blackberry, cherry and oak flavours. Very New World.*	**£5.75**	SAF, ABY, DBY, WES	**B**
FETZER EAGLE POINT PETITE SIRAH 1991 California	*Minty fresh fruit balanced by dark soft tannins and lively, peppery spice. Full-bodied.*	**£5.99**	OD	**B**
BEAULIEU VINEYARDS BEAUTOUR CABERNET SAUVIGNON 1991 California	*Young, elegant and fruity, with fine clear bouquet. Rich, ripe fruit with good balance and depth.*	**£6.00**	JS	**S**
MONTEVINA CABERNET SAUVIGNON 1991 Amador County	*Some fruit on the palate. Dry, really complex, with tannic back and mid-palate.*	**£6.20**	GRO, TP, H&H	**B**

BEL ARBORS MERLOT, FETZER VINEYARDS 1992 California	*Intense cherries on nose, with nice mixture of supple fruit that develops well on palate.*	**£6.37**	VW, AB	**B**
VILLA MT EDEN CABERNET SAUVIGNON 1990 California	*Maturing blackcurrant fruit on nose with berry and violet aromas. Good, clean and chewy.*	**£6.95**	JFE, HOH	**B**
PINOT NOIR 'LA BAUGE AU-DESSUS', AU BON CLIMAT 1991 California	*Fine, delicate nose of light fruits. Good weight of strawberries on the palate.*	**£6.99**	ACH, M&V, SAN, HAR	**B**
FETZER VALLEY OAKS CABERNET SAUVIGNON 1991 California	*Deep ruby-red colour. Delicate, perfumed-fruit nose. Youthful, fruity palate with lots of tannin.*	**£6.99**	OD, W, WL, VW, AB	**S**
FETZER VALLEY OAKS CABERNET SAUVIGNON 1990 California	*Attractive cedar nose, delicate fruit aroma refelected in stylish palate. Good at price.*	**£6.99**	CWS	**G**
GEYSER PEAK CABERNET SAUVIGNON 1992 Sonoma County	*Excellent balance of fruit, alcohol, acid and oak.*	**£7.46**	AUL	**B**
MONTEVINA CABERNET SAUVIGNON 1990 Amador County	*Oak and ripe raspberry well knit on nose. Similar palate, with young fruit and tannin.*	**£7.50**	WMK	**B**
FETZER BARREL-SELECT ZINFANDEL 1991 California	*Spiced chocolate-box fruit, balanced by new oak, vanilla and soft tannins.*	**£7.90**	LAV, WIN	**S**
EAGLE PEAK MERLOT, FETZER VINEYARDS 1992 California	*Superb blackberry fruit, with good cedary nose. Good fruit and balance of tannins. Will improve.*	**£8.37**	LAV, WIN, ABY	**S**

CLOS DU VAL ZINFANDEL 1989 Napa Valley	*Hedgerous and ripe berry fruit, mixed with cedar to produce fine wine made in classic style.*	£8.40	RD, BEN, HEY, DBY	**B**
RAVENSWOOD VINTNERS BLEND ZINFANDEL 1992 Sonoma	*The clean, ripe raspberry fruit of this wine is joined by the vanilla hint of a full oak style.*	£8.50	JAR	**B**
FETZER BONTERRA RED TABLE WINE 1991 California	*Jammy nose lifted by green tannins and some refreshing, zesty fresh fruit acidity.*	£8.98	OD, SAF, LAV	**B**
FIRESTONE CABERNET SAUVIGNON 1991 Santa Barbara	*Nice vanilla oak with good fruit. A medium weight wine with good tannins on the finish.*	£8.99	TH, MWW, CWS	**B**
GARNET PINOT NOIR, SAINTSBURY 1992 Carneros	*Light and sweet, with a touch of toast on the palate. Fresh, juicy fruit gives weight on the length.*	£9.15	BI, ADN, GEL, HHC, CHF, FUL	**S**
SWANSON VINEYARDS MERLOT 1990 Napa Valley	*A classy wine with a spicy fruit nose; and good oak with length. Good depth and style.*	£9.24	AV, WCS	**B**
MERRYVALE HILLSIDE CABERNET SAUVIGNON 1991	*Youthful and with good viscosity. Intense, sweet nose; ripe fruit, still very young.*	£9.79	ABY	**B**
VITA NOVA CABERNET SAUVIGNON 1990 Santa Barbara	*Deep ruby. Spicy and cedary on nose, with soft vegetal aromas. Soft sweet fruit and fine finish.*	£9.90	ACH, M&V	**S**
VOSS VINEYARDS ZINFANDEL 1991 California	*Fresh plummy fruit with scented spices, soft wood tannins and a warm, lingering finish.*	£9.99	LAV	**B**

BERINGER NAPA VALLEY CABERNET SAUVIGNON 1989 Napa Valley	*Good deep colour; rich fruit bouquet. Nice fruit on palate, with good length.*	£9.99	PAG, ROB, GRT, BWC	B
NIEBAUM COPPOLA CABERNET FRANC 1990 Napa Valley	*Cherries, redcurrants and cassis on nose with smoky cedarwood, blackcurrant and oak on palate.*	£9.99	LEA, RD, PON, HOL, LV	S
VOSS VINEYARDS NAPA VALLEY MERLOT 1991 Napa Valley	*Eucalyptus, blackcurrant and oak nose. Deep rich concentration of cassis.*	£9.99	LAV	S
DUXOUP CHARBONO 1991 Sonoma	*Great depth of colour, youthful fruit flavours and soft tannins. Will benefit from ageing.*	£10.00	BI	B
FETZER VINEYARDS BARREL-SELECT CABERNET SAUVIGNON 1991 California	*Brightly coloured wine with warm mint and cedar nose. Obvious, straightforward style;*	£10.28	LEA, BH, ABY	B
FROG'S LEAP ZINFANDEL 1991 Napa Valley	*Clean, sweet upfront fruit ranging from cough-candy to exotic orange peel. Medium tannins.*	£10.49	L&W, BOO, DBY	S
ROBERT MONDAVI PINOT NOIR RESERVE 1991 Napa Valley	*Clean, plummy nose with fairly full-bodied palate of sweet fruits and cedary vanilla oak.*	£10.50	F&M	S
DRY CREEK VINEYARD CABERNET SAUVIGNON 1991 California	*Good fruit aromas. Plentiful blackcurrant fruit. Full weighty flavour.*	£10.51	BH, W, SHB	B
CENTRAL COAST PINOT NOIR, CALERA VINEYARDS 1991 California	*Smoothly textured with herbal aromas and fresh plum flavours. Fruit-gum finish.*	£10.99	MWW, H&H, LV	B

WILLIAM HILL MERLOT 1991 Napa Valley	*Deep and gutsy with lots of power. Ripe berry fruit aroma with mint. Excellent structure.*	£11.25	LAV, WIN	**S**
ATLAS PEAK RESERVE NAPA SANGIOVESE 1992 Napa Valley	*Oaky, burnt nose. Lush, spicy, cherry and black-currant fruit. Depth and complexity.*	£11.35	LAV, WIN	**S**
SANFORD PINOT NOIR 1992 Santa Barbara	*Complex nose. Vegetal, spicy and peppery with soft oak overtones. Big and generous on palate.*	£11.75	BLS, BEN, CAC, VW, BH, DBY	**G**
MORGAN CABERNET SAUVIGNON, CARMEL VALLEY 1990 Carmel Valley	*Sweet mint and fruit bouquet; lots of depth on palate. Oaky and fruity.*	£11.98	BI	**B**
SHAFER MERLOT 1991 Napa Valley	*Deliciously rounded, minty, jammy style. Straight-forward and well-balanced.*	£11.99	WTR, HLV	**B**
MORGAN PINOT NOIR 1992 California	*Clean chocolatey nose. Medium-dry with spicy fruit. Elegant and minty with good acidity.*	£12.00	BI	**B**
CLOS DU VAL CABERNET SAUVIGNON 1989 Napa Valley	*Some spice and nice structure to this jammy wine. Nice acidity and length.*	£12.75	WSO, RD, BEN, HEY, DBY	**B**
SHAFER CABERNET SAUVIGNON, STAG'S LEAP 1990	*Intense and young with lots of nice fruit. Good fruit and tannin balance.*	£12.79	WTR	**B**
RIDGE VINEYARDS MATARO 1991 California	*Delicious spice, mint and peppery nose. Good balance and peppery finish.*	£12.95	ADN	**B**

BEAULIEU VINEYARDS GEORGES DE LATOUR PRIVATE RESERVE CABERNET SAUVIGNON 1989 California	*Very refined. Cedary and minty on nose with masses of vibrant New World fruit in mouth. Good extract.*	£12.99	PF	B
SAINTSBURY PINOT NOIR 1991 Carneros	*Fruity nose with spicy character. Becomes sweeter and riper on palate. Full of young red fruits.*	£12.99	ADN, GEL, HHC, WSO, BI	B
NEWTON UNFILTERED MERLOT 1991 Napa Valley	*Full nose of almost overripe fruit. Powerful fruit in mouth and big tannic bite.*	£12.99	CHF, BOO, RAM, WWG	S
BONNY DOON VINEYARD CINSAULT 1992 Santa Cruz	*Lively fruit-driven style makes for an easy drinking wine. Further ageing will add depth.*	£13.20	ADN	S
CLOS DU VAL MERLOT 1990 Napa Valley	*Good herbaceous and tobacco nose. Soft ripe fruit on palate.*	£13.50	RD, LEA, CEB, BEN, HEY, DBY	B
TREFETHEN CABERNET SAUVIGNON 1989 Napa Valley	*Deep blackcurrant colour and soft aromas. Full palate with bright clean fruit.*	£13.82	ADN, WSO	S
CHATEAU ST JEAN CABERNET SAUVIGNON 1989 Sonoma	*Classy, vanilla/oak nose. Elegant fruit palate, ripe and with intense fruit flavours.*	£13.99	WWT	S
HESS COLLECTION CABERNET SAUVIGNON 1990 Napa Valley	*Light, elegant nose; some tannin and cedary wood.*	£14.16	JAR	B
JOSEPH PHELPS CABERNET SAUVIGNON, BACKUS VINEYARD 1991 Napa Valley	*Strong mint, eucalyptus, fruit and oak nose. Blackcurrant, sweet fruit palate.*	£14.50	LAV, WIN	G

NORTH AMERICA • CALIFORNIA RED

GEYSER PEAK RESERVE ALEXANDRE 1990 Sonoma	*Lighter style with some blackberry bouquet. Full of wood with powerful fruit and tannin finish.*	**£14.65**	AUL	**S**
NEWTON VINEYARD CABERNET SAUVIGNON 1990 Napa Valley	*Hot, spicy fruit and herbal character with soft palate, of good length and fruit.*	**£14.95**	ADN, CHF, SOM, UBC, POP	**S**
JOSEPH PHELPS CABERNET SAUVIGNON 1991 Napa Valley	*Big stewed blackberry nose. Good, sweet fruit and tannin structure with a long aftertaste.*	**£14.99**	LEA, BEN	**B**
CLOS DU BOIS BRIARCREST CABERNET SAUVIGNON 1990 Sonoma	*A big fruity mouthful, warm, country rich and mature. Firm stalky, minty, berry character.*	**£15.00**	LAV, WIN	**S**
RIDGE SANTA CRUZ CABERNET SAUVIGNON 1992 Santa Cruz	*Tight yet pungent minty flavours; cherries and rich Cabernet depth to palate. Berry fruit finish.*	**£15.00**	OD, F&M, H&H	**S**
CABERNET SAUVIGNON LES PAVOTS, PETER MICHAEL WINERY 1989 Sonoma	*Good, rich, classic Bordeaux nose. Masses of blackcurrant fruit and tannin.*	**£15.64**	L&W	**S**
RIDGE GEYSERVILLE 1992	*Tart, spicy, damson fruit, married with rich tannins, giving good depth and long finish.*	**£15.75**	OD, BVL, F&M, HAR, ADN, H&H, DBY	**G**
CORISON CABERNET SAUVIGNON, CATHY CORISON 1990 California	*Purpley wine; dense with cedar/blackberry fruit nose. Lots of fruit from behind tannins.*	**£15.99**	WL	**B**
RIDGE SANTA CRUZ MOUNTAINS CABERNET 1991 Santa Cruz	*Colour of octopus ink! A rich stew of blackberries and soft red fruits with a dash of oak.*	**£16.90**	ADN	**S**

CLOS DU BOIS MARLSTONE 1990 Sonoma	*Delicate and well-balanced, spicy and sweet fruit. Good depth of berry flavours and firm tannins.*	**£17.19**	LAV, WIN	B
ROBERT MONDAVI CABERNET SAUVIGNON RESERVE 1990 Napa Valley	*Deep red coloured wine, leafy with blackcurrant bouquet. Tannins and fruit on palate.*	**£19.50**	LV	B
NIEBAUM COPPOLA RUBICON 1982 Napa Valley	*Sweet strawberry essence on nose. Medium bodied, sweet porty palate. Good length.*	**£19.75**	LEA, PON, CEB, SAN	B
BERINGER HOWELL MOUNTAIN MERLOT 1989 Napa Valley	*Herb, spice and caramel nose. Good fruit, oak and tannin balance.*	**£20.45**	PAG, ROB, GRT, BWC	S
BERINGER PRIVATE RESERVE CABERNET SAUVIGNON 1989 Napa Valley	*Delectable smoky sweet oak and cherry fruits. Formidable flavours and complexity.*	**£21.00**	PAG, ROB, GRT, BWC	S
FAR NIENTE CABERNET SAUVIGNON 1989 Napa Valley	*Plump, oak rich bouquet; slight liquorice flavour. Ripe fruit and smoky middle palate.*	**£27.25**	AV	S
JOSEPH PHELPS INSIGNIA 1990 Napa Valley	*Coriander and herbaceous bouquet; very soft approachable fruit, quite open.*	**£27.97**	RIB, SK	S
OPUS ONE, ROTHSCHILD/MONDAVI 1990 Napa Valley	*Deeply coloured wine with ripe mint and berry aromas. Firm and intense. Good potential.*	**£45.00**	JTD, ABY, JAG, HN, BWI	G

Pinpoint who sells the wine you wish to buy by turning to the stockist codes. If you know the name of the wine you want to buy, use the alphabetical index. If price is your motivation, refer to the invaluable price guide index; red and white wines under £5 and sparkling wines under £10. Good hunting!

DRY WHITE

BEL ARBORS CHARDONNAY, FETZER VINEYARDS 1992 Mendocino County	*Fruity on the nose, with a biscuit flavour on the palate. A wine of good balance and length.*	**£4.36**	LAV, WL, ABY	B
DUNNEWOOD CHARDONNAY 1992 North Coast	*Vegetal, buttery nose; oaky flavours with good fruit and long finish.*	**£4.49**	A	B
CHARDONNAY, CARTLIDGE & BROWNE	*Big and generous with appley fruit flavours. Good finish and high acidity.*	**£4.99**	U	B
MONTEVINA FUME BLANC 1992	*Delicate spicy nose with hints of gooseberries. Soft, elegant and mature.*	**£5.79**	OD, LWL, H&H	B
FETZER GEWURZTRAMINER 1993 California	*Very spicy, lots of fruit and long lasting, with a peach bouquet, and full round lychee palate.*	**£5.94**	BLS, CAC, SHB, HAR	B
MONTEVINA CHARDONNAY 1991 Amador County	*Beautifully crafted with complex and earthby biscuity lemon flavours, and a crisp finish.*	**£6.20**	WMK, H&H	S
BERINGER FUME BLANC 1992 California	*Creamy and soft, with flavours of lime and woody spice.*	**£6.59**	PAG, SEL, ROB, GRT, BWC	S
COTES DE SONOMA CHARDONNAY, PELLEGRINI FAMILY VINEYARD 1992 Sonoma Valley	*Fresh tangerines on the nose, apple fruit and Muscatty flavours on the palate - a delicious wine.*	**£6.79**	WTR	B
GEYSER PEAK SAUVIGNON BLANC 1993 California	*A well-made, modern wine with a lovely bubblegum, melon and pineapple nose.*	**£6.84**	AUL	B

Villa Mount Eden Chardonnay 1991	*Citrus and tropical fruits, with defined but mellow oak flavour.*	£6.95	W, JFE, HOH	B
Geyser Peak Chardonnay, Geyserville 1992 Sonoma County	*Lemony floral nose, not too oaky. Good fresh fruit. Clean and straightforward.*	£7.46	AUL	B
Ca Del Solo Malvasia Bianca, Bonny Doon 1992 California	*Grapey, rich superb picnic wine. Grapey, but 'interestingly', lovely peary flavours.*	£7.75	SAN, POR, HN, NY, M&V, DBY, LV	S
Dry Creek Vineyard Barrel-Fermented Chardonnay, Sonoma County 1992 Sonoma County	*Big fruit flavours with good weight and depth. Strong oak character. Slightly peachy, elegant drinking.*	£7.79	LEA, W, THP	B
Fetzer Vineyards Barrel Select Chardonnay 1992 Mendocino County	*An elegant wine with citrus/tropical fruit nose. Good balance of fruit and use of oak.*	£8.59	ABY, BEN, HOU	B
Firestone Vineyards Chardonnay 1990	*Refined flavours, with lots of oak and ripe fruit. Excellent balance and a good fresh finish.*	£8.79	MWW, WES	S
Carmenet Sauvignon Blanc/Semillon, The Chalone Group 1987 California	*Rich, full flavour of ripe sweet Sauvignon, with heavy asparagus, pineapple and gooseberry.*	£8.99	MWW	B
Fetzer Vineyards Bonterra Chardonnay 1992 Mendocino County	*Fresh, fruity citrus wine. Well-balanced, with delicate oak character.*	£8.99	LAV, SAF, OD	B
Beringer Chardonnay, Napa Valley 1991 Napa Valley	*Full style; ripe, rich, fruity flavours with good weight and balance. Tropical/citrus nose.*	£9.50	PAG, ROB, GRT, BWC	B

NORTH AMERICA • CALIFORNIA WHITE

CALLOWAY VINEYARD & WINERY CALLA-LEES CHARDONNAY 1992 Temecula, So.	*An elegantly light Chardonnay, with supple, clean fruit character and longlasting flavours.*	£9.52	LAV, WIN	S
VOSS VINEYARDS SAUVIGNON BLANC 1993 California	*A lovely fresh grassy nose, with lots of zingy, slightly honeyed, gooseberry fruit.*	£9.99	LAV	B
VOSS VINEYARDS CHARDONNAY, NAPA VALLEY 1991 Napa Valley	*Classic Chardonnay nose. Soft initial palate, and well-balanced fruit and oak flavours.*	£9.99	LAV	S
CRICHTON HALL CHARDONNAY, NAPA VALLEY 1991 Napa Valley	*Wonderful pineappley nose, spicy greengage/ apple-fruit hot long finish.*	£10.12	FUL, PAT	B
WENTE BROTHERS ESTATE RESERVE CHARDONNAY, LIVERMORE VALLEY 1991 California	*Lemony, herbaceous nose. Lean style with good wood character and soft finish.*	£10.50	BBR, BAR, DVY, JAR	B
SAINTSBURY CARNEROS RESERVE CHARDONNAY 1991 Carneros	*A round, full character, savoury on the palate. Well-balanced finish.*	£10.50	ADN, GEL, HHC, W S, BI	G
SWANSON VINEYARDS CARNEROS CHARDONNAY 1991 Napa Valley	*Soft, fruity, clean finish, with an excellent woody character. Full,ripe and flavoursome.*	£10.50	AV, WCS	G
GEYSER PEAK ALEXANDER VALLEY RESERVE CHARDONNAY 1992 Sonoma	*Fresh, tropical nose; good acid and fruit on mid palate. Clean fruit salad character.*	£10.70	AUL	B
NEWTON VINEYARD CHARDONNAY, NAPA VALLEY 1991 Napa Valley	*Good tasty, savoury style with fresh, lemony, fruit flavours.*	£10.95	ADN, TDS, ECK, NI	S

CENTRAL COAST CHARDONNAY, CALERA VINEYARDS 1991 California	*Gentle creamy style of Chardonnay. Clean, slightly sweet fruit and nutty character.*	£10.99	MWW, H&H, LV	B
SANFORD BARREL-SELECT CHARDONNAY 1991 Santa Barbara County	*A wine of excellent weight and texture, with a tasty, oak flavour. Well-balanced, cool edge.*	£10.99	LAV, WIN	G
HESS COLLECTION CHARDONNAY, HESS WINERY 1991 Napa Valley	*Fine, well-intergrated wine, with a lovely light palate. Possibly worth keeping for a few years.*	£11.25	JAR	S
SHAFER BARREL-SELECT CHARDONNAY 1992 California	*Quite a powerful wine with creamy-rich, long fruit flavours.*	£11.49	WTR, HLV, DIO	S
SAINTSBURY CARNEROS CHARDONNAY 1992 Carneros	*Fresh, soft berry fruits, laced with citrus flavours. Good cutting acidity and long finish.*	£11.65	ADN, GEL, HHC, WSO, DBY, BI	B
MARIMAR TORRES CHARDONNAY, DON MIGUEL VINEYARD 1991 Sonoma	*Rich, ripe, flavour-packed wine. Deliciously complex and fruity.Good Chardonnay style.*	£11.95	BTH, PEY, CDM, FSW, GRT, DBY	G
AU BON CLIMAT CHARDONNAY 1992 Santa Barbara	*Hot, ripe bouquet, with intense citrus flavours that soften on the palate.*	£12.00	ACH, PAV, HAR, HN, NY, DBY	B
MORGAN CHARDONNAY 1992 Monterey County	*Warm, oaky nosed wine with very rich and fresh palate.*	£12.00	BI	B
VITA NOVA CHARDONNAY 1992 Santa Barbara	*Barley sugar bouquet, with full and quite powerful, toasty flavours.*	£12.50	ACH, M&V	B

SANFORD CHARDONNAY 1992 Santa Barbara County	*Rich, savoury fruit and tropical flavours complete this wine's buttery aromas. Perfect finish.*	£12.95	CAC, CWS, F&M	S
NEWTON VINEYARD UNFILTERED CHARDONNAY, NAPA VALLEY 1991 Napa Valley	*Lovely tropical bouquet, with good texture and long, crisp, fruity finish. Nice oak treatment.*	£13.25	ADN, RAM, NY, BH, SOM	B
RIDGE SANTA CRUZ MOUNTAINS CHARDONNAY 1991 Santa Cruz Mountains	*Attractive light golden coloured wine with lemony, sweetish nose. Good weight of fruit. Great food wine.*	£14.49	OD, MWW, BEN, LEA	B
JOSEPH PHELPS CHARDONNAY 1992 Carneros	*Elegantly restrained wine, with depth of fruit. Good oak character.*	£14.66	LAV, WIN	B
BERINGER PRIVATE RESERVE CHARDONNAY 1992 Napa Valley	*Fresh, clean, well integrated butter and honey nose. Lively fruit flavours of good length.*	£15.00	PAG, ROB, GRT, BWC	S
PETER MICHAEL CLOS DU CIEL CHARDONNAY 1991 Napa Valley	*Interesting nose; slight buttery toasty character. Good acidity and nice balance.*	£15.25	L&W	B
CLOS DU BOIS CHARDONNAY, CALCAIRE VINEYARD 1992 Sonoma	*Fresh, lemony bouquet, with a touch of new oak. Bright, lunchy style with a nice richness.*	£16.50	LAV, WIN	G
STAG'S LEAP WINE CELLARS CHARDONNAY RESERVE, NAPA VALLEY 1991 Napa Valley	*Elegantly restrained aromas. Soft and luscious fruit. A wine of very good balance and length.*	£17.75	WTR	B

E & J GALLO RESERVE CHARDONNAY, NORTHERN SONOMA 1991 Sonoma	*Warm bananas and cream aroma. Ripe fruit flavours, with a long, rich palate.*	**£21.00**	VW, LV	**G**

SWEET WHITE

ELYSIUM, QUADY WINERY 1993 California	*Fresh violet and blue-berry nose; light and extremely refreshing blueberry/herbal style.*	**£5.99**	VW, MWW, BBR, JS, THP, DBY, NRW	**B**
WENTE BROTHERS LATE-HARVEST RIESLING 1989 Livermore Valley	*Fresh and grapey with a direct, intense style, and long, lingering, distinctive fruity palate.*	**£10.60**	BAR	**B**

ROSE

TESCO CALIFORNIAN ZINFANDEL, STRATFORD WINERY	*Well-balanced with ripe strawberry fruit and a raspberry perfume.*	**£4.29**	TO	**B**
CARTLIDGE & BROWN WHITE ZINFANDEL, STRATFORD WINERY California	*Lovely vibrant pink with a fresh grapey aroma. Good full fruit with hints of cherry and apple.*	**£4.39**	WL	**B**

SPARKLING

CODORNIU NAPA PINOT NOIR/CHARDONNAY Napa Valley	*Yellow and mellow; sharp, clean fruit with matching acidity.*	**£9.89**	WL, BVL, HD, DBY	**B**
DOMAINE CARNEROS BRUT METHODE TRADITIONELLE, CHAMPAGNE TAITTINGER California	*Fairly tight mousse. Good fruit with yeasty characteristics, yet vibrant and clean with good acid and depth.*	**£12.00**	PF	**B**
J SCHRAM, SCHRAMSBERG 1988 California	*Fine-beaded mousse on a wine that is lovely and toasty on the nose. Fresh, light and long.*	**£28.66**	F&M	**G**

FORTIFIED

STARBOARD BATCH 88, QUADY California	*Orange-chocolate spice aroma, with a sweet raisin flavour. Large, ripe finish.*	£4.99	VW	**B**
STARBOARD (BATCH 88), QUADY WINERY 1988 California	*Attractive, medium-sweet. Citrusy, complex style. Spirity with good, plummy fruit.*	£8.99	MWW, WRW	**S**
STARBOARD, QUADY WINERY 1989 California	*Slight elderberry nose with whiffs of salt. Rich chocolate and butter-scotch. Excellent finish.*	£12.99	LYN, NY	**B**

— OREGON —

RED

PINOT NOIR, DOMAINE DROUHIN OREGON 1990 Oregon	*An open, aromatic nose, and flavour which is long and sweet. A pleasant, easy drink.*	£18.50	OD, CEB, LV	**G**

DRY WHITE

WILLAMETTE VALLEY VINEYARDS OREGON MULLER THURGAU 1992 Willamette Valley, Oregon	*Some sweetness fruit with light grapefruit flavour. Good acidity.*	£6.49	LWE, M6	**B**
ARGYLE BARREL AGED CHARDONNAY, THE DUNDEE WINE COMPANY 1991 Willamette Valley, Oregon	*Clean and fresh fruit, nice oak and good balance. Medium length finish with a slight limey character.*	£7.98	LAV, WIN	**B**

SPARKLING				
ARGYLE BRUT, THE DUNDEE WINE COMPANY 1989 Willamette Valley, Oregon	*Quite pale, with a floral, Muscat-like note in smell. Full, rich fruit, with fine length and balancing acidity.*	**£11.75**	OD	**B**

—WASHINGTON STATE—

RED				
COLUMBIA MERLOT, COLUMBIA WINERY 1988 Washington State	*Ripe blackcurrant taste with good weight and developed fruit flavours.*	**£7.50**	BAR, SEL, F&M	**B**
PINOT NOIR WOODBURNE CUVEE, COLUMBIA WINERY 1992 Washington State	*Soft plum and peach nose, caramel flavours on the palate, with a delicate touch of sweetness. A dry finish.*	**£12.50**	BAR	**B**

PORTUGAL

A PART FROM SUCH UNIQUE PILLARS of vinous history as Port and Madeira, Portugal boasts one of the world's most interesting ranges of grape varieties. Sadly, until recently, conservative winemaking has done much to obscure their potential. A new generation of Portuguese producers (at companies like Sogrape and JM da Fonseca) and highly committed young Australians are together beginning to create exciting new styles unparalleled anywhere else in the world.

RED				
SAINSBURY'S DO CAMPO TINTO, PETER BRIGHT	*Ripe cherry fruit, quite jammy with hints of chocolate. Very forthcoming and attractive.*	**£2.99**	JS	**S**
LEZIRIA TINTO, VEGA CO-OPERATIVA ALMEIRIM Almeirim	*Lovely, juicy refreshing, easy going wine. Brilliant value.*	**£2.69**	SMF, G	**G**
TERRAS D'EL REI, COOPERATIVA AGRICOLA DE REGUENGOS 1992 Alentejo	*Light peppery nose. Supple fresh and fruit. Easy-drinking wine, full of summer appeal.*	**£3.15**	SMF, G	**B**
CO-OP BAIRRADA TINTO, SOGRAPE 1989 Bairrada	*Ripe cherry and mint flavours with spicy pluminess and gentle tannins show it has arrived.*	**£3.29**	CWS, VDP	**B**
BORBA, ADEGA CO-OP DE BORBA 1991 Alentejo	*Real class. This has excellent balance of fruit, structure, length of flavour and lift.*	**£3.35**	TO	**S**
BAIRRADA, LUIS PATO 1990 Bairrada	*Warm, spicy fruit on nose. Ripe gentle raspberry/blackberry fruit with creaminess of bananas.*	**£3.49**	TH, WR, BU	**B**

MONTE VELHO, FINAGRA 1992 Alentejo	*Deliciously soft, immediately appealing. Young berry fruit and smooth texture. Great value.*	£3.79	TH, BU, WR	B
QUINTA FOLGOROSA RED, CARVALHO RIBEIRO & FERREIRA 1989 Torres Vedras	*Sweet strawberries and dark cherries abound. Attractive spiciness adds a vibrant warming feel.*	£3.99	SD, LEA, RWW, WH, BIW	B
CISMEIRA RESERVA, QUINTA DA CISMEIRA 1990 Douro	*Intense spiced plum nose with hints of liquorice. Attractive, well integrated new wood.*	£3.99	MRT, BOO	B
FORAL DOURO RESERVA, CAVES ALIANCA 1991 Douro	*Restrained on nose but bursting with rich plummy fruit in mouth. Attractive savoury rustic character.*	£3.99	BP	S
BAIRRADA, CARVALHO RIBEIRO & FERREIRA 1988 Bairrada	*Characterful and well-balanced. Excellent length, weight and value for money.*	£4.00	SD, WH, BIW	B
ALENTEJO, CARVALHO RIBEIRO & FERREIRA 1991 Alentejo	*Gentle plummy fruit gives way to dried fruits backed by some tannins. Excellent value.*	£4.00	VIW, WH, BIW	B
QUINTA DE LA ROSA, DOURO 1992 Douro	*Rich peppery fruit gives warm feeling in mouth. Strong tannins support rich fruit. Concentrated.*	£4.50	HAM, SAN, POR	S
DUQUE DE VISEU, SOGRAPE 1991 Dao	*Excellent nose of liquorice, fruit and cinnamon. Good now, better over next two years.*	£4.79	SAF	B
TINTO VELHO, J M DA FONSECA 1987 Alentejo	*Almost Italian in style. An individual wine with characterful, slightly rustic richness.*	£4.99	MWW	S

DOURO, BRIGHT BROTHERS 1992 Douro	*Richly flavoured. Spiced plum nose with whiff of smoke and an enticing tarry aspect.*	£4.99	TH	S
JOAO PATO, LUIS PATO 1990 Bairrada	*Raisins and stewed plums on nose. Sweetish soft jammy fruit. Elegant style ready for drinking.*	£5.40	WF	B
QUINTA DE PANCAS, SOCIEDADE AGRICOLA PORTA DA LUZ 1990 Estremadura	*Rich, spicy wood nose. Ripe fleshy cherry/plum fruit. Firm tannin gives structure and vigour.*	£5.45	SMF, G	B
QUINTA DE PANCAS, ESTREMADURA CABERNET SAUVIGNON 1991 Estremadura	*Rich in fruit flavour - cherries, plums and damsons. Elegant. Great now, better with time.*	£5.45	SAF	S
VINHA DO MONTE, SOGRAPE 1991 Alentejo	*Rich, quite thick wine with distinctive dry plummy/spicy fruit and sweet vanilla.*	£5.49	GI, NI, VDP, SPR	S
ESPORAO, FINAGRA 1989 Alentejo	*Gentle, slightly smoky oak and refined fruit make for complex wine with a velvety texture.*	£5.69	TH	B
ESPORAO, FINAGRA 1990 Alentejo	*Soft, plummy fruit with some gentle oak make for a most appealing wine.*	£5.69	TH	B
JOAO PATO SPECIAL SELECTION, LUIS PATO 1992 Bairrada	*Retaining youthful vigour and an excellent match for rich, meaty dishes. Will improve.*	£5.90	WF	B
BEIRA MAR GARRAFEIRA RESERVA, ANTONIO BERNADINO 1980	*Ripe smooth fruit aromas. Rich fruit flavours on palate with attractive meaty savouriness.*	£5.99	U	S

Quinta da Bacalhoa, Joao Pires 1990	*Ripe cherry/blackcurrant aromas. Soft, jammy character gives great all-round appeal.*	**£5.99**	MWW	**B**
Tinto da Anfora, J P Vinhos 1990 Alentejo	*Excellent rich nose. Soft, rounded and easy-going. Beautifully clean cedary flavours.*	**£6.00**	SAF	**S**
Cartuxa, Fundacao Eugenio de Almeida 1990 Alentejo	*Youthful but its rich berry fruit does provide good foil for food now. Exciting potential.*	**£6.10**	REY	**B**
Duas Quintas Douro Tinto, Ramos Pinto 1991 Douro	*Appealing warm spicy fruit on nose. Ripe smooth textured berry fruit in mouth.*	**£6.25**	JN	**B**
Joao Pato Tinto, Luis Pato 1989 Portugal	*Intensely fruity with aromas of elderberries, bilberries and plums. Good use of oak.*	**£6.39**	TH, WR, BU, WF	**B**
Alabastro, Caves Alianca 1992 Alentejo	*Fresh, juicy cherry/damson fruit nose, quite sweet and spicy with toffee aspect.*	**£6.50**	BP	**B**
Cartuxa, Fundacao y Almeida 1989 Alentejo	*Ripe blackcurrants with sweet cherry and plum jam overtones. Classy.*	**£6.95**	TH, WR, BU	**B**
Valle Pradnhos, Pinto de Azeudo 1990 Valpacos	*Quite a chewy texture backed by some rich tannins. Needs another two years or so.*	**£6.99**	DBY	**B**
Bairrada, Luis Pato 1988 Bairrada	*Melange of fruit flavours. Complex bitter fruits – should develop well. Deep, dark, mysterious.*	**£6.99**	TH, BU	**S**

QUINTA DO CARMO, DOMAINES BARON DE ROTHSCHILD 1988 Alentejo	*Rich, ripe, rounded fruit with good use of oak to add complexity. Berry fruit flavours in mouth.*	£8.50	TH	B
GARRAFEIRA TE, JOSE MARIA DA FONSECA SUCCS. 1988 Arrabida	*Complex, fascinating cross between French and Portugese with spicy, ripe fruit.*	£8.55	RWC, BAB	G
BARCA VELHA, FERREIRA 1985 Douro	*Excellent nose of warm vanilla, liquorice and cherries. Ripe fruit and soft texture in mouth.*	£24.99	OD, GI, VDP	S

WHITE

SAINSBURY'S DO CAMPO BRANCO, PETER BRIGHT FOR J SAINSBURY	*Gooseberry and lime nose with crisp, tart acidity on the palate. Lovely honeyed finish.*	£2.99	JS	B
SANTA SARA, FERNAO PIRES, JP VINHOS 1993 Terras do Sado	*Fragrant lime blossom aroma. Light touch of lemony oak with honeyed tropical fruit and spices.*	£3.95	JS	B
BAIRRADA BRANCO, QUINTA DE PEDRALVITES, SOGRAPE 1993 Bairrada	*Good, rounded fruit and character from contact with the lees. A good wine.*	£5.99	OD, GI, VDP	B
SETUBAL SUPERIOR MOSCATEL, JOSE MARIA DA FONSECA SUCCS 1966 Azeitao	*Intense oaky nose; full and nutty character with wood flavours coming through.*	£15.00	TAN, F&M	S

PORT

MOAT HOUSE VINTNERS DOUBLE KEYS FINE RUBY PORT, SILVA & COSENS Douro	*Youthful raspberry fruit with hints of spice. Soft, round and mellow. Great value for money.*	£5.39	MHV	S

SAFEWAY FINE RUBY PORT, CALEM Douro	*Soft fruit on nose. Tastes of rich fruitcake, with crisp acidity and aggressive finish.*	**£5.41**	SAF	B
ASDA VINTAGE CHARACTER PORT, SMITH-WOODHOUSE	*Ripe, sweet nose, with some orange fruit present. Hot, baked, spirituous fruit.*	**£5.99**	A	B
SKEFFINGTON RUBY PORT Douro	*Delicate nose and good balance between fruit and alcohol. Good tannin; kick on finish.*	**£5.99**	MWW	B
SAINSBURY'S VINTAGE CHARACTER PORT, TAYLOR FLADGATE & YEATMAN Douro	*Rich nose. Dark and powerful with plenty of weight and well-balanced spirit.*	**£6.09**	JS	S
FINE RUBY, MARTINEZ Douro	*Fruitcake and good marzipan flavours. Generally well-balanced with rich finish.*	**£6.29**	HAM,WAW, PHI, RIB	B
TESCO LBV PORT, SMITH-WOODHOUSE Douro	*Dark in colour with a good, clean, ripe and jammy nose. Strong, ripe, fruit flavours.*	**£6.59**	TO	B
SAINSBURY'S LATE-BOTTLED VINTAGE PORT, CROFT 1987 Douro	*Rich aromas with spicy flavours. Excellent balance between fruit and age; long aftertaste.*	**£6.59**	JS	S
ASDA LBV PORT, SMITH-WOODHOUSE Porto	*Full fruity nose with some eucalyptus. Rich and sweet with good spirit/fruit balance.*	**£6.65**	A	B
CALEM FINE RUBY PORT Douro	*Elegant and balanced, full and creamy. Touches of Christmas cake.*	**£6.75**	ABY, TBW, BGC	B

MOAT HOUSE VINTNERS DOUBLE KEYS LATE-BOTTLED VINTAGE PORT, SILVA & COSENS 1987 Douro	*Extremely good, rich, sweet, raisiny nose. Well-balanced with good tannin; excellent, late-bottled vintage.*	**£7.39**	MHV	**S**
QUINTA DAS CARVALHAS PORT, REAL COMPANHIA VELHA Douro	*Light in colour, sweet and fruity with a fine nose. Quite spirity and simple, yet elegant.*	**£7.49**	TO	**B**
ROYAL OPORTO LBV PORT 1987 Douro	*Ripe, opulent aroma of strawberries and spice. Flavours of cherries and chocolate on the palate.*	**£7.49**	MRS	**B**
DELAFORCE SPECIAL WHITE PORT Douro	*Sweetish, but with enough acidity for a clean, dry finish.*	**£7.49**	SEL, MRN, TH	**B**
CALEM FINE WHITE PORT Douro	*Spirit on nose is delicately fragranced. Palate is more complex, sweet and concentrated.*	**£7.75**	DN, BGC	**B**
SMITH WOODHOUSE LBV, SMITH WOODHOUSE 1988 Douro	*Full, fat and ripe nose. More elegant on the palate with firm, plum fruit and good weight.*	**£7.99**	U	**B**
MERCHANT VINTNERS VINTAGE CHARACTER PORT, FONSECA Douro	*Herbal-fruit nose with rich, intense currany fruit on palate; soft, rich, ripe.*	**£7.99**	HOT	**B**
WARRE'S WARRIOR FINEST RESERVE PORT Douro	*Sweet, ripe figs with high alcohol and acidity. A good finish; powerful stuff.*	**£7.99**	TH, TO, SAF, VW, A	**B**
NOVAL LB PORT, QUINTA DO NOVAL Douro	*Nuts and spirit on nose with warm, ripe fruit on palate. Powerful stuff.*	**£7.99**	PTR, JEH, FUL, W, P&R	**B**

CALEM LBV PORT 1987 Douro	*Plummy nose and supple, well-integrated fruit on palate. Balanced with good follow-through.*	**£8.16**	WIN, CNL, HSL, ABY	**B**
GOULD CAMPBELL, 10-YEAR-OLD TAWNY PORT Douro	*Smoothness and cinna-mon on palate, with some rich fruit. Lighter style with tangy finish.*	**£8.90**	MCC, P&R, H&H	**B**
CHURCHILL'S FINEST VINTAGE CHARACTER PORT, CHURCHILL GRAHAM Douro	*Deep ruby colour. Caramelised rich, unc-tuous fruit with choco-late and cedar tones.*	**£8.99**	CPW, WSC, EE, IRV, IH, WCS, SEB, D	**B**
SANDEMAN IMPERIAL AGED TAWNY PORT Douro	*Light in colour, but quite big, weighty and alcoholic with a fine, tawny nose.*	**£8.99**	HAR, CVF	**B**
ST. MICHAEL 10-YEAR-OLD PORT, MORGAN BROS Douro	*Medium body with quite prominent alcohol and tannin. Ripe fruit with good length.*	**£9.49**	M&S	**B**
TESCO 10-YEAR-OLD TAWNY PORT, SMITH WOODHOUSE Douro	*Tawny-coloured. Clean, sweet and straightfor-ward, with good fruit and alcohol.*	**£9.49**	TO	**B**
FORTNUM & MASON LBV PORT, BURMEISTER 1989 Douro	*Deliciously sweet mouth-ful with good weight, fruit and balancing tannins.*	**£9.75**	F&M	**S**
NIEPOORT LBV PORT 1987 Douro	*Showing some age with good, rich, fruit aroma. Bags of plummy fruit and chocolate in mouth.*	**£9.75**	BTH, WGW, CHF, S&J	**S**
FONSECA FINE RESERVE BIN 27 PORT Douro	*Apricot, orange peel and spicy pepper on nose. Full in mouth and long on finish. Excellent.*	**£9.99**	W, MRN, MZ	**B**

QUARLES HARRIS 20-YEAR-OLD TAWNY Douro	*Some spiciness and vanilla oak on nose, with hot raisins that linger on the palate.*	£9.99	WWT	**B**
DOW'S CRUSTED PORT 1987 Douro	*Good bottle age on nose. Fruit and tannins good, with nice grip. Showing some smoothness.*	£10.00	SAF, SEB	**B**
NIEPOORT SENIOR PORT Douro	*Light-bodied with good, fiery alcohol. Sweet cinnamon fruit with silky-smooth, refined finish.*	£10.00	EE, CWS, BGC	**B**
QUINTA DO NOVAL COLHEITA 1976 Douro	*Nuts and spice form a smoothness and richness in the mouth; even, elegant and complex.*	£10.95	F&M, SEL, SB	**S**
GRAHAMS CRUSTED PORT Douro	*Aromatic nose with some volatility. Full and fruity with tannins, forming good structure.*	£10.99	TO, MWW, PLA, CNL, DVI	**B**
QUINTA DE LA ROSA VINTAGE PORT 1988 Douro	*Deep, young colour with a good nose. Chocolatey and spicy with a hot finish.*	£10.99	HC, OLS, M&V	**B**
GRAHAMS SIX GRAPES Douro	*Creamy, intense and lingering with a good structure; fine and elegant.*	£10.99	OD, VD, ES, JWL, S&J, NRW	**G**
CALEM COLHEITA 1986 Douro	*Mellowed, nutty-wood nose. Tastes of fruit, butterscotch and chocolate digestive biscuits.*	£11.65	WIM, RAC, AMA, AV, CNL	**S**
DELAFORCE HIS EMINENCE' CHOICE 10-YEAR-OLD TAWNY PORT Douro	*Quite complex and multi-dimensional with attractive length and a nutty finish.*	£11.99	CWN, RAC	**B**

GRAHAMS 10-YEAR-OLD TAWNY PORT Douro	*Good tawny colour with complex, rich and nutty nose. Intense on the palate.*	£12.95	SEL, VD, SOH, ES, WGT	S
SMITH WOODHOUSE TRADITIONAL LATE-BOTTLED VINTAGE PORT 1981 Douro	*Berry fruit on the nose. A soft and smooth, medium style with good spirit and length.*	£12.99	C&B, AV, JWL, GNW, S&J	B
THE SOCIETY'S CELEBRATION 20-YEAR-OLD TAWNY PORT, MARTINEZ GASSIOT Douro	*Old oak and marzipan on a relatively volatile nose; bitter-sweet caramel and raisins.*	£13.50	WSO	B
DOW'S 10-YEAR-OLD TAWNY PORT Douro	*Smells of oak and toffee, with some interesting fruit, nuts and depth.*	£13.60	TO, SAF, BU, OD, CWS, GRT	B
CHURCHILL'S QUINTA DA AGUA ALTA VINTAGE PORT, CHURCHILL GRAHAM 1983 Douro	*Sugary and rich with spicy aroma. Youthful, round and attractive with peppery finish.*	£13.89	DBY, EE, WSV, L&W, HW, WCS, SEB	B
WARRE'S TRADITIONAL LATE-BOTTLED VINTAGE PORT 1981 Douro	*Slightly peppery nose with sweet, caramelised fruit and a spirity finish. Very enjoyable.*	£13.90	JS, OD, HHC, W, ADN	B
WARRE'S SIR WILLIAM TAWNY PORT Douro	*Light and clean, but complex. Rich peppery fruit and good spice on the palate.*	£14.39	CNL, GRT, SWS, EM, AV	B
CHURCHILL'S QUINTA DA AGUA ALTA VINTAGE PORT, CHURHILL GRAHAM 1987 Douro	*Fine, deep, vintage colour. Chocolatey palate with good spirit. Rich and concentrated.*	£14.50	TAN, WDW, DBY, WSC, MRT, WCS	B
CALEM QUINTA DA FOZ 1982 Douro	*Light and sweet.Warm plums and redcurrants give some full, rich fruit.*	£14.50	F&M, MCK, HSL	B

QUINTA DE LA ROSA VINTAGE PORT 1991 Douro	*Dark in colour with jammy nose. Some raspberry on palate. Elegant and subtle.*	**£14.95**	M&V	**B**
NIEPOORT COLHEITA 1983 Douro	*Good raisiny nose and lots of rich fruit in mouth. Lemon acidity and pleasant finish.*	**£14.98**	BTH	**S**
FONSECA QUINTA DO PANASCAL PORT 1984	*Well-made, with depth and good finish. Burnt-sugar nose with liquorice/toffee flavours.*	**£14.99**	TH, L&W, MZ	**B**
QUINTA DA EIRA VELHA, MARTINEZ GASSIOT 1987 Douro	*Good length and balance; complex. Soft tastes of figs, spices, mint, cedar and chocolate.*	**£14.99**	VW	**G**
GRAHAMS MALVEDOS VINTAGE PORT 1979 Douro	*Lovely balance of fruit, nuts and tannins, with nose which opens up in glass. A fine old wine.*	**£14.99**	OD, WR, BU, SAF, MRN	**G**
CALEM 20 YEAR OLD TAWNY PORT Douro	*Quite spirity on the nose, with good orange peel and spices. Some sweet, nutty complexity.*	**£15.87**	ABY, ND, HWL	**B**
DELAFORCE VINTAGE PORT 1985	*Classic style - full chocolate, spice and honeyed fruit. Good finish.*	**£15.99**	AV	**B**
GOULD CAMPBELL VINTAGE PORT 1980 Douro	*Baked fruit and caramel spice. Complex, with great depth and length. Exceptional in 20 years.*	**£16.50**	THP, BBR, H&H	**G**
TAYLOR'S QUINTA DE VARGELLAS PORT 1982	*Well-made with depth, balance and length. Bitter-sweet mint chocolate and good fruit.*	**£16.99**	TH, MZ	**B**

WARRE'S QUINTA DA CAVADINHA PORT 1984 Douro	Eucalyptus and mint on nose. Taste of Christmas pudding and nuts. Drinking well now.	£16.99	THP, GRT, D	B
QUINTA DO NOVAL VINTAGE PORT, QUINTA DO NOVAL 1982 Douro	Classy port. Well-balanced with rich, raisiny fruit and some tannins. Very long, excellent.	£16.99	ZAC, TH, THP, SEL, F&M	B
DELAFORCE CURIOUS AND ANCIENT 20-YEAR-OLD TAWNY PORT Douro	Showing some age with good richness, raisin fruit and nuttiness on palate. Complex.	£16.99	SEL	S
QUINTA DO NOVAL PORT 1982 Douro	Rich figgy, raisiny nose, with softish fruit and chocolate tones on the palate. Nicely balanced.	£16.99	VW	S
FERREIRA QUINTA DO SEIXO VINTAGE PORT 1983 Douro	Soft and elegant, with a good mixture of hot spice and soft, figgy fruit. Quite light.	£17.50	BP	B
FERREIRA VINTAGE PORT 1985 Douro	Baked nose with lots of spirit and hints of vanilla. Tastes of caramel and sweet, stewed fruit.	£17.50	BP	B
DELAFORCE VINTAGE PORT 1977	Excellent liquorice fruit with long, chewy finish. Showing its age, but still some liveliness on palate.	£17.99	SEL, THP, OD	G
FONSECA GUIMARAENS VINTAGE 1978	Warm oranges and spice on nose. Masses of blackberry fruit in the mouth. Delicious.	£17.99	TH, MZ	B
SMITH WOODHOUSE VINTAGE PORT, 1991 Douro	Good colour with masses of sweet, rich fruit. Fat with good body and weight. Fine quality.	£17.99	WR, BBR, J&B, SUM, THP	S

DOW'S VINTAGE PORT 1980 Douro	*Dark, deep and fat with heavy fruit, chocolate and figs on the palate. Powerful.*	**£18.00**	WON, S&D, TWC, D	**B**
COCKBURN VINTAGE PORT, 1985 Douro	*Plums, blackcurrants and cedar on nose. Quite sweet and concentrated.*	**£18.00**	VW, THP, D	**S**
TAYLOR'S VINTAGE PORT 1980	*Nice damson and cherry fruit with good balance, soft; easy-drinking at present.*	**£18.99**	TH, THP, H&H, D, MZ	**B**
FONSECA GUIMARAENS VINTAGE PORT 1967 Douro	*Well-balanced plummy fruit aroma with tinges of peppermint. Quite sweet, but elegant.*	**£18.99**	VW, MZ	**S**
NIEPOORT VINTAGE PORT 1987 Douro	*Soft raspberry fruit and aniseed nose. Round mouthful with caramel, spirity finish and grip.*	**£19.00**	REY	**S**
WARRE'S VINTAGE PORT, 1980 Douro	*Clean, fragrant and stylish, with hints of cedar and spicy cream on nose; well-balanced.*	**£19.95**	TO, OD, GMV, BC, WON, TBW, D	**S**
FONSECA GUIMARAENS VINTAGE PORT 1976	*Positive fruit, figs and chocolate in mouth. Large, powerful, rich and complex.*	**£19.99**	SAF	**B**
SKEFFINGTON VINTAGE PORT 1977 Douro	*Light in colour, with a raisiny nose and aged wood coming through. Light, developed style.*	**£19.99**	TH, WR, BU	**B**
SMITH WOODHOUSE VINTAGE PORT, 1980 Douro	*Aromatic, tea-leaf nose with opulent, sweet fruit in mouth. Sweet and full. Enjoyable now.*	**£19.99**	OD	**B**

GRAHAMS VINTAGE PORT 1980 Douro	*Deep garnet, with old wood and smoky fruit on nose. Full finish; ready in five years.*	£19.99	OD, BU, WON, T&W, COE, H&H, D	S
WARRE'S VINTAGE PORT 1991 Douro	*Heavy, intensely sweet style. Great depth and concentration – terrific! Keeps well.*	£19.99	WR, OD, U, FJ&B, THP, D	S
QUARLES HARRIS VINTAGE PORT 1980 Oporto	*Young, fruity bramble and blackcurrant nose. Sweet and rich. Needs 10 more years.*	£19.99	HOW, WWT	G
WARRE'S VINTAGE PORT 1983 Douro	*Good inky colour. Slightly burnt nose with plum taste. Acidity and tannins well-balanced.*	£19.99	VW, THP, ABY, D	G
CROFT VINTAGE PORT 1982 Douro	*Lovely nose and a deliciously long, fruity finish. The spirit is balanced with good grip.*	£20.00	VW, D	B
DOW'S VINTAGE PORT, 1985 Douro	*Vegetal nose with burnt caramel and plums in mouth. Quite tough and chewy.*	£20.00	VW, THP, GRT, BGC, D	B
GRAHAMS VINTAGE PORT 1985 Douro	*Medium brick-red colour. Sweet fruit, spicy and stylish with good weight.*	£20.00	VW, TBW	S
FONSECA VINTAGE PORT 1985 Douro	*Good Douro nose. Rich, fat and ripe, but still classy. Masses of spicy fruit.*	£20.00	VW, THP, D	G
FONSECA VINTAGE PORT 1980 Douro	*Clean, spicy, tobacco and cedary nose. Fruity on palate with some tangy acidity.*	£21.00	TH, VW, MZ, D	S

GRAHAMS 20 YEAR-OLD TAWNY PORT Douro	*Light and rather stylish. Lots of alcohol on nose. Rich, hot and good complexity.*	**£21.95**	SEL, VD, HAR, WBK, FEN	**B**
QUINTA DO VESUVIO VINTAGE PORT 1991 Douro	*Dark with intensely sweet plummy character on nose and good tannins. Fantastic.*	**£21.99**	WR, OD, ADN, BBR, J&B, THP, SEB, D	**S**
TAYLOR'S VINTAGE PORT 1977	*Aromatic nose with slight mintiness and good fruit. Great balance and length.*	**£22.00**	TH, H&H, THP, TBW, MZ, D	**G**
QUINTA DO NOVAL VINTAGE PORT 1975 Douro	*Some good chewy fruit and nuttiness; quite full, spirity, sweet and mature.*	**£22.69**	VW	**B**
DOW'S 20-YEAR-OLD TAWNY PORT Douro	*Deep walnut-brown colour. Fat and well-balanced with considerable age.*	**£22.90**	FRV, GRT, FEN, WAV, LAY, NRW	**G**
DELAFORCE VINTAGE PORT 1975	*Sweets and stewed apricots contribute to aromatic spiciness. Ready to drink.*	**£23.00**	MLG, AV	**B**
FERREIRA DUQUE DE BRAGANCA 20-YEAR-OLD TAWNY PORT Douro	*Masses of woody nuts, fruit and spices; good body, structure and long, clean finish.*	**£23.99**	BP	**S**
NIEPOORT COLHEITA 1978 Douro	*Rich, well-balanced and medium-sweet with clean, good, long finish. The fruit is good.*	**£25.00**	BOO, MFL	**S**
CALEM COLHEITA PORT 1978 Douro	*A restrained nose with good flavours and some richness; a mature, sweeter-style port.*	**£25.25**	WIM	**B**

TAYLOR'S 20-YEAR-OLD TAWNY PORT	*Very brown colour, with hot, Douro smell. Slight nuttiness. Round, smooth, spicy and rich.*	£25.99	TH, TBW, MZ, ABY	B
NIEPOORT 20-YEAR-OLD PORT Douro	*Clean and well-structured with soft toffee, nuts and caramel with a lovely finish.*	£27.50	REY	S
DOW'S VINTAGE PORT 1966 Douro	*Deep damson and ripe fruit nose. Fat, full and soft with pleasant roundness on palate.*	£35.75	D	S

MADEIRA

GRAHAMS VINTAGE PORT 1966 Douro	*Lovely nose with good fruit and aroma of peppermints; excellent structure – a classic.*	£49.00	JEF, J&B	G
FINEST MADEIRA, MADEIRA WINE COMPANY Madeira	*Medium-brown colour. Rich with good acidity for clean finish; excellent value for money.*	£6.99	TO	S
RUTHERFORD & MILES, OLD ARTILLERY MALMSEY Madeira	*Pale orangey-brown, with hints of vanilla and raisins.*	£8.49	GRO, LKN, ROD, EX, MAR	B
BLANDYS DUKE OF CLARENCE RICH MADEIRA Madeira	*Ripe, cooked fruit on nose. Good caramel flavour with sweet apricots on palate. Balanced.*	£8.99	W, G, A, MWW, BC, THP, GRT, TBW, D	B
HENRIQUES & HENRIQUES, FINEST FULL RICH 5-YEAR-OLD Madeira	*Nutty, rich, ripe and brandied on the palate, with high alcohol and a slightly burnt quality.*	£9.49	BEC, KEL, HAR, MLG, IRV, VEX	B
COSSART GORDON 5-YEAR-OLD MALMSEY MADEIRA Madeira	*Excellent chestnutty character with a rich, ripe and long palate.*	£10.99	Widely Available	S

COSSART GORDON 10-YEAR-OLD VERDELHO Madeira	*Rich, raisiny and full, with browned-almond nose. Moderate length and concentration.*	£13.99	BU, DIR	**B**
COSSART GORDON RESERVE 10-YEAR-OLD MALMSEY MADEIRA Madeira	*Intense bonfire-toffee and walnut aroma. Palate shows rich, concentrated flavours.*	£14.95	BU, WR, BBR, AV, GMV	**S**
BLANDYS 10-YEAR-OLD MALMSEY MADEIRA Madeira	*Sweet, rich, caramelised raisins on palate. Intense, full, complex. Balanced with amazing character.*	£14.99	TO, W, WR, OD, TBW, GRT	**S**
HENRIQUES & HENRIQUES, 10-YEAR-OLD MEDIUM DRY VERDELHO Madeira	*A moderate nose with good acidity, and toasty, smoky tones on the finish.*	£15.00	SD, SP, GEL, RDV, VEX	**B**
COSSART GORDON 15-YEAR-OLD RICH MALMSEY MADEIRA Madeira	*Rich, coffee nose. Bags of sweet fruit, with acidity for clean finish. Rich and elegant, brilliant!*	£19.99	BU, WR, DIR	**S**
COSSART GORDON VINTAGE MALMSEY MADEIRA, MADEIRA WINE COMPANY 1965 Madeira	*Huge fruit nose and rich, burnt, honey flavour. Fat and concentrated. Delicious.*	£39.95	DIR	**G**
RUTHERFORD & MILES JUBILEE SELECTION VERDELHO 1952 Madeira	*Complex caramel, chocolate and coffee on nose. Old, rich, finely-balanced and elegant.*	£39.95	BU	**G**
RUTHERFORD & MILES SERCIAL VINTAGE MADEIRA 1969 Madeira	*Copper with lighter centre. Nice, rich fruit with high alcohol and acidity; lots of character.*	£49.00	BU	**B**
BLANDYS VINTAGE MALMSEY MADEIRA 1964 Madeira	*Classically balanced and rich with high acidity giving a clean finish.*	£63.00	F&M	**S**

BLANDYS VINTAGE BUAL 1954 Madeira	Medium depth in colour. Rich lemon on palate with clean acid and fruit. Fullish-bodied.	£65.00	BU, WR, WAV, JWL	B
BLANDYS SERCIAL MADEIRA 1940 Madeira	Lovely dark, golden colour, salty tang to nose; elegant and stylish with fantastic length.	£85.00	JEF, PGR	G

PERSONAL TASTING NOTES

SIGHT	
	Clear Bright Hazy Cloudy Colour
SMELL	
	Fresh Musty Floral Fruit Vegetal Animal Wood/Oak Others
TASTE	
	Weight Sweetness Dryness Acidity Fruit Vegetal Wood/Oak Balance
SUMMARY	
	Age Maturity Location Vintage

SOUTH AFRICA

Emerging from political isolation, South Africa is fighting to regain the position it held in the 1970s as one of the winemaking leaders of the New World. Despite the handicap of a shortage of Chardonnay vines and new oak barrels, the industry is evolving astonishingly quickly. Although some styles - principally the Pinotages - are old-fashioned when compared with Australia, New Zealand and California, there are some remarkably successful, European-style wines being produced.

RED					
Pinotage, Matthew Clark Stellenbosch	*An attractive fruit-driven style of fresh confiture makes an obviously easy-drinking wine.*	**£3.21**	A, W, MAK	**B**
Cape Selection Pinotage, Vinimark Trading 1993 Stellenbosch	*Rich ripe fruit and Southern French spices combine with tannins to produce some complexity.*	**£3.79**	SMF, G	**B**
Tesco International Winemaker Cabernet Sauvignon Merlot, Vinfruco Stellenbosch	*Light red fruit aromas and a soft velvety texture.*	**£3.99**	TO	**B**
Simonsvlei Classique Reserve 1993 Paarl	*Plummy aromas, jammy. Good grassy character. Will age well.*	**£3.99**	WST	**B**
Simonsvlei Pinotage 1993 Paarl	*Up-front, jammy fruit makes for voluptuous wine held together with dryer tannins and good acid.*	**£3.99**	SAF	**B**
Landskroon Pinotage 1991 Paarl	*Deep ruby colour gives soft fruit flavours with accessible tannins.*	**£3.99**	A	**B**

KAPSFONTEIN PINOTAGE 1993 Swartland	Rich colour with ripe berry-fruit nose mixes with full tannins and good acidity for full length.	£3.99	AVA, RWV	S
CAPEVIEW MERLOT, K MILNE 1994 Paarl	Light, juicy, plummy wine. Well made modern European style.	£4.29	VW	B
CRICKET HILL PINOTAGE 1991 Paarl	Stalky, vegetal characteristics on nose give way to soft berry fruit flavours. Good value.	£4.39	SUP	B
BAY VIEW PINOTAGE, DU PREEL & LAUBSER 1991 Coastal Region	Good young spicy wine with some lovely pinot noir and raspberry flavour.	£4.69	SUP, LPI	S
BACKSBERG CABERNET SAUVIGNON 1991 Western Cape	Fresh colour; quite attractive fruit on nose. The blackcurranty style has good intensity.	£4.99	G&M, HCC, CAP, A&A	B
ST MICHAEL MERLOT/ CABERNET SAUVIGNON, JAN COETZEE/NEIL ELLIS 1993 Stellenbosch	Herbaceous, fresh and grassy bouquet; fruit flavours with some richness. Elegant style.	£4.99	M&S	B
DROSTDY HOF MERLOT 1991 Coastal Region	Lightly perfumed bouquet. Attractive fruit on palate. Will improve.	£5.25	NGF	B
SIMONSIG PINOTAGE 1991 Stellenbosch	Full rich colour and sweet, spicy fruit accompanied by finely balanced oak and acidity.	£5.25	W, BFI, JOH, BFF, EOR	S
FAIRVIEW ESTATE CABERNET SAUVIGNON 1993 Paarl	Solid red, very glycerinny. Quality nose, sweet, spicy and richly fruity.	£6.45	FW, CAP, GRT	S

BLAAUWKLIPPEN ZINFANDEL 1989 Stellenbosch	*Mature wine with good plummy, spicy flavour. Ready to drink.*	**£6.84**	FW, VIL, WOI, NGF	B
MIDDLEVLEI PINOTAGE 1989 Stellenbosch	*Mature, quite traditional South African wine with quite rich earthy flavours.*	**£6.90**	QR, NGF	B
UITERWYK PINOTAGE 1991 Stellenbosch	*Interesting mulberry and pepper flavours. Maturing attractively.*	**£6.95**	L&W	S
LONGRIDGE CABERNET SAUVIGNON, DU PREEL & LAUBSER 1990 Stellenbosch	*Deep colour. Soft, easy fruits on nose and in mouth. Vanilla creaminess, firm tannins.*	**£6.99**	SUP	B
FAIRVIEW ESTATE SHIRAZ 1992 Paarl	*Fresh, light with clean blackcurrant fruit, black pepper spice, soft tannins and a minty finish.*	**£6.99**	A, VAU, IRV, HAM, THP, GRT	B
HAMILTON RUSSELL PINOT NOIR 1992 Walker Bay	*Ripe, sweet perfumed fruit set off by rich new oak. Complex, full bodied, will develop well.*	**£6.99**	AV	S
CLOS MALVERNE PINOTAGE 1991 Stellenbosch	*Typical pinotage but with richer fruit flavour than most.*	**£7.49**	LWE, HOL, CTH	B
HAMILTON RUSSELL PINOT NOIR 1991 Walker Bay	*Delicately balanced scented violet nose beginning to develop some vegetal character.*	**£7.49**	SAF	B
VRIESENHOF CABERNET SAUVIGNON 1988 Stellenbosch	*Medium-deep garnet coloured wine with good oaky/blackcurrant character.*	**£7.85**	NGF	B

KANONKOP PINOTAGE 1991 Stellenbosch	*A big wine, really impressive combination of ripe banana fruit and sweet new oak. Keep for 2-3 years.*	**£7.99**	WEP	S
RUSTENBERG CABERNET SAUVIGNON 1991 Stellenbosch	*Deep brick colour to this wine of good ripe, concentrated fruit flavours. High tannins.*	**£8.00**	AV	S
WILDEKRANS PINOTAGE 1993 Walker Bay	*Aromatic cedarwood nose with ruby colour of full fruit produce. Fine balance with gutsy finish.*	**£8.25**	FW, CEW	S
ALTO ESTATE CABERNET SAUVIGNON 1986 Stellenbosch	*Deep, rich nose, packed with maturing cedar spice and dry red fruit. Reaching its peak.*	**£8.65**	NGF	B
SIMONSIG CABERNET SAUVIGNON, SIMONSIG ESTATES 1988 Stellenbosch	*Medium-deep garnet colour to this wine with a herbacious grassy nose.*	**£8.85**	FSW, NGF	B
STELLENRYCK CABERNET SAUVIGNON, THE BERGKELDER 1987	*Strongly oaked wine. Excellent blackcurrant fruit structure hides substantial tannins. Needs time.*	**£8.99**	QR, NGF	G
LA MOTTE CABERNET SAUVIGNON 1987 Franschhoek	*Some rich fruit and good mid palate. Quite dry with good balance and finish.*	**£9.70**	NGF	B
KANONKOP CABERNET SAUVIGNON 1988 Stellenbosch	*Sweet, jammy, cassis nose. Good depth of fruit, rubber and tar with enough tannin to give backbone.*	**£9.89**	WEP	B
KANONKOP PAUL SAUER 1990 Stellenbosch	*Mint, blackcurrant and eucalyptus. Full bodied blackcurrant flavours. Good balance.*	**£9.90**	JS	B

SOUTH AFRICA • WHITE

WELLINGTON RED, CLARIDGE 1991 Wellington	*Dark blackberry coloured wine; up-front, powerful fruit flavours.*	**£9.95**	L&W, SEB	**B**
RUSTENBERG GOLD 1990 Stellenbosch	*Sweet mature nose. Soft, chewy, cherry and damson fruit, with good oak balance. Will keep.*	**£9.95**	AV, L&W, IRV	**S**
MEERLUST RUBICON 1988 Stellenbosch	*Blackcurrant and oak. Complex, concentrated fruit structure to palate. Dry and tannic.*	**£9.95**	F&M, QR	**S**
DRY WHITE				
ROSENVIEW EARLY RELEASE WHITE, VINFRUCO 1994 Stellenbosch	*Really nice, clean nose. Quite rich, of medium concentration, fruity and with a good finish.*	**£2.49**	SAF	**B**
WINELANDS CHENIN BLANC, VINFRUCO 1993 Stellenbosch	*Light, grapey and aromatic, floral nose. Good fruit on mid-palate and good length.*	**£3.49**	TH, WR, BU	**B**
TESCO SWARTLAND SAUVIGNON BLANC, SWARTLAND CO-OP 1993 Swartland	*Grassy nose, reminiscent of fresh gooseberries. On palate, flavours of melons, mangoes and apples.*	**£3.79**	TO	**B**
ST MICHAEL CRAIGHALL CHARDONNAY/ SAUVIGNON 1993 Stellenbosch	*A lemony nose on this rich, very full wine. Clean, fresh fruit and fair finish.*	**£3.99**	M&S	**B**
CHARDONNAY SUR LIE, DANIE DE WET 1993 Robertson	*Subtle and delicate gooseberry aromas unfold with melons and citrus fruits on palate.*	**£4.29**	SAF, NGF, OD	**B**
STELLENZICHT SAUVIGNON BLANC 1993 Stellenbosch	*Grassy, gooseberry fool nose; fruit flavour is soft and concentrated, showing steely, mineral edge.*	**£4.95**	W	**B**

DANIE DE WET GREY LABEL CHARDONNAY 1993 Robertson	*Toasty, honey and marzipan aromas. Well balanced; lovely fruit and feel in mouth.*	**£4.99**	JS	**S**
KLEIN CONSTANTIA SAUVIGNON BLANC 1994 Constantia	*Pale yellow with pinky tinge; has tropical aroma with suggestion of pear. Sweetly aromatic.*	**£5.69**	AV	**B**
BACKSBERG CHARDONNAY 1992 Paarl	*Rich, classic, buttery Chardonnay. Mid-weight. Elegant and well rounded.*	**£5.95**	G&M, HCC, CAP, A&A, CHH, ABY	**B**
STELLENRYCK CHARDONNAY, THE BERGKELDER 1992	*Nice, clean fresh bouquet; not too oaky. Light fruit flavours.*	**£6.32**	NGF	**B**
BOSCHENDAL GRAND CUVEE SAUVIGNON BLANC 1993 Paarl	*Yeasty and marked by subtle use of sweet oak. Light, elegant, steely wine, well-balanced.*	**£6.49**	TO, MYS, WHK, GRT	**B**
DIEU DONNE CHARDONNAY 1993 Franschhoek	*Gentle boiled sweet character; redcurrants and leafy. Rounded fruit flavours on palate.*	**£6.50**	PLA, JFE, CAG, CAP, PAT, D	**B**
CHAMONIX WINERY CHARDONNAY 1993 Franschhoek	*Really impressive deep butterscotchy nose. Concentrated, elegant and long.*	**£6.95**	TO	**B**
LONGRIDGE CHARDONNAY, DU PREEL & LAUBSER 1992 Stellenbosch	*Full, nice smoky nose, light buttery fruit bouquet. Soft, creamy character. Quite good length.*	**£6.99**	SUP	**B**
MULDERBOSCH BARREL-FERMENTED SAUVIGNON BLANC 1993 Stellenbosch	*Pleasing balance of soft, ripe fruit and warm, toasty vanilla oak. Lovely acidity.*	**£7.17**	JAR	**B**

BOSCHENDAL CHARDONNAY 1993 Paarl	*Big boned, muscular Chardonnay with fruit flavour and wood to match.*	**£7.35**	JS, ROD, GRT	**B**
MULDERBOSCH BARREL-FERMENTED SAUVIGNON BLANC 1992 Stellenbosch	*Fabulously intense Sauvignon character. Full and rich with lots of length and flavour.*	**£8.00**	JAR	**B**
WELTEVREDE CHARDONNAY 1992 Robertson	*Well-balanced, with good fruit flavour and hints of apple.*	**£8.00**	NY, SNO, PIM, CC, LWE	**S**
SIMONSIG CHARDONNAY 1992 Stellenbosch	*Subtle, elegant Chardonnay with good cross between old and new world style.*	**£8.98**	PAL	**B**

SWEET WHITE

STELLENZICHT WEISSER RIESLING NOBLE LATE HARVEST 1992 Stellenbosch	*Deep-straw colour. Intense apricot and citrus aroma. Nutty, raisiny nose, full, with dried fruit palate.*	**£3.99**	VW	**G**
VIN DE CONSTANCE, KLEIN CONSTANTIA ESTATE 1989 Constantia	*Wonderfully mature raisiny marmalade and quince fruit balanced by an opulent sweetness.*	**£10.66**	AV, JTD, GON, NGF	**B**

ROSE

BOSCHENDAL BLANC DE NOIRS 1993 Paarl	*Pale orange in colour. Fresh, round, ripe fruit, well-balanced and quite long. Good for picnics.*	**£6.45**	C&A, MYS	**B**

SPARKLING

LE GRAND PAVILLON, BOSCHENDAL Paarl	*Good mousse; a tangy, lemony flavour, with rich, creamy follow through. Pleasant dry taste.*	**£6.49**	SAF	**B**

KRONE BOREALIS BRUT, TWEE JONGE GEZELLEN 1988 TULBAGH	*Good bubbles in strong, swirling mousse. Lemon and lime nose with nutty tones on palate.*	**£7.95**	W	**B**
BOSCHENDAL BRUT 1990 Paarl	*Clean, biscuit-nosed with lemon-citrus zest that lingers to the finish. Even better with time.*	**£7.99**	GRT	**S**
PONGRACZ, BERGKELDER 1991	*Attractive nose of yeast, biscuit and lemon tones. Good acidity balances Chardonnay taste.*	**£8.10**	NGF	**S**
KAAPSE VONKEL BRUT, SIMONSIG ESTATES 1991 Stellenbosch	*Pale gold, with lemon nose. Nutty, tasty flavours with good fruit, lasting for medium length.*	**£9.99**	BFI, LWE, NGF	**B**

SOUTH AMERICA

THE WINEMAKING REVOLUTION has only really taken effect in Chile over the last decade, following the introduction of stainless steel equipment by Miguel Torres. Today, the wines are principally made using such classic varieties as Chardonnay, Sauvignon, Cabernet and Merlot. On the other side of the Andes in Argentina, the industry has been slower to develop but may benefit from such unusual grape varieties such as the Torrontes and Malbec.

— ARGENTINA —

RED				
GAUCHOS LURTON CABERNET SAUVIGNON, J & F LURTON Mendoza	*Good open nose reeking of sweet new oak. Youthful palate with firm, ripe plummy fruit.*	**£5.50**	IWS	B
COLLECTION PRIVADA, BODEGA J E NAVARRO CORREAS 1988 Mendoza	*Nice full fruit; cherry and berry flavours with nice mid palate. Good finish, dry and tannic.*	**£7.00**	LV, MYS, PLA, BTH, BWI	B
MENDOZA CABERNET SAUVIGNON, EDMUNDO J. CORREAS, 1988,	*Soft, attractive and old-fashioned Spanish-style wine.*	**£8.27**	MYS	B

DRY WHITE				
TORRONTES, LA AGRICOLA 1994 Mendoza	*Greengage and pineapple fruit on the palate and young crushed apples on the nose.*	**£3.75**	T&T	B
CAFAYATE TORRONTES, ARNALDO ETCHART SA 1993 Cafayate	*Pale Sweet mango taste, soft, with a slightly smoky complexity. Dry finish.*	**£4.00**	WTR, EGL, PEA, CEN, CDE, CAX	S

CHARDONNAY 'OAK CASK'RESERVE, TRAPICHE 1993 Mendoza	*Clean, fresh nose; sweet, wooded style with good fruit concentration.*	£4.50	JS, GI	B

— CHILE —

RED				
ASDA CHILEAN CABERNET MERLOT, VINICOLA LAS TAGUAS 1993 Mataquito	*Big, sweet, chunky, plummy palate; a fine body and super-long, elegant finish.*	£3.49	A	S
TOCORNAL CABERNET SAUVIGNON MERLOT, VINA TOCORNAL 1993 Cachapoal Valley & Colchagua	*Deep cherry colour; a soft, ripe, minty, jammy nose. Sweet juicy fruit on the palate with a good herbal tone.*	£3.49	OD, FUL	S
CALIBORO CABERNET SAUVIGNON, VINA SEGU-OLLE 1993 Maule Valley	*Spice and mint bouquet and cherry fruit. Good fat flavours and finish. Light and enjoyable.*	£3.79	G, EOR, IRV, WAC, CWL	B
CANEPA UNOAKED CABERNET SAUVIGNON 1993 Maipo	*A simple, light, fresh character may be found in this youthful, purple-coloured wine.*	£3.99	T&T	B
VINA CARMEN CABERNET SAUVIGNON 1993 Maipo	*Deep colour with excellent fruit and depth on palate. Nice vanilla character and good finish.*	£3.99	OD, DBY	S
PORTAL DEL ALTO MERLOT 1993 Maipo	*Blackcurrant and slightly toasty fruit nose followed by oaky fruit palate. Good flavour and length.*	£4.49	HOT	B
CONO SUR PINOT NOIR 1993 Rapel	*Cooked raspberry nose, good fruit palate and a strong, tannic structure.*	£4.49	OD, FUL	B

CABERNET MERLOT, CARTA VIEJA 1992	*Herbaceous, minty, leafy nose followed by good flavours, juice and tannins. Slightly sweet finish.*	£4.69	FBG	**B**
SANTA RITA MERLOT RESERVA 1992 Maipo	*New World oak flavours; clean fruit, blackcurrants and brambles. Pleasant middle palate.*	£4.75	BI, MAR, ABY	**B**
VINA UNDURRAGA CABERNET SAUVIGNON RESERVA 1990 Maipo	*Cassis and vanilla on the nose. Touch of blackcurrants and velvety cherry flavour.*	£4.79	AV, FUL, GNW, SHJ, IRV, DBY	**B**
CABERNET SAUVIGNON, JOSE CANEPA 1992 Maipo	*Nice, deep, purply-red colour. Aroma of stewed currants and a hint of cigar box.*	£4.79	T&T	**S**
SANTA RITA RESERVA CABERNET SAUVIGNON 1989	*A lovely, minty/ blackcurranty bouquet. The finish is tannic. Quite a strong wine but good.*	£4.99	SMF, G, NRW, DBY, BI, TO	**B**
MONTENUEVO OAK-AGED CABERNET SAUVIGNON, VINICOLA MONDRAGON 1991	*Heavily extracted, cooked blackcurrant fruit with clean distinct oak and solid tannins.*	£4.99	MWW	**B**
SANTA RITA CABERNET SAUVIGNON RESERVA 1990 Maipo	*Red fruit bouquet; blackcurrants. Touch of complexity, nuttiness and spice. Well structured.*	£4.99	TO, SMF, BI MWW, WSO, BC, NRW, ABY	**B**
MONTES CABERNET MERLOT SPECIAL CUVEE, DISCOVER WINES 1992 Curico	*Nice nose of concentrated fruit. Soft, balanced and well developed. Clean fruity. Hurrah!*	£4.99	SV	**B**
ROWAN BROOK CABERNET SAUVIGNON RESERVA, CANEPA 1991 Mataquito	*Big, sweet nose with rich, smoky oak. Plenty of tannin in the mouth and lots of sweet fruit.*	£4.99	A	**S**

Cono Sur Cabernet Sauvignon Selection Reserve 1992	Opaque purple-black colour. a good mouthful of juicy, ripe plums, mint and sweet oak.	£5.00	OD, SSM, UWM, FUL	**S**
San Pedro Cabernet Sauvignon 1992	Good colour and raspberry fruit bouquet; smooth, light bodied. Juicy fruit and mild tannins.	£5.29	SAF	**S**
Seleccion Del Directorio, Santa Helena 1991 Curico	Good, deep colour, with firm, raisiny fruit. Nice combination of oak, fruit and age.	£5.29	CTH, UWM, THP, CTH, WMP, CTH	**S**
Santa Carolina Cabernet Sauvignon Special Reserve 1990 Maipo	Light and easy blackcurrant juice style yet with plenty of tannin.	£5.49	WRW, G&M, HOU, ECA	**B**
Gato Negro Cabernet Sauvignon, San Pedro 1992 Lontue	Typically blackcurranty and damsony with a hint of oak.	£5.59	MRN	**B**
Santa Rita Medalla Real Cabernet Sauvignon 1991 Maipo	Interesting cassis nose with smokey and grapey aromas. Full, blackcurrant flavour.	£5.99	SAF, BI, HAR, CWW, MAR	**B**
Cono Sur Selection Reserve Pinot Noir 1993 Rapel	Fruity and sweet, jammy and plummy flavours, lots of body, softness and character.	£5.99	OD, SSM, UWM, FUL	**B**
Caliterra Estate Cabernet Sauvignon Reserva, Vina Caliterra 1991	Good, deep colour. Very attractive, herbal, apple and blackberry nose. Spicy, slightly herbal.	£5.99	OD, T, BSC, DBY	**S**
Cousino Macul Antiguas Reserva Cabernet Sauvignon 1989 Maipo	Mature, minty character to nose; good cabernet fruit flavours and length. Classy finish.	£6.30	W, AB, BOO, ADN, CWM, RWV, WCS, DBY	**B**

MIGUEL TORRES MANSO DE VELASCO VINEDO DEL GOBERNADOR CABERNET SAUVIGNON 1989 Curico	*Quite complex, intense fruit flavours; fruit spice and cherries. Firm fruit and acid on palate. Slightly dry.*	£6.45	DBY	**B**
DON MAXIMIANO CABERNET SAUVIGNON SPECIAL RESERVA, ERRAZURIZ ESTATE 1991 Aconcagua Valley	*Ruby red wine of medium depth; characterful and complex. Good clean, oaky middle. Full, vibrant finish.*	£6.99	DBY	**B**
SANTA CAROLINA CABERNET SAUVIGNON GRAN RESERVA 1990 Maipo	*Well-balanced, well-made wine with a stalky, herbaceous bouquet. Medium weight, with soft fruit.*	£6.99	ECA	**B**
SANTA CAROLINA CABERNET SAUVIGNON GRAN RESERVA 1989 Maipo	*Oaky, sweet blackcurrant nose with lovely sweet middle and plenty of fruit on palate.*	£6.99	OD, G&M, HOU, ECA, DIO	**S**
MONTES ALPHA CABERNET SAUVIGNON 1990 Curico	*Rich soft fruit nose; violets and blackberries. Nice velvety fruit, soft tannins and good oak.*	£7.99	DBY, TO	**B**
MAGNIFICUM CABERNET SAUVIGNON, JOSE CANEPA 1990 Maipo	*Young red currant aroma on bouquet and on palate. Simple fruit flavours, medium bodied with tannic finish.*	£10.49	T&T	**B**
	DRY WHITE			
SANTA RITA 120 SAUVIGNON BLANC 1994 Maipo	*Grassy herbaceous gooseberry nose; a fresh and zippy wine with hints of citric fruits.*	£3.99	OD, VW, AB, CEL, BI, DIO, DBY	**B**
VILLA MONTES SAUVIGNON BLANC, DISCOVER WINES 1994 Curico	*Pears, tropical fruit and some elderflower and herbal notes. Plenty of fresh crisp spritzy fruit.*	£4.00	EOR, L&W, PLA, TDV, HD	**B**

CANEPA CHARDONNAY 1993 Maipo	*Limey green apples on the nose. Opulent yet refined. This is truly seductive.*	**£4.49**	T&T	**S**
PORTAL DEL ALTO CHARDONNAY 1993 Maipo	*Lemony aromas. Hint of ripe camembert, on nose with fresh fruit salad and smoky tones on palate.*	**£4.65**	HOT, L&W, MVN	**B**
MONTES CHARDONNAY, CUVEE RYMAN/MONTES 1993 Curico	*Clean and lemony with earthy tones, this shows rich, honeyed fruit and fine balance.*	**£4.99**	WR, TH, TO	**B**
CALITERRA ESTATE CASABLANCA CHARDONNAY 1993	*Ripe, soft sweet fruit palate with subtle wood character. Good length and finish.*	**£4.99**	WHC, D, DBY	**B**
SANTA CAROLINA CHARDONNAY 1993 Maipo	*Light, fresh lemon nose. Well-knitted flavours to this wine.*	**£4.99**	OD, G&J, BWL, G&M, HOU, ECA, CWS	**B**
SANTA RITA MEDALLA REAL CHARDONNAY 1993 Maipo	*Rich, creamy, young, pineappley wine.*	**£6.49**	JS, BI, CWW, MAR	**S**
CASABLANCA SANTA ISABEL ESTATE CHARDONNAY 1992 Casablanca Valley	*Balanced ripe fruit and subtle oak. Silky with nice acid and complex tropical and citrus fruit.*	**£7.95**	JS	**B**

ROSE

MIGUEL TORRES CABERNET SAUVIGNON ROSE 1993 Curico	*Gorgeously dry wine with ripe fruit on the nose and fresh well-balanced flavours*	**£4.79**	CC, GWI, MCC, PIM, DBY	**B**

SPAIN

Despite some of the most conservative attitudes in the wine world, Spain is quietly undergoing the early phases of a quiet revolution. Top class wines are beginning to emerge from previously underperforming regions, while new styles are being produced in traditional areas like Rioja. Much remains to be done, particularly with sparkling wines, but Spain has more to offer today's wine drinkers than ever before.

RED				
DON HUGO RED, BODEGAS VITORIANAS Northern Spain	*Plenty of soft raspberry/ cherry fruit with subtle new oak.*	£2.79	W, G	**B**
MORRISONS RIOJA RED, BODEGAS NAVAJAS 1992 Rioja	*A complex nose combining ripe vanilla fruit and subtle oak. Clean and uncomplicated.*	£2.99	MRN	**B**
VINA DEL CASTILLO, VINICOLA DE CASTILLA 1993 La Mancha	*A pale purple colour, with an excellent depth of raspberry fruit. Very drinkable.*	£2.99	TO	**B**
ST MICHAEL VALENCIA, SCHENK 1991 Valencia	*A mixture of cherries, chocolate and spices with a touch of pepper and good, soft tannins.*	£2.99	M&S	**B**
SANTARA CONCA DE BARBERA DRY RED, HUGH RYMAN & BODEGAS CONCAVINS 1993 Conca de Barbera	*Light wine with soft, summery redcurrant fruit. Clean and crisp palate.*	£2.99	MWW, SSM	**B**
CASA DE LA VINA CENCIBEL, VALDEPENAS 1992 Valdepenas	*Young wine, packed with raspberries and plums. Stylish and rounded with depth.*	£3.25	SAF, NRW, FUL, BUT	**B**

CASA DE LA VINA VALDEPEÑAS CENCIBEL 1993 Valdepeñas	*Youthful in appearance, this is a young wine with lots of style, full of great fruit.*	**£3.25**	CEL, DBY, NRW
VIÑA ALBALI VALDEPEÑAS CABERNET SAUVIGNON, BODEGAS FELIX SOLIS 1991 Valdepeñas	*Rich strawberry and cherry fruit flavours rounded out with smooth creamy oak.*	**£3.29**	PEC
SAFEWAY OAK-AGED VALDEPEÑAS, FELIX SOLIS 1987	*Rich nose, dominated by vanilla oak, but combined on the palate with lots of fruit.*	**£3.39**	SAF
RIOJA VEGA CRIANZA, BODEGAS MUERZA 1989 Rioja	*Ripe cherry, vanilla and blackcurrants evident on the nose.*	**£3.46**	Widely Available
RIOJA BERBERANA TEMPRANILLO CRIANZA 1990 Rioja	*A big and powerful wine, clean and fresh, which shows maturity and complexity.*	**£3.49**	FUL
ALBOR RIOJA, CAMPO VIEJO 1992 Rioja	*Aromas of cherries and violets, accompanied by a little pepper. Very well-balanced.*	**£3.49**	Widely Available
NAVAJAS RIOJA BLANCO SIN CRIANZA 1992 Rioja	*This pale red, subtle wine has a lovely balance of spicy oak and creamy fruit.*	**£3.49**	WL, TBW
VINADRIAN RIOJA TINTO, BODEGAS GURPEGUI 1993 Rioja	*Light purple-red in colour, this youthful wine is full of crisp berries and banana.*	**£3.50**	RWW
MALT HOUSE VINTNERS RIOJA TINTO, BODEGAS FUENTORO 1992 Rioja	*Full of youthful red fruit flavour with lively tones of cherries. Well-balanced.*	**£3.65**	MHV

RIOJA LATURCE TINTO, BODEGAS LATURCE 1992 Rioja	*A meaty wine with plenty of oak and lots of mature well-knit fruit. Most enjoyable.*	£3.69	D	B
SOMERFIELD RIOJA TINTO ALMENAR 1990 Rioja	*Promising wine with a perfumed nose. Exhibits a good degree of complexity and length.*	£3.79	SMF, G,	B
CO-OP RIOJA TINTO, BODEGAS ALMENAR 1990 Rioja	*Full red in colour, this quaffable wine is full of rich and complex oak and ripe fruit flavours.*	£3.79	CWS	B
RIOJA ORLA DORADA, FAUSTINO RIVERO ULECIA 1993 Rioja	*Light, cherry-and-raspberry nose with tones of macerated strawberries and fresh, leafy aromas.*	£3.98	TAN, SHJ	B
RIOJA BERBERANA OAK-AGED TEMPRANILLO 1992 Rioja	*Full of damsons, leather and liquorice, with a touch of smoky oak. A lovely, chewy texture.*	£3.99	SAF	G
NAVAJAS RIOJA SIN CRIANZA 1992 Rioja	*Mature and smooth, this elegant wine with delicious raspberry has a lingering finish.*	£3.99	WL, VTH, PMR, WCE, TPW, TBW, FUL	S
RIOJA BERBERANA OAK-AGED TEMPRANILLO 1992 Rioja	*Deeply coloured with a concentrated American oak nose underpinned by ripe cherry.*	£3.99	SAF, FUL, DBY	G
SOLANA VALDEPENAS CENCIBEL, CASA DE LA VINA & DON LEWIS 1993 Valdepenas	*Soft raspberry nose, rich garnet colour. Ripe, spicy, full cherry taste. Good balance.*	£3.99	OD, MRN, WMK	G
RIOJA SANTA DARIA TINTO, COOPERATIVA VINICOLA DE CENICERO 1992 Rioja	*Succulent black cherry and plum fruit offset by vegetal tones and hints of leather and liquorice.*	£4.08	LAV, WIN	B

CHIVITE RESERVA, CHIVITE 1989 Navarra	*Delicious cherry fruit makes this a seductive proposition. Elegant and well-balanced oak.*	**£4.49**	VW	**B**
LANGUNILLA RIOJA CRIANZA, BODEGAS LAGUNILLA 1988 Rioja	*Orangey red hues indicating good development and maturity. A rich and nutty wine.*	**£4.49**	WAV, WOI	**B**
PALACIO DE GRAJAL, RIBEIRO DEL DUERO, BODEGAS VINOS DE LEOZ 1992 Leoz	*Luscious damson and cherry nose with good initial berry fruit. Soft, long finish.*	**£4.50**	PEC	**B**
MALT HOUSE VINTNERS CORTESIA RIOJA RESERVA, BODEGAS FUENTORO 1988 Rioja	*A rich, ripe strawberry nose overlies a palate of wild strawberry, tobacco and spice.*	**£4.65**	MHV	**B**
RIOJA COSME PALACIO Y HERMANUS, BODEGAS PALACIO 1990 Rioja	*Rich scents of vanilla and coconut with raisiny, tarry fruit. An elegant wine.*	**£4.65**	OD, W, GSH, T&W, OHI, FUL	**S**
AGRAMONT TINTO, BODEGAS PRINCIPE DE VIANA SA 1990 Navarra	*Ripe berry fruit on the nose overlying a rich palate of crunchy raspberry and warm oak.*	**£4.75**	W, SAF, WTR, BBR	**B**
RIOJA CRIANZA, FAUSTINO RIVERO ULECIA 1990 Rioja	*An elegant wine with lots of fruit and Italian-style tannins.*	**£4.79**	U, FUL	**B**
MARQUES DE CACERES RIOJA CRIANZA TINTO, UNION VITI-VINICOLA 1990 Rioja	*A good jammy nose is followed by a huge fruit flavour on the palate. Youthful and lively.*	**£4.95**	DBY, CEB, D	**B**
MARQUES DE CACERES RIOJA CRIANZA TINTO, UNION VITI-VINICOLA 1989 Rioja	*A deep rich red colour, full of rounded plummy fruit and spicy vanilla wood flavours.*	**£4.95**	TBW, D, WES, DBY	**B**

CONDE DE VALDEMAR RIOJA CRIANZA, MARTINEZ BUJANDA 1988 Rioja	*Light garnet in colour. Lots of juicy fruit and soft smoky oak with hints of liquorice.*	**£4.99**	TH, WR, BU, TDS, VEX	**B**
CAMPILLO RIOJA CRIANZA, BODEGAS CAMPILLO 1988 Rioja	*Forceful strawberry fruit aroma, very well-bal-anced with soft oak flavours.*	**£4.99**	OD, A	**B**
TESCO VINA MARIA RIOJA RESERVA, BODEGAS ARISABEL 1987 Rioja	*A delicate nose of oak, raspberry, vanilla and tomato. An elegant and lively wine.*	**£4.99**	TO	**S**
DON JACOBO RIOJA CRIANZA TINTO, BODEGAS CORRAL 1989 Rioja	*A developed, complex bouquet and lots of clean, Bordeaux-style fruit. Great balance.*	**£5.19**	LAV, WIN	**B**
ARTADI VINAS DE GAIN RIOJA CRIANZA, COSECHEROS ALAVESES 1991 Rioja	*Rich oaky and spicy, with a lovely full vanilla oak nose. Soft and mel-low in the mouth.*	**£5.49**	CNL, WSO, SEL, BOO	**B**
SIGLO RIOJA RESERVA, BODEGAS AGE 1985 Rioja	*A mature, fruity style, showing muted straw-berry flavours and some sweet, softly spicy oak.*	**£5.79**	A+A, CTL, MHC, MCC, RWV	**S**
GRAN COLEGIATA TORO RESERVA, BODEGAS FARINA 1987 Toro	*Terrific mature nose of sweet vanilla, buttered toast, fruit jam and stewed plums.*	**£5.85**	MWW	**B**
PRIORATO NEGRE SCALA DEI, CELLERS DE SCALA DEI 1988 Priorato	*This red shows a pro-nounced cherry-and-mint character in a rus-tic, baked fruit.*	**£5.89**	WL, DBY	**B**
RAIMAT TEMPRANILLO 1990 Penedes	*A deep ruby colour with buckets of soft, ripe fruit. Rich warm and rather good.*	**£5.89**	BVL, DBY	**B**

SENORIO DE LAZAN SOMONTANO RESERVA, BODEGA COOPERATIVA COMARCAL DEL SOMOTANO 1988 Somontano	*Pronounced vanilla and American oak nose. Oaky, traditional Rioja style wine. Tangy and fruity.*	£5.99	BOD, MWS	B
SENORIO DE NAVA RIBERA DEL DUERO CRIANZA 1989 Ribera del Duero	*Deep red in colour, this has a rich perfumed fruit aroma. Full-bodied with great potential.*	£5.99	A, SPR, SAF, CWS	S
BERBERANA RIOJA RESERVA 1987 Rioja	*This pale ruby wine combines tarry fruit with spicy oak.*	£5.99	Widely Available	B
TORRES GRAN SANGREDETORO 1989 Penedes	*A vibrant, purple/red wine which contains heaps of ripe cherries and spicy tannins.*	£6.19	WR, OD, U, LWL, BU, GRT, NRW, SEB	S
VINA ALBERDI RIOJA CRIANZA, LA RIOJA ALTA 1989 Rioja	*Soft, berry fruit and rich, spicy oak with tones of liquorice.*	£6.49	DBY, WR, BU, L&S, THP	B
CONDE DE VALDEMAR RIOJA RESERVA, MARTINEZ BUJANDA 1987 Rioja	*Vibrant jammy aroma; a wine full of ripe sweet berries with hints of tar and plenty of tannin.*	£6.85	TH, WR, BU	B
MARQUES DE CACERES RIOJA RESERVA, UNION VITI-VINICOLA 1986 Rioja	*A light easy-drinking wine, packed with sweet peppery fruit and a hint of leaves and spices.*	£6.89	DBY, HHC	B
OCHOA NAVARRA RESERVA 1982 Navarra	*Mature blackberry with creamy vanilla. Smooth and ripe with an evocative dusty finish.*	£6.95	REW, JSN, LKN, WCH, TAN, DWS	B
TINTO CALLEJO RIBERA DEL DUERO CRIANZA 1989 Ribera del Duero	*Soft coconut aromas. Beautifully balanced wine with rich, chewy fruit and mellow oak.*	£6.95	WSO	B

MARQUES DE RISCAL RIOJA RESERVA 1989 Rioja	*This strongly oaked wine combines flavours of light, cherry fruit and rich tannins.*	£6.99	VW, DBY	**B**
CAMPILLO RESERVA RIOJA, BODEGAS CAMPILLO 1985 Rioja	*Gamey fruit and heavy toasty oak. Rich and soft in the mouth. Approaching maturity.*	£6.99	GI	**B**
SENORIO DE SARRIA NAVARRA CABERNET SAUVIGNON CRIANZA, BODEGA DE SARRIA 1987 Navarra	*Lovely perfumed nose. Warm sweet vanilla, figs and cassis combine in this velvety wine.*	£6.99	TH, WR, BU	**B**
NEGRE SCALA DEI PRIORAT PRIORATO, CELLERS DE SCALA 1991 Priorato	*Ripe, rich spritzy cherry fruit and attractive light dusty tannins with a hint of coconut oak.*	£6.99	WL, HAR, WIN, WCE, DBY	**B**
NAVAJAS RIOJA TINTO RESERVA 1985 Rioja	*Orange-red colour indicates plenty of age. Warm and long.*	£6.99	MG, MRS, MRT, NIC, GRO, FUL	**B**
MONTECILLO VINA MONTY RIOJA GRAN RESERVA 1986 Rioja	*A velvety smooth wine with a hint of vanilla on the nose. Good ageing potential.*	£7.00	OD, BAR, WG	**B**
RAIMAT CABERNET SAUVIGNON 1990 Penedes	*Spicy, maturing aromas of gently stewed summer fruit, cinnamon toast and marscapone.*	£7.09	TO, BVL, TH	**B**
MARQUES DE MURRIETA RIOJA TINTO RESERVA 1988 Rioja	*A warm oaky nose underpinned by a good weight of fleshy fruit and ripe tannins.*	£7.49	MWW, TBW, FUL, DBY, TH, THP, OD	**B**

Pinpoint who sells the wine you wish to buy by turning to the stockist codes. If you know the name of the wine you want to buy, use the alphabetical index. If price is your motivation, refer to the invaluable price guide index; red and white wines under £5 and sparkling wines under £10. Good hunting!

PAGO DE CARRAOVEJAS RIBERA DEL DUERO 1992 Ribera del Duero	*A magnificent nose of blackcurrant and mint offset by tones of stewed fruit and rhubarb.*	£7.95	BWC, PTR, MRT, LEA, GRT	G
VINA REAL RIOJA CRIANZA, CVNE 1989 Rioja	*A rich mid-red colour, with spicy peppery fruit and a touch of vanilla oak on the nose.*	£7.99	Widely Available	B
VINA REAL RIOJA RESERVA, CVNE 1986 Rioja	*Rich and earthy warm fruit with lovely toasty oak; hints of lead pencils and spices.*	£7.99	FSW, GRT, WCA, WIW, DWS, DBY	S
TORRES GRAN CORONAS CABERNET SAUVIGNON RESERVA 1988 Penedes	*Packed full of straw-berries and raspberries with a firm, gently tannic backbone.*	£7.99	AVA, DIR, GRT	B
JEAN LEON CABERNET SAUVIGNON 1987 Penedes	*Nice fruity nose; rich and soft. Flavour on mid palate and tannins at back.*	£8.35	L&S	B
VINA ARANA RIOJA RESERVA, LA RIOJA ALTA SA 1986 Rioja	*A big and juicy wine with fleshy fruit, com-plex character and good firm tannins.*	£8.75	F&M, DBY, WSO, L&S, DBY	B
CAMPILLO RIOJA GRAN RESERVA, BODEGAS CAMPILLO 1982 Rioja	*Wonderful complexity, full and rich. Leave this two more years and then treat yourself.*	£9.99	TO	B
VINA ARDANZA RIOJA RESERVA, LA RIOJA ALTA SA 1986 Rioja	*Fine and elegant wine showing lovely maturity. Bags of rich fruit and soft, cedary spicy oak.*	£10.25	SAF, G, BBR, TH, ADN, L&S, DBY, CEB	S
MONTE-VANNOS RIBERO DEL DUERO RESERVA 1987 Ribera del Duero,	*Pale garnet colour indi-cates maturity. Oaky vanilla flavour with ripe fruit and firm tannins.*	£10.36	CWS, WIN, DBY	B

CONDE DE VALDEMAR RIOJA GRAN RESERVA, MARTINEZ BUJANDA 1985 Rioja	*Dark cherry red with rich aromas of vegetal, old-style wood. Packed with sweet, fresh fruit.*	**£10.49**	TH, WR, BU, VEX	**B**
PESQUERA RIBERA DEL DUERO TINTO, ALEJAN- DRO 1990 Ribera del Duero	*Excellent black cherry and ripe plum fruit given great complexity by rich smoky oak.*	**£11.00**	JAR, L&S, DBY	**B**
CONDE DE LA SALCEDA RIOJA GRAN RESERVA, VINA SALCEDA 1985 Rioja	*Vibrant ruby with a cinnamon, strawberry and coconut bouquet and a creamy vanilla taste.*	**£11.00**	TAN, SHJ, WIC, ADN, L&W	**S**
CONDE DE VALDEMAR RIOJA GRAN RESERVA, MARTINEZ BUJANDA 1982 Rioja	*Good fruity nose, full of complex aromas and a whiff of the farmyard. A lingering finish.*	**£11.99**	TH, WR, BU, VEX, DBY	**B**
MARTINEZ BUJANDA RIOJA RESERVA EXCEPCIONEL 1987 Rioja	*Characterful spicy wine full of sweet blackcurrant. Could use another year or two of ageing.*	**£11.99**	VEX, WR, BU	**S**
PRADO ENEA RIOJA GRAN RESERVA, BODEGAS MUGA 1985 Rioja	*Rich farmyard flavour with blackcurrant flavours backed up by spicy coconut oak.*	**£11.99**	WBR, IRV, A&A, DBY	**S**
MONTE REAL RIOJA GRAN RESERVA, BODEGAS RIOJANAS 1982 Rioja	*Packed with earthy dark cherry aromas and classic Rioja-style vanilla and chocolate oak.*	**£12.46**	ABY	**B**
PROTOS RESERVA, RIBERA DEL DUERO 1987 Ribera del Duero	*Young, tarry fruit and tones of cedar and vanilla. Needs some time to mature.*	**£12.80**	BN, MAR	**B**
GRAN RESERVA 904, LA RIOJA ALTA SA 1983 Rioja	*Mature colour and a cheesy nose point to a well-aged wine with aristocratic elegance.*	**£14.50**	Widely Available	**B**

DRY WHITE

CASTILLO IMPERIAL BLANCO, BODEGAS Y BEBIDAS Galicia	*A clean, crisp wine with hints of apricots and spice. Fresh and balanced.*	**£2.49**	SMF, G	**S**
LAZARILLO, LA MANCHA BLANCO, COOPERATIVE JESUS DEL PERDON 1993 La Mancha	*Fresh, with an appley floral nose, a touch of carbon dioxide, and a slight nuttiness.*	**£2.75**	VW	**B**
TESCO MOSCATEL DE VALENCIA, GANDIA Valencia	*Subtle palate with a touch of sweetness. Light and long.*	**£2.99**	TO	**B**
SANTARA DRY WHITE, CONCA DE BARBERA, CONCAVINS/HUGH RYMAN 1993 Conca de Barbera	*A lemony nose on this dry, fresh wine. A delicious finish that ends with tastes of melon.*	**£2.99**	MWW, SSM	**S**
SAFEWAY MOSCATEL DE VALENCIA, GANDIA Valencia	*Honeyed, fruity aromas.*	**£3.19**	SAF	**B**
SOMERFIELD MOSCATEL DE VALENCIA, GANDIA Valencia	*Marmalade character with a touch of grapefruit; rich, flavoursome.*	**£3.25**	SMF, G	**B**
DUC DE FOIX BLANCO SECO JOVEN, COVIDES LTDA 1993 Penedes	*Slightly smoky on the nose, with lovely buttery, lemony fruit on the palate.*	**£3.25**	STB	**B**
RUEDA SAUVIGNON BLANC, HERMANOS LURTON 1993 Rueda	*Floral, vaguely herby, aroma with tones of citrus fruit and gooseberry. Well-balanced.*	**£3.29**	JS	**B**

Pinpoint who sells the wine you wish to buy by turning to the stockist codes.
If you know the name of the wine you want to buy, use the alphabetical index.
If price is your motivation, refer to the invaluable price guide index; red and
white wines under £5 and sparkling wines under £10. Good hunting!

CASAL DA BARCA, BODEGAS ALANIS 1993 Ribeiro	*Grapey, grassy, cool, fermented nose. Fresh clean citrus fruit on the palate. Dry and light.*	**£3.29**	TH, DBY	**S**
MOSCATEL DE VALENCIA, GANDIA Valencia	*Well balanced with good structure to the palate.*	**£3.49**	TH, WR, BU, TDS, FUL	**B**
FRUIT DE VI, VALLFORMOSA Penedes	*Soft, fragrant, grapey fruit make this medium-sweet wine spicy, attractive and fresh.*	**£3.99**	MTL	**B**
HERMANOS LURTON RUEDA SAUVIGNON, J & F LURTON 1993 Rueda	*Nose of gooseberry and grapefruit. The flavour reveals blackcurrant, capsicum and cut grass.*	**£4.10**	OD, JS, FUL	**S**
SOLANA BLANCO, BODEGAS ALANIS / DON LEWIS 1993 Ribeiro	*Hints of orange blossom on the nose. Young and well-balanced taste. A good all-rounder.*	**£4.25**	OD, MRN, WMK	**B**
MONTENOVO BLANCO, VALDEORRAS BODEGAS SENORIO SAT 1992 Galicia	*Soft nuts and apples on the nose. Well-balanced, with good length and weight. Will keep well.*	**£4.49**	L&S	**S**
TORRES GRAN VINA SOL 1993 Penedes	*Dry, light but elegant; pineapple and rhubarb, spritzy and lean with a balanced clean finish.*	**£5.00**	GRT, TO, OD, WR, CC	**B**
BORNOS SAUVIGNON BLANC, BODEGA DE CRIANZA DE CASTILLA LA VIEJA 1993 Rueda	*Rich and oily ripe Sauvignon showing some asparagus and gooseberry character.*	**£5.80**	GER, RWW	**B**
VINOS DEL VERO CHARDONNAY 1992 Somontano	*Light, fresh and stylish with soft, ripe fruit, biscuity characters and tangy lemon acidity.*	**£5.90**	RTW, EWG, EX, DBY, CWS, DWS, GRT	**B**

RIOJA BLANCO, CONDE DE VALDEMAR, MARTINEZ BUJANDA 1992 Rioja	*A stylish wine with depth and weight; the soft wood flavours make it easy to drink.*	£6.75	LKN, RIC, GS, VEX, DBY	B
MARQUES DE ALELLA CHARDONNAY, PARXET SA 1993 Alella	*An aromatic, limey nose with honeyed pineapple fruit on the palate.*	£6.77	WCS	B
ALBARINO MARTIN CODAX, VILARINO Y CAMBADOS 1992 Rias Baixas	*An interesting nose, rich and attractive on the palate with a long, fruity finish.*	£7.10	WIM	B
TORRES FRANSOLA GRAN VINA SOL 1992 Penedes	*A rich biscuity creamy oak nose, balanced on the palate with subtle Sauvignon fruit.*	£7.29	FSW, A&A, RBS, TAN	B
MALAGA, MOSCATEL PALIDO, SCHOLTZ HERMANOS Malaga	*Copper-coloured wine with a burnt toffee nose. Rich flavour of caramel with a touch of orange.*	£7.79	WDW, CAV, CNL, GWI, L&S	S
LAGAR DE CERVERA, ALBARINO, RIAS BAIXAS, LAGAR DE FORNELOS SA 1992 Rias Baixas	*Mineral and creamy tinges on the nose married with soft fruit and a pleasant aftertaste.*	£7.95	TH, TAN, L&W, WTR, SOM, L&S	B
MORGADIO, ALBARINO, RIAS BAIXAS, AGROMINO SL 1993 Rias Baixas	*A classy nose with hints of orange and oak. Well-rounded with a good finish.*	£8.62	ADN	B

ROSE

ROSADO MARQUES DE CACERES RIOJA 1993 Rioja	*Rose pink wine with hint of watermelon and bubblegum. Fruit and acidity are well-balanced.*	£4.49	DBY	B

SPARKLING

SOMERFIELD CAVA, CONDE DE CARALT Penedes	*Easy-going and drinkable with a fresh nose. One of the best-value cavas.*	£4.99	SMF	**B**
DUC DE FOIX CAVA BRUT, COVIDES Penedes	*A nose of fruit, butter and yeast, and a palate that is clean with the merest hint of cream.*	£5.25	STB	**B**
SEGURA VIUDAS CAVA BRUT RESERVA Cava/Penedes	*A fruity tinge to the nose which is clean and zippy. Austere palate with a biscuity edge, excellent value.*	£5.99	WR, OD, ES, WRW, EX	**B**
ANNA DE CONDORNIU, CODORNIU SA 1989 Penedes	*Bags of lemon and fizz. The pale gold colour doesn't prepare you for the full, fruity taste.*	£7.39	TH, SAF, W, HD	**B**
PARXET CHARDONNAY CAVA 1990 Cava	*Creamy, yeasty nose with a good biscuity taste and some useful weight.*	£7.93	WCS	**B**
TORRE DEL GALL, GRAN RESERVA BRUT, CAVA CHANDON 1990 Penedes	*Clean, citrus aromas with matching taste make this a refreshing drink.*	£7.99	VW, M&C	**B**

FORTIFIED

CARTA BLANCA FINO, AGUSTIN BLAZQUEZ Jerez	*Pleasantly crisp with good length.*	£2.89	WRT, MRS	**B**
TESCO SUPERIOR MANZANILLA, SANCHEZ ROMATE Jerez	*Good clean, tangy character to nose. Clean with a good crisp finish.*	£2.99	TO	**B**

TESCO SUPERIOR OLOROSO SECO, SANCHEZ ROMATE Jerez	*An open, fruity nose with salty, nutty flavours. Soft and syrupy with a long, dry finish.*	£2.99	TO	**S**
SAINSBURY'S PALO CORTADO, FRANCISCO GONZALEZ FERNANDEZ Jerez	*Sweet, light and soft style. Good fruity flavours with a hint of sweetness.*	£3.39	JS	**B**
SOMERFIELD FINO SHERRY, LUIS CABALLERO Jerez	*Soft fruity flavours, nutty and concentrated.*	£3.89	SMF, G, FG	**B**
BOOTHS MEDIUM AMONTILLADO, EMILIO HIDALGO Jerez	*Good nose, clean and winey. Clean, rich flavours.*	£3.95	BTH	**B**
TESCO SUPERIOR PALO CORTADO, SANCHEZ ROMATE Jerez	*Rich, golden colour with honey caramel character. Crisp acid and clean finish.*	£3.99	TO	**B**
WM LOW CREAM, PEREZ MEGIA Jerez	*A dry, coffee and toffee nosed wine. Hints of caramel with rich nutty flavours on the palate.*	£3.99	WL	**S**
WISDOM & WARTER PALE CREAM Jerez	*Nut brown colour. Quite smooth with lots of fruit and length.*	£4.15	HOT, MRN, LTW, MYS, LWL, BEF,	**B**
WAITROSE FINO SHERRY, LUIS CABALLERO SA Jerez	*Appley fruit bouquet; firm acidity and light fruit flavours. Long finish.*	£4.35	W	**B**
WAITROSE AMONTILLADO SHERRY, ANTONIO ROMERO Jerez	*An excellent nutty nose with toffee aromas. Rum and raisins in the mouth, soft and creamy.*	£4.35	W	**S**

WAITROSE CREAM SHERRY, ANTONIO ROMERO Jerez	*A light, orangey nose. Treacle and walnut flavour with butterscotch tones.*	£4.35	W	**G**
DON CAVALA CREAM, BODEGA M MORALES RODRIGUEZ Jerez	*Smoky, caramel nose followed by rich caramel flavours. Very smooth, but dry finish.*	£4.39	TH, WR, BU, TDS	**B**
SAINSBURY'S AMONTILLADO, FRANCISCO GONZALEZ Jerez	*Orange/gold colour with light bouquet. Nutty fruit flavours. Creamy soft, quite sweet.*	£4.39	JS	**B**
SAFEWAY CREAM SHERRY, BODEGAS GARCIA DE LEANIZ Jerez	*A toffee bouquet, followed by weighty caramel flavours and a hint of marmalade.*	£4.39	SAF	**B**
SAFEWAY CREAM SHERRY, EMILIO LUSTAU Jerez	*Amber colour, light intensity. Fabulous, smoky caramel nose. Superb long finish.*	£4.39	SAF	**B**
SAINSBURY'S OLOROSO, MORGAN BROS. Jerez	*Fine and fresh, with a caramel nose hinting of olive oil. Elegant and woody, a dry aftertaste.*	£4.39	JS	**S**
TESCO FINEST SOLERA FINO SHERRY, SANCHEZ ROMATE Jerez	*Faint, floral character, fine flavour with crisp, salty tang. Long and elegant.*	£4.92	TO	**B**
HIDALGO AMONTILLADO NAPOLEON Jerez	*Rich, honey bouquet. Quite soft palate, nice structure and length.*	£5.19	MWW	**B**
LUSTAU OLD DRY OLOROSO, LUSTAU Jerez	*Attractive soft style; elegant with plenty of oak. Salty fine and dry with nutty wood flavours.*	£5.25	SAF	**B**

LA CONCHA AMONTILLADO, GONZALEZ BYASS Jerez	*Golden brown colour with sharp bouquet. Very good.*	**£5.25**	SB, TO, G, W, TDS, TBW	**B**
ELEGANTE FINO, GONZALEZ BYASS Jerez	*Soft flavours; pleasant and long.*	**£5.25**	SB, TO, SAF, G, A, TBW	**B**
SUPERIOR CREAM, GONZALEZ BYASS Jerez	*An intense nose of figs and currants. Light and refreshing; fresh acidity and fruity flavours.*	**£5.39**	G, MRS, TBW	**S**
CAPATAZ ANDRES CREAM, EMILIO LUSTAU SA Jerez	*Complex nutty, caramel bouquet. Sweet rich, complex structure. Massive length.*	**£5.99**	HN, RIV, FSW, DWS	**B**
BOOTHS MANZANILLA, EMILIO HIDALGO Jerez	*Almondy nose, slightly salty, very elegant on the palate; nutty and tangy. Lots of character.*	**£6.15**	BTH	**S**
FORTNUM & MASON AMONTILLADO, LUSTAU Jerez	*Orange nose. Excellent nutty flavour and lots of length. Good dry style; grows classy with age.*	**£6.45**	F&M	**G**
ALFONSO OLOROSO SECO, GONZALEZ BYASS Jerez	*Broad, delicate, nutty character with depth of fruit on palate. Good length, slightly salty.*	**£6.53**	OD	**B**
TIO PEPE FINO, GONZALEZ BYASS Jerez	*Soft, clean character. Good style.*	**£6.99**	SB, TO, SAF, G, A, TBW	**B**
OLOROSA VIEJO, MANUEL DE ARGUESO SA Jerez	*A pungent, chocolate and fig nose. Nutty on the palate with tones of banana flambé.*	**£7.45**	SV, PUG, P, PLA, NY	**S**

MALAGA SOLERA 1885, SCHOLTZ HERMANOS SA Malaga	*Nutty nose with orange peel tones. Intense with a luscious fruit and cake flavours.*	**£7.77**	W, WSO, L&W, SEL, DBY, L&S	**G**
VIEJO OLOROSO DULCE 30-YEAR-OLD, VALDESPINO Jerez	*Deeply coloured with figs, dates and raisins on bouquet. Sweet with strong alcohol on palate.*	**£7.95**	WSO	**B**
CREAM OF CREAM SHERRY, PEDRO XIMENEZ, ARGUESO VALDESPINO	*Toffee and muscovado nose. Creamy and sweet with fruit and raisins on the palate.*	**£8.99**	SAF	**G**
DON ZOILO VERY OLD AMONTILLADO Jerez	*Good nutty bouquet with richer palate and good length. Vanilla character. Wistful and assertive.*	**£9.15**	WRK, RBS, BEC, F&M, LV	**B**
DON ZOILO CREAM Jerez	*Bonfires and toffee-apples on the nose. Full-bodied, marmaladey, nutty, soft and attractive.*	**£9.45**	WRK, B&B, GHS, LV	**G**
PEDRO XIMENEZ SOLERA SUPERIOR, VALDESPINO Jerez	*Dark, treacle colour. Very rich and sweet. Superb smoothness, lengthy with curranty flavours.*	**£9.50**	LEA	**G**
DOS CORTADOS OLOROSO, WILLIAMS & HUMBERT Jerez	*Pale gold colour with a nutty/fruit flavour. Good, ripe woody concentration.*	**£10.45**	WBR, SEL, GNW	**B**
BARBADILLO OLOROSO SECO Jerez	*Aromatic with a fresh, salty nose. Rich, fruity and oaky. Medium-bodied with a bone-dry finish.*	**£11.50**	BEL, AR, MG, GMV, LF, GRT, SEB	**G**
MATUSALEM OLOROSO MUY VIEJO, GONZALEZ BYASS Jerez	*Full of Christmas pudding flavours. A well-balanced, elegant sherry. Finishes long and clean.*	**£17.80**	TO, SAF, TDS, OD	**G**

ALONSO EL SABIO OLOROSO, OSBORNE Y CIA Jerez	*Tawny brown/orange. Chocolate, figs; quite a heavy style with some sweetness. Elegant finish.*	**£22.00**	BAR	**B**
OLOROSO SOLERA BC 200, OSBORNE Y CIA Jerez	*Interesting nutty character. Rich, chocolatey fruit but clean firm finish with some acidity.*	**£22.00**	BAR	**B**

PERSONAL TASTING NOTES

SIGHT	
	Clear Bright Hazy Cloudy Colour
SMELL	
	Fresh Musty Floral Fruit Vegetal Animal Wood/Oak Others
TASTE	
	Weight Sweetness Dryness Acidity Fruit Vegetal Wood/Oak Balance
SUMMARY	
	Age Maturity Location Vintage

A N INCONGRUOUS GATHERING OF VERY diverse wine-producing countries. Israel, Greece and Cyprus are all individually beginning to modernise a wine industry, for too long handicapped by tradition. Neighbouring Lebanon has a one-winery success story in the shape of Chateau Musar, while India is proving to be surprisingly good at making good sparkling wine.

— CYPRUS —

BLEND				
GRAND COMMANDARIA, ETKO Limmasol	*Lovely mahogany-amber colour. Quite high alcohol and nice, juicy length.*	**£3.99**	GER, AMA, ML	**S**
COMMANDARIA ST JOHN, KEO	*Lovely, rich old colour. A rich and treacly palate. Clean and burnished flavour to finish.*	**£4.69**	U, VW, MOJ, TBW	**B**

— GREECE —

RED				
NEMEA, BOUTARI 1991 Meme, Pelopponese	*Jammy, brambly forset fruit nose.*	**£3.99**	Widely Available	**B**
CAVA HATZIMICHALI, HATZIMICHALIS 1990 Atalanti	*Richly coloured with some rustic character and loads of sweet, ripe fruit offset by rich oak.*	**£8.50**	GWC, RAC	**S**
DOMAINE HATZI MICHALIS MERLOT 1992 Atalanti	*Slightly tarry, menthol and blackberry nose. Similar in the mouth with almost aniseed.*	**£12.50**	GWC, RAC	**B**

DRY WHITE

RETSINA OF ATTICA, D KOURTAKIS SA Attica	*Good and fresh retsina-styled wine. Would go well with oily food.*	**£3.49**	MRN, W, TH, VW, OD	**B**
HATZIMICHALIS, D HATZIMICHALIS 1992 Atalanti	*Very pale green, dry, mid-weight wine. Clean, floral, lemon nose, sherbet palate.*	**£7.00**	GWC, RAC	**S**
AMBELON, HATZIMICHALIS 1992 Atalanti	*Bright, young, greenish colour. Pleasing lemony nose with a hint of vanilla.*	**£7.00**	GWC, RAC	**S**

— INDIA —

SPARKLING

OMAR KHAYYAM, INDIAN SPARKLING WINE 1987 Maharashira Hills	*Fruity, biscuity and mouthfilling; nice acid giving a pleasant zing on an aged taste.*	**£7.99**	CWS, MRS, FUL, AR, GRO, NRW, DBY	**B**

— ISRAEL —

DRY WHITE

YARDEN MUSCAT, GOLAN HEIGHTS WINERY Galilee 1990	*Concentrated raisiny nose; has depth and lusciousness to palate. Good fruit.*	**£4.99**	WBR, JFD, SEL, AG, SU, DBY	**B**

FORTIFIED

PARTOM, SCV/CARMEL 1983	*Heavy, cooked nose with lots of sweet fruit on the palate. Caramel and some toffee-orange.*	**£6.27**	AG	**B**

— LEBANON —

RED

CHATEAU MUSAR, SERGE HOCHAR 1987 Bekaa Valley	*Maturing, rich, plummy, spicey interesting wine.*	**£7.99**	SMF, G, THP, TBW, ABY, GRT	**B**

PERSONAL TASTING NOTES

SIGHT	
	Clear Bright Hazy Cloudy Colour
SMELL	
	Fresh Musty Floral Fruit Vegetal Animal Wood/Oak Others
TASTE	
	Weight Sweetness Dryness Acidity Fruit Vegetal Wood/Oak Balance
SUMMARY	
	Age Maturity Location Vintage

PERSONAL TASTING NOTES

SIGHT

Clear   Bright   Hazy   Cloudy   Colour

SMELL

Fresh   Musty   Floral   Fruit   Vegetal   Animal   Wood/Oak   Others

TASTE

Weight   Sweetness   Dryness   Acidity   Fruit   Vegetal   Wood/Oak   Balance

SUMMARY

Age   Maturity   Location   Vintage

PERSONAL TASTING NOTES

SIGHT

Clear Bright Hazy Cloudy Colour

SMELL

Fresh Musty Floral Fruit Vegetal Animal Wood/Oak Others

TASTE

Weight Sweetness Dryness Acidity Fruit Vegetal Wood/Oak Balance

SUMMARY

Age Maturity Location Vintage

PERSONAL TASTING NOTES

SIGHT	
	Clear Bright Hazy Cloudy Colour
SMELL	
	Fresh Musty Floral Fruit Vegetal Animal Wood/Oak Others
TASTE	
	Weight Sweetness Dryness Acidity Fruit Vegetal Wood/Oak Balance
SUMMARY	
	Age Maturity Location Vintage

PERSONAL TASTING NOTES

SIGHT	
	Clear Bright Hazy Cloudy Colour
SMELL	
	Fresh Musty Floral Fruit Vegetal Animal Wood/Oak Others
TASTE	
	Weight Sweetness Dryness Acidity Fruit Vegetal Wood/Oak Balance
SUMMARY	
	Age Maturity Location Vintage

PERSONAL TASTING NOTES

SIGHT

Clear Bright Hazy Cloudy Colour

SMELL

Fresh Musty Floral Fruit Vegetal Animal Wood/Oak Others

TASTE

Weight Sweetness Dryness Acidity Fruit Vegetal Wood/Oak Balance

SUMMARY

Age Maturity Location Vintage

PERSONAL TASTING NOTES

SIGHT	
	Clear Bright Hazy Cloudy Colour

SMELL	
	Fresh Musty Floral Fruit Vegetal Animal Wood/Oak Others

TASTE	
	Weight Sweetness Dryness Acidity Fruit Vegetal Wood/Oak Balance

SUMMARY	
	Age Maturity Location Vintage

PERSONAL TASTING NOTES

SIGHT	
	Clear Bright Hazy Cloudy Colour
SMELL	
	Fresh Musty Floral Fruit Vegetal Animal Wood/Oak Others
TASTE	
	Weight Sweetness Dryness Acidity Fruit Vegetal Wood/Oak Balance
SUMMARY	
	Age Maturity Location Vintage

PERSONAL TASTING NOTES

SIGHT	
	Clear Bright Hazy Cloudy Colour
SMELL	
	Fresh Musty Floral Fruit Vegetal Animal Wood/Oak Others
TASTE	
	Weight Sweetness Dryness Acidity Fruit Vegetal Wood/Oak Balance
SUMMARY	
	Age Maturity Location Vintage

PERSONAL TASTING NOTES

SIGHT	
	Clear Bright Hazy Cloudy Colour
SMELL	
	Fresh Musty Floral Fruit Vegetal Animal Wood/Oak Others
TASTE	
	Weight Sweetness Dryness Acidity Fruit Vegetal Wood/Oak Balance
SUMMARY	
	Age Maturity Location Vintage

Nagyrede Rouge, Szoloskert Co-operative 1993	£1.99	B
Cabernet Sauvignon/Merlot Country Wine, Vincom Burgas	£2.49	B
Squinzano, Mottura	£2.59	S
Leziria Tinto, Vega Co-operativa Almeirim	£2.69	G
Montepulciano d'Abruzzo, Cortenova 1992	£2.74	B
Asda Corbieres, Val d'Orbieu	£2.75	B
Oriachovitza Vintage Blend Reserve Merlot/Cabernet 1990	£2.75	B
Don Hugo Red, Bodegas Vitorianas	£2.79	B
Spar Cabernet Sauvignon & Cinsault Country Wine	£2.79	B
Asda St Chinian, Val d'Orbieu	£2.85	B
Safeway Young Vatted Merlot 1993	£2.85	B
Asda Merlot Vin de Pays d'Oc, Skalli	£2.89	B
Malt House Vintners Valpolicella, Sartori 1993	£2.89	B
Domaine Bouche Vin de Pays de Vaucluse 1990	£2.95	S
Merlot, Minosegi, Szaraz Voros Bor 1993	£2.95	B
St-Chinian, Jean d'Almon, RMDI 1992	£2.95	B
Cabernet Sauvignon/Merlot Reserve, Lovico Suhindol 1989	£2.99	B
Lovico Suhindol Reserve Merlot1990	£2.99	B
Morrisons Rioja Red, Bodegas Navajas 1992	£2.99	B
Sainsbury's do Campo Tinto, Peter Bright	£2.99	S
Safeway Romanian Special Reserve Pinot Noir 1989	£2.99	B
Sainsbury's Faugeres, Domaines Virginie	£2.99	B
Santara Conca de Barbera Dry Red, Hugh Ryman, 1993	£2.99	B
Somerfield Montereale Rosso, Calatrasi	£2.99	B
St Michael Valencia, Schenk 1991	£2.99	B
Vina del Castillo, Vinicola De Castilla 1993	£2.99	B
Waitrose Good Ordinary Claret, Ginestet	£2.99	B
Barbera del Piemonte San Orsola, Fratelli Martini 1993	£3.00	B
Val du Torgan, Tuchan	£3.00	B
Terras d'el Rei, Cooperativa Agricola de Reguengos 1992	£3.15	B
Somerfield Australian Dry Red, Penfolds	£3.19	B
Syrah Vin de Pays d'Oc, Maison Jean Jean 1991	£3.19	B
Pinotage, Matthew Clark	£3.21	B
Casa de la Vina Cencibel, Valdepenas 1992	£3.25	B
Casa de la Vina Valdepenas Cencibel 1993	£3.25	B
Co-Op Bairrada Tinto, Sogrape 1989	£3.29	B
Sliven Bulgarian Cabernet Sauvignon, Vini Sliven 1989	£3.29	B
St. Michael Duboeuf Selection Rouge, Georges Duboef	£3.29	B
Vin de Pays des Cevennes, Vin de Pays de l'Herault	£3.29	B
Vina Albali Valdepenas Cabernet Sauvignon 1991	£3.29	B
Borba, Adega Co-op de Borba 1991	£3.35	S
Co-Op Costieres de Nimes, RMDI	£3.35	B
Safeway Oak-Aged Valdepenas, Felix Solis 1987	£3.39	S
Rioja Vega Crianza, Bodegas Muerza 1989	£3.46	B

Albor Rioja, Campo Viejo 1992	£3.49	B
Asda Chilean Cabernet Merlot, Vinicola Lastaguas 1993	£3.49	S
Bairrada, Luis Pato 1990	£3.49	B
Chateau de Belesta Cotes du Roussillon Villages 1992	£3.49	S
Chateau La Foret, Barton & Guestier 1993	£3.49	S
Domaine du Soleil Vegetarian Syrah, Vin de Pays de l'Aude 1993	£3.49	B
Lazio Merlot/Sangiovese, Casale del Giglio 1993	£3.49	B
Montepulciano d'Abruzzo, Cantina Tollo 1992	£3.49	B
Navajas Rioja Blanco Sin Crianza 1992	£3.49	B
Rioja Berberana Tempranillo Crianza 1990	£3.49	S
Ryans Creek Shiraz/Cabernet, Yalumba	£3.49	B
Spar Fitou, Val d'Orbieu	£3.49	B
St Michael Domaine Roche Blanche, Vin de Pays d'Oc	£3.49	B
St Michael Fitou, Caves du Mont Tauch 1991	£3.49	B
Tocornal Cabernet Sauvignon Merlot, Vina Tocornal 1993	£3.49	S
Domaine des Salices Merlot, Vin de Pays d'Oc 1993	£3.50	B
Syrah Rouge, Vin de Pays d'Oc, Georges Duboeuf 1993	£3.50	B
Vinadrian Rioja Tinto, Bodegas Gurpegui 1993	£3.50	B
Bestvin Fitou, Les Chais Beaucairois	£3.59	B
Copertino Cantine Sociale Copertino Puglia 1990	£3.59	B
Geminian Cabernet Sauvignon, Vin de Pays d'Oc 1993	£3.59	B
Sainsbury's Copertino Riserva, Cantina Sociale 1991	£3.59	B
Malt House Vintners Rioja Tinto, Bodegas Fuentoro 1992	£3.65	B
Asda South Australian Shiraz Angoves 1991	£3.69	B
Ca'Vit Merlot del Trentino, I Mastri Vernacoli 1991	£3.69	B
Domaine Grange du Pin, Jean Jean 1993	£3.69	B
Fitou Terroir de Tuchan, Tuchan 1991	£3.69	B
Rioja Laturce Tinto, Bodegas Laturce 1992	£3.69	B
Rocca Suena, Amarone Recioto della Valpolicella 1986	£3.69	B
Cotes Du Roussillon Rouge, Arnaud de Villeneuve 1990	£3.75	B
Minervois Abbaye de Tholomies, Jeanjean 1991	£3.75	B
Berloup Prestige St-Chinian, Coop de Berlou 1992	£3.79	B
Co-Op Rioja Tinto, Bodegas Almenar 1990	£3.79	B
Caliboro Cabernet Sauvignon, Vina Segu-Olle 1993	£3.79	S
Cape Selection Pinotage, Vinimark Trading 1993	£3.79	B
Monte Velho, Finagra 1992	£3.79	B
Somerfield Rioja Tinto Almenar 1990	£3.79	B
Winzerhaus Blauer Zweigelt, Niederosterreichischer 1993	£3.85	B
Domaine de Thelin Vin de Pays D'Oc Syrah 1991	£3.90	B
Cotes du Rhone, Chateau St Maurice, Valat 1991	£3.95	B
Rioja Orla Dorada, Faustino Rivero Ulecia 1993	£3.98	B
Buzet, Domaine de la Croix, Tesco Les Domaines 1989	£3.99	B
Canepa Unoaked Cabernet Sauvignon 1993	£3.99	B
Cellier Des Dauphins Cotes du Rhone Prestige Rouge 1992	£3.99	B

Chateau Pesquie, Coteaux des Valerianes, 1993	£3.99	B
Ciro Rosso Classico, Librandi 1990	£3.99	B
Cismeira Reserva, Quinta da Cismeira 1990	£3.99	B
Cotes Du Roussillon Rouge, Arnaud de Villeneuve 1993	£3.99	S
Domaine des Henrys, Vin de Pays des Cotes de Thongue 1993	£3.99	B
Domaine Fouletiere, Coteaux du Languedoc 1991	£3.99	B
Dry Plains Shiraz Cabernet, Berri Estates 1993	£3.99	B
Figaro Rouge, Vin de Pays de l'Herault 1993	£3.99	B
Foral Douro Reserva, Caves Alianca 1991	£3.99	S
Fortant de France Merlot, Skalli 1993	£3.99	S
Gutturnio Rossi, Colli Piacentini, Cantine 4 Valli	£3.99	B
Kapfonstein Pinotage 1993	£3.99	S
Landskroon Pinotage 1991	£3.99	B
Lovico Suhindol Reserve Merlot 1990	£3.99	B
Monastere de Trignan, Coteaux du Languedoc 1992	£3.99	S
Navajas Rioja Sin Crianza 1992	£3.99	S
Nemea, Boutari 1991	£3.99	B
Peter Lehmann Barossa Valley Grenache 1989	£3.99	B
Phillippe De Baudin Cabernet Sauvignon 1992	£3.99	B
Quinta Folgorosa Red, Carvalho Ribeiro & Ferreira 1989	£3.99	B
Rioja Berberana Oak-Aged Tempranillo 1992	£3.99	G
Simonsvlei Classique Reserve 1993	£3.99	B
Simonsvlei Pinotage 1993	£3.99	B
Solana Valdepenas Cencibel, Casa de la Vina 1993	£3.99	G
Somerfield Australian Cabernet Sauvignon, Penfolds	£3.99	B
St Michael Domaine Mont Rose Syrah-Cabernet	£3.99	B
Teroldego Rotaliano i Mesi, Casa Girelli 1991	£3.99	B
Tesco Australian Mataro, Kingston Estate	£3.99	B
Tesco Californian Zinfandel, Stratford Winery	£3.99	B
Tesco Chianti Classico, Ampelos, San Casciano 1991	£3.99	S
Tesco International Winemaker Cabernet Sauvignon Merlot	£3.99	B
Vina Carmen Cabernet Sauvignon 1993	£3.99	S
Bairrada, Carvalho Ribeiro & Ferreira 1988	£4.00	B
Barbera del Piemonte, Giordano 1992	£4.00	B
Chianti Rufina, Villa di Vetrice 1991	£4.00	B
Rosso Conero, Umani Ronchi 1992	£4.00	B
Rioja Santa Daria Tinto, Cooperativa Vinicola de Cenicero 1992	£4.08	B
Macon Rouge Superieur Les Truffieres, Honore Lavigne 1992	£4.15	B
Lambrusco Grasparossa di Modena Secco 1993	£4.19	B
Capeview Merlot, K Milne 1993	£4.29	B
Domaine des Combelles, Minervois 1991	£4.29	G
Cricket Hill Pinotage 1991	£4.39	B
Hardy's Nottage Hill Cabernet Sauvignon 1992	£4.39	B
McWilliams Hanwood Cabernet Sauvignon 1991	£4.39	B
Penfolds Bin 35 Shiraz/Cabernet 1992	£4.39	B

Cuvee Du Cepage Cabernet Sauvignon, Vin de pays d'Oc 1992	£4.40	G
Phillippe De Baudin Merlot, Vin de Pays d'Oc 1992	£4.45	B
Somerfield Oak-Aged Claret, Louis Eschenauer 1990	£4.45	B
Chivite Reserva, Chivite 1989	£4.49	B
Cono Sur Pinot Noir 1993	£4.49	B
Langunilla Rioja Crianza, Bodegas Lagunilla 1988	£4.49	B
Portal Del Alto Merlot 1993	£4.49	B
Ryecroft Flame Tree Cabernet Shiraz 1993	£4.49	S
Sainsbury's Chianti Classico, Cecchi 1991	£4.49	B
Teroldego Rotaliano, Ca'Vit 1992	£4.49	S
Chateau de Caraguilhes Corbieres 1990	£4.50	B
Palacio de Grajal, Ribeiro del Duero 1992	£4.50	B
Quinta de la Rosa, Douro 1992	£4.50	S
Minervois Domaine Sainte Eulalie, M Blanc 1991	£4.55	B
Vacqueyras, Vieux Clocher, Arnoux et Fils 1990	£4.59	S
Vacqueyras, Vieux Clocher, Arnoux et Fils 1991	£4.59	G
Macon Superior les Epillets, Cave de Lugny 1993	£4.65	B
Malt House Vintners Cortesia Rioja Reserva 1988	£4.65	B
Rioja Cosme Palacio y Hermanus, Bodegas Palacio 1990	£4.65	S
Ciro Rosso Classico, Librandi 1992	£4.67	B
Bay View Pinotage, Du Preel & Laubser 1991	£4.69	S
Cabernet Merlot, Carta Vieja 1992	£4.69	B
Agramont Tinto, Bodegas Principe de Viana SA 1990	£4.75	B
Penfolds Bin 2 Shiraz-Mourvedre 1992	£4.75	B
Penfolds Rowlands Brook Shiraz 1991	£4.75	B
Santa Rita Merlot Reserva 1992	£4.75	B
Waitrose Special Reserve Claret, Ginestet 1990	£4.75	B
Cabernet Sauvignon, Jose Canepa 1992	£4.79	S
Corbieres Chateau Grand Moulin 1991	£4.79	B
Duque de Viseu, Sogrape 1991	£4.79	B
Minervois, Chateau de Violet Cuvee Clovis 1992	£4.79	B
Rioja Crianza, Faustino Rivero Ulecia 1990	£4.79	B
Vina Undurraga Cabernet Sauvignon Reserva 1990	£4.79	B
Chateau Les Ollieux, Surbezy-Cartier 1991	£4.80	B
Chianti Classico, Conti Serristori 1990	£4.85	S
Crozes-Hermitage Domaine Barret 1992	£4.90	S
Chais Baumiere Cabernet Sauvignon, Vin de Pays d'Oc 1992	£4.95	B
Fiori d'Inverno, Ca'Vit 1992	£4.95	B
Marques de Caceres Rioja Crianza Tinto, Union Viti-Vinicola 1989	£4.95	B
Marques de Caceres Rioja Crianza Tinto, Union Viti-Vinicola 1990	£4.95	B
Rosemount Cabernet Sauvignon/Shiraz 1993	£4.95	G
Vacqueyras Cuvee Du Marquis de Fonseguille 1991	£4.95	B
Backsberg Cabernet Sauvignon 1991	£4.99	B
Campillo Rioja Crianza, Bodegas Campillo 1988	£4.99	B

Carignano Del Sulcis, C S Santadi 1991	£4.99	B
Chais Baumiere Cuvee Proprietaire, Vin de Pays d'Oc 1990	£4.99	B
Chateau les Pins, Cotes de Roussillon Villages 1991	£4.99	B
Chateau Meaume, Bordeaux Superieur, Alan Johnson-Hill 1990	£4.99	B
Chateau Mingot, Cotes de Castillon, Yvon Mau 1990	£4.99	B
Chateau Saint Robert, Graves, Credit Foncier 1988	£4.99	B
Chianti Rufina Riserva, Villa di Vetrice 1990	£4.99	B
Collection Anniversaire, Special Reserve Claret, Yvon Mau 1990	£4.99	B
Conde de Valdemar Rioja Crianza, Martinez Bujanda 1988	£4.99	B
Corbieres, Chateau de Luc, Eleve en Futs de Chene 1991	£4.99	B
Corbieres, Chateau de Lastours, Cuvee Simones Descamps 1991	£4.99	B
Cotes du Rhone Reserve La Vieille Ferme, J P & F Perrin 1992	£4.99	S
Cotes du Rhone, Vignoble de la Jasse, Daniel Combe 1992	£4.99	B
Deakin Estate Cabernet Sauvignon, Katnook 1992	£4.99	B
Domaine de la Baume, Vin de Pays d'Oc, Chais Baumiere 1991	£4.99	S
Douro, Bright Brothers 1992	£4.99	S
Franciacorta Rosso Villa Padule, Villa Padule 1992	£4.99	B
Lindeman's Bin 50 Shiraz 1992	£4.99	B
Mildara Church Hill Shiraz/Cabernet 1991	£4.99	B
Minervois, Carignanissime de Centeilles, Boyer-Domergue 1992	£4.99	S
Montana Cabernet Sauvignon 1991	£4.99	B
Montenuevo Oak-aged Cabernet Sauvignon 1991	£4.99	B
Montepulciano d'Abruzzo, Conte di Bordino 1990	£4.99	B
Montes Cabernet Merlot Special Cuvee, Discover Wines 1992	£4.99	B
Notarpanaro Rosso Del Salento, AZ AG Taurino 1985	£4.99	B
Parrot's Hill Shiraz, BRL Hardy Wine Co/Valley Growers 1992	£4.99	B
Pewsey Vale Vineyard Cabernet Sauvignon, S Smith & Son 1990	£4.99	B
Roo's Leap Shiraz Cabernet, Mildara 1992	£4.99	S
Rosemount Shiraz/Cabernet Sauvignon 1993	£4.99	B
Rouge Homme Shiraz/Cabernet 1991	£4.99	G
Rowan Brook Cabernet Sauvignon Reserva, Canepa 1991	£4.99	S
Salice Salentino, Candido 1989	£4.99	B
Santa Rita Cabernet Sauvignon Reserva 1990	£4.99	B
Santa Rita Reserva Cabernet Sauvignon 1989	£4.99	B
St Michael Beaujolais Villages, Georges Duboeuf 1992	£4.99	B
St-Joseph La Pilatte, Michel Mourier 1991	£4.99	B
St. Michael McLaren Vale Shiraz, Andrew Garrett 1992	£4.99	B
St Michael Merlot/Cabernet Sauvignon 1993	£4.99	B
Tesco Vina Maria Rioja Reserva, Bodegas Arisabel 1987	£4.99	S
Tinto Velho, J M da Fonseca 1987	£4.99	S
Tollana Black Cabernet Sauvignon, Penfolds 1991	£4.99	B
Tollana Black Shiraz, Penfolds 1991	£4.99	S

Kwik-Save Morio Muskat, St. Ursula 1993	£2.29	B
Bereich Nierstein, St Gertrudis-Kellerei GmbH 1992	£2.39	B
Rosenview Early Release White Vinfruco 1994	£2.49	B
Castillo Imperial Blanco, Bodegas Y Bebidas	£2.49	S
Lazarillo, La Mancha Blanco, Cooperative Jesus del Perdon 1993	£2.75	B
St Ursula Morio Muscat QbA 1993	£2.79	B
Muscat, Vin de Pays Collines de la Maure, Hugh Ryman 1993	£2.99	B
River Duna Sauvignon Blanc, Neszmely 1993	£2.99	B
Sainsbury's do Campo Branco, Peter Bright for J Sainsbury	£2.99	B
Santara Dry White, Conca de Barbera, Hugh Ryman 1993	£2.99	S
Sauvignon Blanc, Hincesti 1993	£2.99	B
St Michael Chardonnay Del Veneto, Girelli	£2.99	B
Tesco Moscatel De Valencia, Gandia	£2.99	B
Vin du Pays Du Gers Blanc 1993, Producteurs Plaimont 1993	£2.99	B
Safeway Moscatel de Valencia, Gandia	£3.19	B
Sainsbury Bianco di Custoza, Geoff Merrill / GIV 1993	£3.19	B
Duc De Foix Blanco Seco Joven, Covides Ltda 1993	£3.25	B
Somerfield Moscatel de Valencia, Gandia	£3.25	B
Casal da Barca, Bodegas Alanis 1993	£3.29	S
Rueda Sauvignon Blanc, Hermanos Lurton 1993	£3.29	B
Sainsbury's Pinot Grigio Atesino, GIV, 1993	£3.29	B
St Michael Italian Chardonay, Fratelli Martini 1993	£3.29	S
Tesco Domaine Saint Alain, Vin de Pays de Cotes de 1993	£3.29	B
Bellefontaine Terret, Vin de Pays des Cotes de Thau 1993	£3.30	B
Co-Op Spatlese Rheinpfalz, GWG Rietburg 1990	£3.49	B
Domaine Brial Muscat de Rivesaltes, Vignerons de Baixas 1993	£3.49	B
Domaine Du Haut Rauly Monbazillac 1990	£3.49	S
Moscatel De Valencia, Gandia	£3.49	B
Retsina of Attica, D Kourtakis SA	£3.49	B
Tollana Dry White, Penfolds 1993	£3.49	B
Winelands Chenin Blanc, Vinfruco 1993	£3.49	B
Sainsbury's Chardonnay delle Treí Venezie, Geoff Merrill	£3.59	B
Chateau Les Vieilles Souches Bordeaux Blanc, Jean Guillot 1993	£3.60	B
Domaine du Biau, Vin de Pays des Cotes de Gasgogne 1993	£3.69	B
Domaine le Puts, Vin de Pays des Cotes de Gascogne 1993	£3.69	S
Le Piat D'Or Dry White, Piat Pere et Fils	£3.69	S
Le Monferinne Chardonnay, Araldica 1993	£3.75	B
Torrontes, La Agricola 1994	£3.75	B
Ca'Madunina Pinot Grigio Friuli, Bidoli / Gaetana 1993	£3.79	B
Chardonnay Teresa Rizzi, Gruppo Italiano Vini 1993	£3.79	B
St Ursula Galerie, Pinot Blanc Dry 1993	£3.79	B
Tesco Swartland Sauvignon Blanc, Swartland Co-op 1993	£3.79	B
Dulong Chardonnay, Vin de Pays d'Oc 1993	£3.80	B
Resplandy Viognier, Vin de Pays d'Oc 1993	£3.90	B

Marquis DíAlban Bordeaux Blanc, Dulong 1993	£3.95	B
Santa Sara, Fernao Pires, JP Vinhos 1993	£3.95	B
Sainsbury's Italian Grechetto, Geoff Merrill/GIV 1993	£3.95	B
Sauvignon Blanc Vino da Tavola, Geoff Merrill/GIV 1993	£3.95	B
Vendange Blanc,Vin de Pays des Cotes Catalanes 1993	£3.95	S
Angelico, Bordeaux Blanc, Calvet 1993	£3.99	S
Chardonnay Del Salento, Cantele 1993	£3.99	B
Chardonnay del Salento, Cantele/K Milne 1993	£3.99	B
Chateau Les Vieilles Souches Bordeaux Sauvignon 1992	£3.99	B
Domaine de la Roche, Cotes de Duras, Hugh Ryman 1993	£3.99	B
Domaine de la Tuilerie Chardonnay, Vins de Pays d'Oc 1993	£3.99	B
Domaine de Petitot, Cotes de Duras, Hugh Ryman 1993	£3.99	B
Domaine des Salices Sauvignon Vin de Pays díOc 1993	£3.99	B
Fruit de Vi, Vallformosa	£3.99	B
La Serre Sauvignon Blanc, Vin de Pays d'Oc 1993	£3.99	G
Nagyrede Sauvignon Blanc, Kym Milne/Nagyrede 1993	£3.99	B
Penfolds Bin 21 Semillon-Chardonnay 1993	£3.99	B
Peter Lehmann Barossa Valley Dry White 1993	£3.99	B
Safeway Rheinpfalz Auslese, St. Ursula 1992	£3.99	B
Sainsbury's Frascati Secco Superiore, Geoff Merrill 1993	£3.99	B
Santa Rita 120 Sauvignon Blanc 1994	£3.99	B
Spar Viognier Cuxac, Val d'Orbieu	£3.99	B
St Michael Chardonnay del Piemonte Vino da Tavola, 1993	£3.99	S
St Michael Craighall Chardonnay/Sauvignon 1993	£3.99	B
St Michael Domaine Mandeville Chardonnay 1993	£3.99	B
Westhofener Bergkloster Auslese, St. Ursula 1992	£3.99	B
Cafayate Torrontes, Arnaldo Etchart SA 1993	£4.00	S
Chardonnay del Piemonte, Araldica 1993	£4.00	B
Fortant de France Sauvignon Blanc, Skalli 1993	£4.00	B
Villa Montes Sauvignon Blanc, Discover Wines 1994	£4.00	B
Hermanos Lurton Rueda Sauvignon, J & F Lurton 1993	£4.10	S
Domaine d'Augeron, Vin de Pays de Terroirs Landais Blanc, Bubola 1992	£4.24	B
La Serre Chardonnay, Vin de Pays d'Oc 1993	£4.25	B
Shawsgate Vineyard Muller Thurgau/Seyval Blanc 1992	£4.25	B
Solana Blanco, Bodegas Alanis / Don Lewis 1993	£4.25	B
Chardonnay Sur Lie, Danie de Wet 1993	£4.29	B
Domaine De Laballe, Vin De Pays De Terroirs Landais 1993	£4.29	B
Cuvee des Fleurs, Jacques Lurton 1992	£4.33	B
Bel Arbors Chardonnay, Fetzer Vineyards 1992	£4.36	B
Sauternes Baron de Fontenilles, Ginestet	£4.39	B
Old Triangle Riesling, S Smith & Son 1993	£4.40	B
Angove's Chardonnay 1993	£4.49	B
Canepa Chardonnay 1993	£4.49	S
Dunnewood Chardonnay 1992	£4.49	B

Montenovo Blanco, Valdeorras Bodegas Senorio SAT 1992	£4.49	S
Tesco Golden Harvest, Zimmermann Graeff 1992	£4.49	B
Bacchus, East Sutton Vine Garden, Bacchus 1992	£4.50	B
Chardonnay Le Veritiere, Gruppo Italiano Vini 1993	£4.50	B
Chardonnay 'Oak Cask' Reserve, Trapiche 1993	£4.50	B
David Wynn, Dry White 1992	£4.50	S
Sauvignon de Touraine, Domaine Gibault 1993	£4.50	B
Mauzac Vin de Pays de l'Aude, La Batteuse, Bernard Delmas 1993	£4.55	S
Scharzhofberger Riesling Kabinett, Rudolf Muller 1990	£4.59	B
Portal Del Alto Chardonnay 1993	£4.65	B
Wyken Bacchus, Wyken Vineyards 1991	£4.65	B
Commandaria St John, Keo	£4.69	B
Jacob's Creek Chardonnay, Orlando Wines 1993	£4.69	B
Muscadet de Sevre et Maine Sur Lie, Domaine 1993	£4.75	B
Ozidoc Chardonnay, Vins de Pays d'Oc, Domaine Virginie 1993	£4.75	B
Ozidoc Sauvignon, Domaine Virginie 1993	£4.75	B
Quelltaler Estate Riesling 1993	£4.75	B
Sainsbury's Chardonnay, Vino Da Tavola, Geoff Merrill/GIV 1993	£4.75	B
Houghton Swan Valley Dry White 1991	£4.79	B
Phillippe De Baudin Sauvignon Blanc 1993	£4.80	S
Chais Baumiere Sauvignon Blanc Vin de Pays d'Oc 1993	£4.95	S
Stellenzicht Sauvignon Blanc 1993	£4.95	B
Bridgewater Mill Riesling 1993	£4.99	B
Caliterra Estate Casablanca Chardonnay 1993	£4.99	B
Chardonnay Blanc de Blanc, Caves Desmoines	£4.99	B
Chardonnay, Cartlidge & Browne	£4.99	B
Chardonnay Vin de Pays d'Oc, Hugh Ryman 1993	£4.99	S
Chateau Bonnet, Entre-deux-Mers, A Lurton 1992	£4.99	B
Chateau de la Jaubertie Bergerac Sec, Henry Ryman 1993	£4.99	B
Chateau de la Jaubertie Bergerac Blanc, Hugh Ryman 1992	£4.99	B
Chateau Grand Moulin, Corbieres Blanc, J N Bousquet 1992	£4.99	B
Chateau Grand Moulin, Corbieres Blanc 1993	£4.99	B
Cooks Discovery Sauvignon Blanc, Cooks NZ Wines 1993	£4.99	B
Cotes de Duras Sauvignon Vieilles Vignes, Berticot 1993	£4.99	B
Danie de Wet Grey Label Chardonnay 1993	£4.99	S
Domaine De Rivoyre Chardonnay, Vin De Pays d'Oc 1992	£4.99	B
Domaine 'Virginie' Chardonnay, Vin de Pays d'Oc 1992	£4.99	B
Heritage Fume, Harvest Wine Group 1993	£4.99	B
Domaine du Petit Paris, Bergerac Sec, Jean Geneste 1993	£4.99	B
Graves Blanc, Collection Anniversaire, Yvon Mau 1993	£4.99	B
Hardy's Moondah Brook Estate Chenin Blanc 1993	£4.99	B
James Herrick Chardonnay, Vin de Pays d'Oc 1993	£4.99	B
Lindeman's Bin 65 Chardonnay 1993	£4.99	B
Marienberg Cottage Classic, Marienberg Wines 1993	£4.99	B

Montes Chardonnay, Cuvee Ryman/Montes 1993	£4.99	B
Muscadet de Sevre et Maine Sur Lie, Domaine des Deux-Rives 1992	£4.99	B
Nutbourne Vineyard, Huxelrebe 1992	£4.99	B
Orlando RF Chardonnay 1992	£4.99	S
Penfolds Koonunga Hill Chardonnay 1993	£4.99	B
Penfolds South Australian Semillon-Chardonnay 1993	£4.99	S
Pinot Grigio, Torre Di Luna, Gaierhof 1993	£4.99	B
Poachers Blend, White, St Hallett 1993	£4.99	B
Red Cliffs Estate Chardonnay 1993	£4.99	B
Santa Carolina Chardonnay 1993	£4.99	B
Sauvignon Blanc, Vin de Pays du Jardin de la Franc 1993	£4.99	B
Scheurebe Dienheimer Tafelstein Kabinett 1993	£4.99	B
Simon Hackett McLaren Vale Semillon 1993	£4.99	S
Somerfield White Burgundy, Georges Desire 1992	£4.99	G
Vouvray Demi-Sec, Domaine De La Mabilliere 1992	£4.99	B
White Burgundy, M. Michelet & Fils 1992	£4.99	B
White Clare, Wakefield Wines 1991	£4.99	B
Wiltinger Klosterberg Riesling Kabinett, Van Volxem 1989	£4.99	S
Yarden Muscat, Golan Heights Winery Galilee 1990	£4.99	B

Morrisons Asti Spumante, Gianni, IVI SpA	£4.59	S
Somerfield Cava, Conde de Caralt	£4.99	B
Killawarra Brut, Penfolds	£5.00	B
Duc de Foix Cava Brut, Covides	£5.25	B
Angas Brut Non-Vintage Cuvee Rose, Yalumba	£5.90	B
Comtesse de Die Clairette de Die Tradition 1992	£5.95	B
Asti Spumante, Araldica	£5.99	B
Segura Viudas Cava Brut Reserva	£5.99	B
Le Grand Pavillon, Boschendal	£6.49	B
Saumur, Vignerons de Saumur	£6.49	B
Seppelt Pinot Rose Cuvee Brut	£7.00	B
Anna de Condorniu, Codorniu SA 1989	£7.39	B
Parxet Chardonnay Cava 1990	£7.93	B
Krone Borealis Brut, Twee Jonge Gezellen 1988	£7.95	B
Boschendal Brut 1990	£7.99	S
Cuvee Prestige Pinot Noir Chardonnay, Yalumba	£7.99	S
David Wynn Brut, Adam Wynn	£7.99	B
Omar Khayyam, Indian Sparkling Wine 1987	£7.99	B
Seaview Pinot Noir-Chardonnay, Penfolds 1990	£7.99	B
Torre del Gall, Gran Reserva Brut, Cava Chandon 1990	£7.99	B
Yaldara Vintage Brut Pinot Noir Chardonnay 1990	£7.99	B
Yalumba Cuvee Prestige Cabernet Sauvignon	£7.99	S
Pongracz, Bergkelder	£8.10	S
Mick Morris Rutherglen Sparkling Shiraz Durif	£8.50	B
Mayerling Cremant d'Alsace, Cave Vinicole de Turckheim	£8.99	B
Nicole D'Auriny Reserve, Union Auboise	£8.99	B
Seppelt Sparkling Shiraz 1990	£8.99	B
Seppelt Sparkling Shiraz 1991	£9.00	B
Carr Taylor NV Sparkling Wine	£9.50	B
Codorniu Napa Pinot Noir/Chardonnay	£9.89	B
Champagne Paul D'Hurville Brut, Champagne de Hours	£9.99	S
Champagne St Honore, Duval-Leroy	£9.99	B
Deutz Marlborough Cuvee, Montana	£9.99	B
Kaapse Vonkel Brut, Simonsig Estates 1991	£9.99	B
Yalumba D 1991	£9.99	B

Every wine in this guide has at least one stockist code beside its entry, identifying where the wine can be sourced. The list below translates the code into the company name, with a telephone number for you to make enquiries direct.

Where the stockists are stated as WIDELY AVAILABLE there are more than 10 outlets which stock this wine. In these cases you should be able to find your wine in most good wine retailers. At the time of going to press all wines were in stock. However, some are in limited supply and may not be available now.

Every effort has been made to list all the stockists with their relevant wines. Should you encounter any problems with finding a wine listed in this guide, then please write to: The International Wine Challenge, Publishing House, 652 Victoria Road, South Ruislip, Middlesex, HA4 0SX.

Code	Name	Phone
A	Asda Stores Ltd	0532 435435
AB	Augustus Barnett Ltd	0283 512550
ABY	Anthony Byrne Fine Wines Ltd	0487 814555
ACH	Andrew Chapman Fine Wines	0235 531452
AD	Adgestone Vineyard	0983 402503
ADN	Adnams Wine Merchants	0502 724222
AFI	Alfie Fiandaca Ltd	081 951 1603
AG	Amazing Grapes	081 202 2631
AK	Arriba Kettle & Co	0386 833024
ALL	Alliance Wine Co Ltd	0505 613215
ALV	A L Vose & Co Ltd	05395 33328
AMA	Amathus	081 886 3787
AMD	Andrew Mead Wines	0547 6268
AMP	P W Amps	0832 273502
AMW	Amey's Wines	0787 77144
AR	Arthur Rackham	0932 351585
ASH	Ashley Scott	0244 520655
AUC	Australian Wine Centre	071 930 1309
AUJ	Aujoux (UK)	08865 555
AUL	Auldman Stewart	081 871 5217
AUS	Australian Wineries	03722 74065
AV	Averys of Bristol	0272 214141
AVA	Ava Wines	0247 465490
AWC	Anthony Wine Cellars	071 722 8576
AWV	Andrew Weir Vintners	0582 35353
A&A	A & A Wines	0483 274666
A&N	Army & Navy Store	071 8341234
B	Benedicts	0983 529596
BAB	Bablake Wines	0203 228272
BAK	Barkham Manor Vineyard	0825 722103
BAL	Ballantynes of Cowbridge	0446 773044
BAR	Barwell & Jones	0473 232322
BBR	Berry Bros & Rudd Ltd	071 396 9600
BC	Booker Cash & Carry	0933 440404
BEC	Beaconsfield Wine Cellars	0494 675545
BEF	Beaminster Fine Wines	0308 862350
BEL	Bentalls of Kingston	081 546 1001
BEN	Bennetts Wine & Spirits Merchants	0386 840392
BES	Bestway Cash & Carry	081 453 1234
BFF	Buffery & Son	0451 30667
BFI	Bedford Fine Wines Ltd	0234 721153
BFV	Bowland Forest Vintners	0200 8640
BGC	Borg Castel	0254 852128
BGV	Berwick Glebe Vineyard	0622 850637
BH	B H Wines	0228 576711

BI	Bibendum Wine Ltd	071 722 5577
BIN	Bin 89 Wine Warehouse	
		0742 755889
BIW	Bright Ideas on Wine	0438 816556
BKT	Bucktrout & Co. Ltd	0481 24444
BKW	Berkeley Wines	0925 444555
BLS	Balls Brothers Ltd	071 739 6466
BLW	Blayneys—Cellar 5	091 548 3083
BN	Bottlenecks	081 520 2737
BN	Bin Ends	0709 367771
BNK	The Bottleneck	0843 861095
BOD	Bodegas Direct	0243 773474
BOO	Booths of Stockport	061 432 3309
BOS	Boschendal Estate Wines	
		0491 577707
BOY	Batleys of Yorkshire	0924 291522
BSC	Ben Shaw's Wine Cellar	0484 516624
BSE	The Barrel Selection Agencies	
		0383 872238
BTH	Booths	0772 251701
BU	Bottoms Up	0707 328244
BUD	Budgens	081 422 3422
BUM	Bumblebee Wholefoods	071 607 1936
BUT	The Butlers Wine Cellar	0273 698724
BV	Bookers Vineyard,	04482 575
BVL	David Burns Vintners Ltd	
		0202 823411
BWC	Berkmann Wine Cellars Ltd/Le Nez Rouge	071 609 4711
BWI	Bute Wines	0700 502730
BWL	Berkeley Wines Ltd	081 683 0494
BWS	The Barnes Wine Shop	081 878 8643
BYV	Byron Vintners	0602 704682
B&B	Bottle & Basket	081 341 7018
CAC	Cachet Wines	0904 690090
CAG	Castang Wine Shippers	0984 40438
CAP	Cape Province Wines	0784 451860
CAR	C A Rookes Wine Merchants	
		0789 297777
CAV	Cavendish House	0242 521300
CAX	Vina santa carolina	0794 516102
CC	Chiswick Cellar	081 994 7989
CD	Camisa Delicatessen	071 437 7610
CDE	Cote D'Or Wines	081 998 0144
CDM	Caves de la Madeleine	071 736 6145
CEB	Croque en Bouche	0684 565612
CEL	Cellar 5 (also Vaux Breweries) Ltd	
		0925 444555
CEN	Centurion Vintners	0453 763223
CEW	Cape Estate Wines Ltd	081 455 9895
CFT	Clifton Cellars	0272 730287
CGW	The Cote Green Wine Company	
		061 426 0155
CHF	Chippendale Fine Wines	0943 850633
CHH	Charles Hennings	0798 872485
CHL	Chateau Lascombes	071 790 1860
CJ	Christopher James & Co.	
		0392 221519
CLP	Clapham Cellars	071 978 5601
CLS	Clissold Wines	071 254 5269
CLW	Classic Wines	081 500 7614
CNL	Connolly's (Wine Merchants) Ltd	
		021 236 9269
COE	Coe of Ilford Ltd	081 551 4966
COK	Corkscrew Wines	0228 43033
COM	Compagnie du Vin	0334 84376
CPW	Christopher Piper Wines Ltd	
		0404 814139
CRG	Cargo Club	081 9469111
CRL	The Wine Centre/Charles Steevenson Wines	0822 615985
CSW	Chislehurst Wines	081 467 4340
CT	Charles Taylor Wines Ltd	0372 728330
CTH	Charterhouse Wine Co	0775 88680
CTL	Continental Wine & Food Ltd	
		0484 538333
CVF	Craven Fine Wines	0905 20215
CVR	The Celtic Vintner Limited	
		0792 206661
CVW	Chiltern Valley Wines	049163 330
CVY	Chanctonbury Vineyard	0903 892721
CWI	(Pigs n' Piglets)	0558 650671
CWL	Charles Wells Ltd	0234 27270
CWM	Cornwall Wine Merchants Ltd	
		0209 715765
CWN	Chasseur Wines	07982 5150
CWS	The Co-operative Wholesale Society	
		0618 34π1 212

CWW	Classic Wine Warehouses Ltd	0244 390 444
C&A	Chennell & Armstrong Ltd	0904 647991
C&B	Corney & Barrow Ltd	071 251 4051
C&H	Cairns & Hickey	0532 459501
D	Davisons Wine Merchants	081 681 3222
DBP	Davis Browning & Partners Ltd	071 408 1438
DBS	Denbies Wine Estate	0306 876616
DBW	David Baker Wines	0656 650732
DBY	D Byrne & Co	0200 23152
DD	Domaine Direct	071 837 1142
DEL	Delicatessen Shop NW3	071 435 7315
DID	Domenico's Italian Deli	0702 463741
DIO	Dionysus	081 874 2739
DIR	Direct Wine Shipments	0232 238700
DN	Deinhard	071 261 1111
DUW	Duncairn Wine Stores	0232 238700
DVC	De Ville & Co	081 543 6677
DVI	Dartmouth Vintners	0803 832602
DVY	Davy & Co Ltd	071 407 9670
DWS	Direct Wine Suppliers	07072 65532
D'A	D'Arcys	0412 264309
EBA	Ben Ellis & Associates Ltd	0737 842160
ECA	Edward Cavendish & Sons Ltd	0794 516102
ECK	Eckington Wines	0246 433213
EE	Eaton Elliot Wine Merchant	0625 582354
EGL	Eagle Wines	
ELV	El Vino	071 353 5384
EM	Ebury Mathiot Wines	071 708 0088
EMV	East Mersea Vineyard	0780 56886
ENO	Enotria Wines Ltd	081 961 4411
EOO	Everton's of Ombersley Ltd	0533 542702
EOR	Ellis of Richmond	081 943 4033
EP	Eldridge Pope & Co plc	0305 251251
ES	Edward Sheldon	0608 661409

ESG	East Sutton Vine Garden	0622 843191
ET	Elliot & Tatham (Fine Wines)	0451 870555
ETV	Eton Vintners	0753 831595
EUR	Europa Stores Ltd	081 845 1255
EVI	Evingtons Wine Merchants	0533 542702
EW	Eldergate Wines	0908 607885
EWC	English Wine Centre	0323 870532
EWD	Euro World Wines	041 649 4544
EWG	European Wine Growers	0524 701516
EX	Exmouth Wines	071 278 8457
FAR	Farr Vintners Ltd	071 828 1960
FDL	Findlater Mackie Todd & Co Ltd	081 543 7528
FEN	Fenwick Ltd	091 232 5100
FFR	F W Francis & Co	0483 502590
FFW	Farthinghoe Fine Wine & Food	0295 710018
FIN	Findlater (Wine Merchants) Ltd	0001 976130
FLM	Ferrers le Mesurier	0832 732660
FNZ	Fine Wines of New Zealand Ltd	071 482 0093
FRI	Friarwood Ltd	071 736 2628
FRV	The Four Vintners	071 739 7335
FS	Francis Stickney Fine Wines	081 201 9096
FSW	Frank E Stainton	0539 731886
FTH	Forth Wines Ltd	0577 863668
FUL	Fuller Smith & Turner plc	081 994 3691
FVW	Fine Vintage Wines	0865 724866
FWF	French Wine Farmers Ltd	071 486 4811
F&M	Fortnum & Mason	071 734 8040
G	Gateway Foodmarkets Ltd	0272 359359
GAR	Garland Wines	0372 275247
GBA	Georges Barbier	081 852 5801
GEL	Gelston Castle Fine Wines	0556 3012
GER	Gerry's Wines & Spirits	071 734 2053

GH	Goedhuis & Co Ltd	071 793 7900
GHL	George Hill Ltd of Loughborough	
		0509 212717
GHS	Gerard Harris Fine Wines	
		0296 631041
GI	Grape Ideas	0865 791313
GMN	Gemini Wines	0753 681328
GMV	GM Vintners	0872 79680
GNW	The Great Northern Wine Co	
		0532 461200
GON	Gauntleys of Nottingham	
		0602 417973
GRO	Grog Blossom	071 794 7808
GRP	G R Pickard	0484 428526
GRT	Great Western Wine Company	
		0225 448428
GS	Gerald Seel	0925 819695
GSH	The Grape Shop	071 924 3638
GSJ	Grants of St James's	0483 302255
GWC	Greek Wine Centre	0743 64636
GWI	General Wine Company	0428 722201
GWM	Guildford Wine Market	0483 575933
G&J	G & J Greenall	0925 50111
G&M	Gordon & Macphail	0343 545111
HAD	Hadleigh Wine Cellars	0473 280275
HAG	The Hanwood Group	0455 556161
HAL	Hall Batson & Co	0603 415115
HAM	Hampden Wine Co	084 421 3251
HAR	Harrods Ltd	071 730 1234
HBV	High Breck Vintners	0420 562218
HC	The Haslemere Cellar	0428 645081
HCC	Henry C. Collison & Sons	
		071 839 6407
HCK	Pierre Henck Wines Ltd	0902 751022
HD	Hollywood & Donnelly	0232 799335
HDR	HDRA	0203 303517
HER	Hermitage Wine Cellars	0235 861060
HEY	Heyman Bros Ltd	071 730 0324
HHC	Hynard hughes & Co Ltd	0116 276 9496
HHR	H & H Ryman	0455 559384
HLV	Halves Ltd	0584 877866
HN	Harvey Nichols	071 235 5000
HOH	House of Hallgarten	0582 22538
HOL	Holland Park Wine Co	071 221 9614
HOT	House of Townend	0482 26891
HOU	Hoult's Wine Merchants	0484 510700
HPD	Harpenden Wines	0582 765605
HS	Hilbre Scatchard Ltd	051 236 6468
HSL	Hanslope Wines	0908 510262
HST	Heath Street Wine Stores	
		071 435 6845
HSV	Hidden Spring Vineyard	04353 2640
HTW	H T White	0323 20161
HV	John Harvey & Sons	0272 275000
HVW	Helen Verdcourt	0628 25577
HW	Hedley Wright & Co Ltd	0279 506512
HWL	Howells of Bristol	0454 294085
HWM	Harvest Wine Group	0734 344290
H&D	Hicks & Don	0258 456040
H&H	Hector & Honorez Wines Ltd	
		0480 861444
IH	Ian G. Howe	0636 704366
IRV	Irvine Robertson Wines Ltd	
		031 553 3521
IT	Italvini	081 997 7030
IVY	Ivy Wines	0243 370280
IWS	International Wine Services	
		0494 680857
JAG	J A Glass	0592 651850
JAR	John Armit Wines	071 727 6846
JAV	John Arkell Vintners	0793 823026
JCK	J C Karn	0242 513265
JEF	John E Fells & Sons Ltd	
		081 749 3661
JEH	J E Hogg	031 556 4025
JFD	John Ford Wines	0273 735891
JFE	James Fearon Wines Ltd	0248 370200
JFR	John Frazier Ltd	021 704 3415
JMC	James E McCabe	0762 333102/7
JN	James Nicholson Wine Merchant	
		0396 830091
JOB	Jeroboams	071 823 5623
JOH	John Liddington Ltd	0536 516466
JS	J Sainsbury Plc	071 921 6420
JSN	John Sarson & Son	0533 891010
JTD	J T Davies (See Davisons)	
		081 686 9989
JWL	J W Lees and Co	0616 432487

J&B	Justerini & Brooks Ltd	071 493 8721
KEL	John Kelly	0937 842965
KF	Kiwi Fruits	071 240 1423
KS	Kwiksave	0745 887111
LAH	Lamberhurst Vineyards	0892 890286
LAV	Les Amis du Vin	081 451 0981
LAY	Laytons Wine Merchants	
		071 388 5081
LCC	Landmark Cash & Carry Ltd	
		081 863 5511
LEA	Lea & Sandeman Co Ltd	071 376 4767
LES	C R S Ltd - Leos	061 832 8152
LF	La Forge	0666 822476
LKN	Luckins	0371 872839
LOL	Louis Latour Ltd	071 409 7276
LS	Laurence Smith & Son	031 667 3327
LTW	Littlewoods Organisation plc	
		051 235 2222
LU	Luigi's Delicatessen	071 352 7739
LUV	Luvians/The Bottle Shop	033 454820
LV	La Vigneronne	071 589 6113
LW	Lurgashall Winery	042 878 292
LWE	London Wine Emporium Ltd	
		071 587 1302
LWL	London Wine Ltd	071 351 6856
LYN	Lyndhurst Wines	0444 454626
L&S	Laymont & Shaw Ltd	0872 70545
L&W	Lay & Wheeler Ltd	0206 764446
M6	M6 Cash & Carry (Blackburn) Ltd	
		0254 582290
MAK	Makro Self Service Wholesalers Ltd	
		061 707 1585
MAR	Marco's Wines	081 871 4944
MAY	F & E May Ltd	071 405 6249
MCC	MCC Vintners	041 643 2282
MCO	Malcolm Cowen Ltd	081 965 1937
MFL	Murrayfield Wines	031 313 5100
MG	Matthew Gloag & Son Ltd	
		0738 21101
MHC	Manor House Wine Merchants	
		0446 775591
MHV	Malt House Vintners	0933 440404
MHW	Mill Hill Wines	081 959 6754
MIT	Mitchells of Lancaster (Brewers) Ltd	
		0524 63773
MJW	Michael Jobling Wines	091 261 5298
MK	McKinley Vintners	081 671 7219
MLG	Milligans of Leeds	0532 668761
MM	Michael Menzel Wines	0742 683557
MMW	Maurice Mason Wine Services Ltd	
		081 841 8732
MOK	Middlemas of Kelso	0573 224471
MON	Mondial Wines	081 335 3455
MOR	Moreno Wine Importers	071 723 6897
MRF	Mark Reynier Fine Wines Ltd	
		071 978 5601
MRN	Wm Morrison Supermarkets	
		0924 821234
MRS	Morrisons	0274 494166
MRT	Martinez Fine Wine	0943 603241
MS	Malpas Stallard	0905 23127
MTL	Mitchells Wine Merchants Ltd	
		0742 745587
MVN	The Merchant Vintners Co Ltd	
		0482 29443
MW	Menai Wines	0248 681568
MWL	Manwood Wines Ltd	0565 54781
MWS	Midhurst Wine Shippers	0730 812222
MWW	Majestic Wine Warehouses	
		0923 816999
MYS	Mayor Sworder & Co Ltd	
		071 735 0385
MZ	Mentzendorff & Co	071 222 2522
M&C	Moet & Chandon	071 235 9411
M&S	Marks & Spencer plc	071 268 8580
M&V	Morris & Verdin Ltd	071 630 8888
NBV	Nutbourne Manor Vineyard	
		071 627 3800
ND	Neville Dennis Wines	0782 615616
NET	Nethergate Wines	0787-277244
NI	Nobody Inn	0647 52394
NIC	Nicolas UK Ltd	071 937 3996
NRW	Noble Rot Wine Warehouse Ltd	
		0527 575606
NUR	Nurdin & Peacock Ltd	081 946 9111
NVN	Nevins	0744 24841

NY	Noel Young Wines	0223 844744
N&P	Nickolls & Perks Ltd	0384 394518
OAT	Oatley Vineyard	0278 671340
OBC	The Old Butcher's Wine Cellar	
		0628 810606
OD	Oddbins Ltd	081 944 4400
OHI	Oakhouse Wine Co	0584 810850
OLS	The Old St Wine Co	071 729 1768
ORG	The Organic Wine Co Ltd	
		0494 446557
P	Parfrements	0203 503646
PAG	Pagendam Pratt & Partners Ltd	
		0937 844711
PAL	Pallant Wines Ltd	0243 788475
PAT	Patriarche UK Ltd	071 381 4016
PAV	Pavilion Wine Co	071 628 8224
PEA	Peake Wine Associates (South & West)	
		0705 529786
PEC	Pechiney UK Ltd	0753 522800
PEP	Peppercorn Wholefoods	071 4311251
PEY	Philip Eyres Wine Merchant	
		0494 433823
PF	Percy Fox & Co Ltd	0279 633140
PGR	Patrick Grubb Selections	0869 40229
PHI	Philglas & Swiggot	071 924 4494
PI	Party Ingredients T/A Nutbourne Vineyard	071 627 3800
PIC	Le Picoleur	071 402 6920
PIM	Pimlico Dozen Ltd	071 834 3647
PLA	Playford Ros Ltd	0845 526777
PLE	Peter Lehmann Wines (UK) Ltd	
		0227 731353
PMR	Premier Wine Warehouse	
		071 736 9073
PO	Peter Osborne	0491 612311
POM	Pomona Wines	0634 235658
PON	Le Pont de la Tour	071 403 2403
POP	The Pipe of Port	0702 614606
POR	Portland Wine Company	
		061 962 8752
PST	Penistone Court Wine Cellars	
		0226 766037
PTR	Peter Green & Co	031 229 5925

PUG	Pugsons of Buxton	0298 77696
PV	Prestige Vintners	0264 335586
P&R	Peckham & Rye	041 3344312
QR	Quellyn Roberts Wine Merchants	
		0244 310455
R	R S Wines	0272 631780
RAC	Rackham's Dept Store	021 236 3333
RAE	Raeburn Fine Wines	031 332 5166
RAM	The Ramsbottom Victuallers Co Ltd	
		0706 825070
RAV	Ravensbourne Wine	081 692 9655
RBS	Roberson Wine Merchant	
		071 371 2121
RD	Reid Wines (1992) Ltd	0761 452645
RDW	Rodney Densem Wines	0270 623665
REM	Remy & Associates	0491 410777
RES	La Reserve	071 589 2020
REW	La Reserva Wines	0484 846732
REY	Raymond Reynolds Ltd	0663 747040
RH	Rodney Hogg Wines	0933 317420
RHV	Richard Harvey Wines	0929 480352
RIB	Ribble Vintners Ltd	0772 884866
RIC	Richard Granger (Personal Wine Merchant)	091 281 5000
RIV	Riverside Wines	0823 324412
RM	Robert Mendelsohn	081 455 9895
		0256 770397
RNW	Richard Nurick	07357 4877
ROB	T M Robertson & Son	031 229 4522
ROD	Rodney Densem Wines	0270 623665
RR	Robert Rolls	071 248 8382
RTW	The Rose Tree Wine Co	
		0242 583732
RWC	Rioja Wine Co Ltd	0824 703407
RWV	Rawlings Voigt Ltd	071 403 9269
RWW	Richmond Wine Warehouse	
		081 948 4196
R&I	Russell & McIver Ltd	071 283 3575
S	S Wines	071 351 1990
SAC	Le Sac a Vin	071 381 6930
SAF	Safeway Stores plc	081 848 8744
SAL	Saltern Wine Co	0202 297270
SAN	Sandiway Wine Co	0606 882101

SAS	Sherston Wine Company (St Albans)	
		0727 858841
SAV	Sava Centre	0734 778000
SB	Sainsbury Brothers	0225 460481
SD	Scatchard Ltd	051 236 6468
SEA	House of Seagram	081 543 6677
SEB	Sebastopol Wines	0235 850471
SEL	Selfridges	071 629 1234
SG	Stevens Garnier	0865 791313
SHA	Shawsgate Vineyard	0728 724060
SHB	Shaws of Beaumaris	0248 810328
SHJ	S. H. Jones & Co Ltd	0295 251177
SK	Seckford Wines	0473 626681
SKA	Skalli Fortant de France	0491 411300
SMF	Somerfield	0272 359359
SMG	Smugglers	0428 54846
SMV	St Martins Vintners	0273 777744
SNO	Snowdonia Wine Warehouse	
		0273 00402
SOB	Stones of Belgravia	071 2351612
SOH	Soho Wine Supply	071 636 8490
SOM	Sommelier Wine Co Ltd	0481 721677
SPR	Spar UK Ltd	081 863 5511
SSM	Stewarts Supermarkets	0232 704434
STB	Stokes Brothers (UK) Ltd	
		0303 252178
SU	Susser Ltd	081 455 4336
SUM	Summerlee Wines Ltd	081 997 7889
SUP	Supergrape Ltd	081 874 5963
SV	Smedley Vintners	0462 768214
SW	Schuler Wine Ltd	0800 890 330
SWS	Stratford's Wine Shippers & Merchants	
		0628 810006
S&D	Saltmarsh & Druce	0993 703721
S&J	Simpkin & James	0533 623132
S&W	Superfood & Wines	081 290 0077
TAN	Tanners Wines Ltd	0743 232400
TBW	Talbot Wines	021 744 5775
TDS	Thresher Drink Stores	0707 328244
TDV	Todd Vintners	0795 532206
TH	Thresher Wine Shops	0707 328244
THP	Thos Peatling	0284 755948
TO	Tesco Stores plc	0992 632222
TOJ	Tony Jeffries Wines	0604 22375
TOS	Trumps of Sidmouth	039 551 2446
TP	Terry Platt Wine Merchant	
		0492 592971
TPW	Topsham Wines	0392 874501
TRE	Tremaynes	0491 575061
TW	Thames Wine Sellers	071 663 6948
TWC	The Wine Cellar	0329 822733
T&T	Thierry's Wine Services	
		0794 515500
T&W	T & W Wines	0842 765646
U	Unwins Wine Merchants	0322 272711
UBC	Ubiquitous Chip	041 334 5007
UWM	United Wine Merchants Ltd	
		0232 231231
VAU	Vaux Breweries Ltd	091 567 6277
VD	Vins Direct	0534 482322
VDP	Vinhos de Portugal (UK) Ltd	
		0865 791315
VDV	Vin du Van	0233 758 727
VER	Vinceremos Wines & Spirits Ltd	
		0532 431691
VEX	Vinexports Ltd	0886 812555
VIL	Village Wines	0322 558772
VIW	Vintage Wines	0602 476565
VLW	Villeneuve Wines Ltd	0721 722500
VR	Vintage Roots	0734 401222
VT	The Vine Trail	0272 423946
VTH	Vintage House	071 4372592
VW	Victoria Wine	0483 715066
V&C	Valvona & Crolla Ltd	031 556 6066
W	Waitrose Ltd	0344 424680
WAC	Waters of Coventry Ltd	0926 888889
WAV	Waverley Vintners Ltd	0738 29621
WAW	Waterloo Wine Co Ltd	071 403 7967
WB	Wine Barrels	071 228 3306
WBK	W H Brakspear	0491 573636
WBR	Wadebridge Wines	0208 812692
WCA	The Wine Case	081 560 5514
WCB	Wine Cellars	0243 577212
WCE	Winecellars	081 871 3979
WCH	Winchcombe Wine Merchants	
		0242 604313

WCO	Wine Company of Scotland	031 346 1113
WCS	Wine Collections	031-667 3955
WDW	Windrush Wines Ltd	0451 860680
WEP	Welshpool Wine Company	0938 553243
WES	Wessex Wines	0308 423400
WF	Wine Finds	0584 875582
WG	Wines Galore	081 858 6014
WGT	Weingott	071 353 7733
WGW	Woodgate Wines	0229 885 637
WH	The Wine House	081 669 6661
WHC	Whiclar & Gordon Wines Ltd	0306 885711
WHO	Wholefoods of Newport	0239 820773
WIA	Whighams of Ayr Ltd	0292 267000
WIC	Wickham & Co Ltd	0237 473292
WIL	Willoughby's of Manchester	061 834 6850
WIM	Wimbledon Wine Cellar	081 540 9979
WIN	The Winery	071 286 6475
WIW	Winchcombe Wine Merchants	0242 604313
WKV	Wyken Vineyard	0359 50240
WL	William Low & Company plc	0382 814022
WMK	Winemark Wine Merchant	0232 746274
WMP	Wine Importers	031 4553 4601
WOA	Wallaces of Ayr Ltd	0292 262330
WOC	Whitesides of Clitheroe Ltd	0200 22281
WOI	Wines of Interest	0473 215752
WON	Weavers of Nottingham	0602 580922
WOT	Wootton Vineyard	0749 890359
WOW	Wines Of Westhorpe	0283 820285
WR	Wine Rack	0707 328244
WRK	Wine Raks	0224 311460
WRT	Winerite Ltd	0532 837651
WRW	The Wright Wine Co	0756 700886
WS	W S Wines	0225 783007
WSC	The Wine Schoppen Ltd	0742 365684
WSG	Walter S. Siegel Ltd	071 627 2720
WST	Western Wines	074 635 411
WSV	Wineservice	081 876 2095
WSW	Westcliffe Wines	0202 294670
WTL	Whittalls Wines	0922 36161
WTP	W T Palmer	0865 247123
WTR	The Wine Treasury Ltd	071 371 7131
WW	Wine World	0923 264718
WWG	Wigglesworth Wines	0435 813740
WWI	Woodhouse Wines	0258 52141
WWN	Wine Winners	0327 300125
WWT	Whitebridge Wines	0785 817229

Compiling such a detailed guide as this involves a small army; from proofers to designers, subs to wine journalists, friends to relatives. The few must thank the many for a tremendous, combined effort. By name, they are:

Willy Lebus at Bibendum, Anthony Whittaker, Philip Reedman at Australia House, Matthew Balken at the German Wine Information Service, Caty Oates, Margaret Harvey, Debbie Collinson, Justin Howard-Sneyd, Harry Dickinson, Sue Pike, David Lindsay, Andy Ward and Jonathan Cahill.

Paul Flint, Jane Hughes, Ruth Arnold, Jamie Ambrose, Sean Rickard, Lorna Crosbie-Smith, Corinna Farrow, Simon Flint, Mat Flint, George Glass.

All the tasters who participated in the 1994 International Wine Challenge, too numerous to list in this small guide, all the Challenge helpers and Simon Woods.

And finally, with special thanks to Robert Joseph and Sophie Wybrew-Bond, for all their energy and determination in making this project a success.

Extra special thanks go to Frances Kiernan, who laboured day and night for longer than she would care to remember – we all hope that she has been reunited with her family. This guide would not be in your hands without her numerous nightshifts.